ANCIENT INDIAN TRADITION AND MYTHOLOGY

Translated by
A BOARD OF SCHOLARS

Edited by
Dr. G.P. Bhatt

VOLUME 30

ANCIENT INDIAN TRADITION AND MYTHOLOGY SERIES

[PURĀṆAS IN TRANSLATION]

Volumes Released

ŚIVA 1-4
LIṄGA 5-6
BHĀGAVATA 7-11
GARUḌA 12-14
NĀRADA 15-19
KŪRMA 20-21
BRAHMĀṆḌA 22-26
AGNI 27-30
VARĀHA 31-32
BRAHMA 33-36
VĀYU 37-38
PADMA 39-48
SKANDA, PARTS I-XXI, 49-69
VĀMANA 72

Volumes Under Preparation

SKANDA, PARTS XXII-XXIII, 70-71
BHAVIṢYA
BRAHMAVAIVARTA
DEVĪBHĀGAVATA
KĀLIKĀ
MĀRKAṆḌEYA
MATSYA
VIṢṆU
VIṢṆUDHARMOTTARA

THE AGNI PURĀṆA

Translated and Annotated by

N. GANGADHARAN

PART IV

MOTILAL BANARSIDASS PUBLISHERS
PRIVATE LIMITED • DELHI

Reprint Edition: Delhi, 2002, ***2007***
First Edition : Delhi, 1987

ISBN: 978-81-208-0306-0

MOTILAL BANARSIDASS
41 U.A. Bungalow Road, Jawahar Nagar, Delhi 110 007
8 Mahalaxmi Chamber, 22 Bhulabhai Desai Road, Mumbai 400 026
203 Royapettah High Road, Mylapore, Chennai 600 004
236, 9th Main III Block, Jayanagar, Bangalore 560 011
Sanas Plaza, 1302 Baji Rao Road, Pune 411 002
8 Camac Street, Kolkata 700 017
Ashok Rajpath, Patna 800 004
Chowk, Varanasi 221 001

UNESCO COLECTION OF REPRESENTATIVE WORKS— Indian Series
This book has been accepted in the Indian Translation Series of the UNESCO Collection of Representative Works, jointly sponsored by the United Nations Educational Scientific and Cultural Organization (UNESCO) and the Government of India

PRINTED IN INDIA

BY JAINENDRA PRAKASH JAIN AT SHRI JAINENDRA PRESS, A-45 NARAINA, PHASE-I, NEW DELHI 110 028 AND PUBLISHED BY NARENDRA PRAKASH JAIN FOR MOTILAL BANARSIDASS PUBLISHERS PRIVATE LIMITED, BUNGALOW ROAD, DELHI 110 007

PUBLISHER'S NOTE

The purest gems lie hidden in the bottom of the ocean or in the depth of rocks. One has to dive into the ocean or delve into the rocks to find them out. Similarly, truth lies concealed in the language which with the passage of time has become obsolete. Man has to learn that language before he discovers that truth.

But he has neither the means nor the leisure to embark on that course. We have, therefore, planned to help him acquire knowledge by an easier course. We have started the series of Ancient Indian Tradition and Mythology in English Translation. Our goal is to universalize knowledge through the most popular international medium of expression. The publication of the Purāṇas in English Translation is a step towards that goal.

PREFACE

This thirtieth volume in the series on *Aucient Indian Tradition and Mythology* forms the fourth and last part of the *Agni Purāṇa.* It contains the English translation of chapters 312-383.

The project of this series was envisaged in 1970 by the late Lala Sundar Lal Jain of Messers Motilal Banarsidass. Thirty-six volumes of the series, including the present one, have so far been published and others are in progress. With the release of this volume complete sets of the translation of ten Mahāpurāṇas, viz. Agni, Bhāgavata, Brahma, Brahmāṇḍa, Garuḍa, Kūrma, Liṅga, Nārada, Śiva and Varāha are now available to the interested readers.

Two attractive and very useful features of this Part of the Agni Purāṇa are: (1) a new Introduction supplementing the one added to Part I and giving additional information about the subject matter discussed in the various chapters of the Purāṇa and its salient points and thus rendering superfluous any attempt to give a summary of the contents of the present Part here, and (2) also a detailed Index covering all the four parts of the Purāṇa.

It is our pleasant duty to put on record our sincere thanks to Dr. R.N. Daṇdekar and the UNESCO authorities for their kind encouragement and valuable help which render this work more useful than it would otherwise have been. We are extremely grateful to Dr. Gangadharan of the Sanskrit Department, University of Madras, for translating the text and contributing the Introduction as well as the Index. We are also thankful to all those who have been helpful in our project.

—*Editor*

CONTENTS

ABBREVIATIONS

Common and self-evident abbreviations such as Ch(s)—Chapter(s), p—page, pp—pages, V—Verse, VV—Verses, Ftn—footnote, Hist. Ind. Philo.—History of Indian Philosophy are not included in this list.

ABORI	*Annals of the Bhandarkar Oriental Research Institute*, Poona
AGP	S. M. Ali's *The Geography of Purāṇas*, PPH, New Delhi, 1973
AIHT	*Ancient Indian Historical Tradition*, F. E. Pargiter, Motilal Banarsidass (MLBD), Delhi
AITM	*Ancient Indian Tradition and Mythology* Series, MLBD, Delhi
AP	*Agni Purāṇa*, Guru Mandal Edition (GM), Calcutta, 1957
Arch.S.Rep.	Archaeological Survey Report
AV	*Atharva Veda*, Svādhyāya Mandal, Aundh
Bd. P.	*Brahmāṇḍa Purāṇa*, MLBD, Delhi 1973
BG	*Bhagavadgītā*
Bh. P.	*Bhāgavata Purāṇa*, Bhagavat Vidyapeeth, Ahmedabad
Br.	*Brāhmaṇa* (preceded by name such as Śatapatha)
BS. P.	*Bhaviṣya Purāṇa*, Vishnu Shastri Bapat, Wai
BV. P.	*Brahma Vaivarta Purāṇa*, GM, 1955-57
CC	*Caturvarga Cintāmaṇi* by Hemādri
CVS	*Caraṇa Vyūha Sūtra* by Śaunaka; Com. by Mahidāsa
DB	*Devī Bhāgavata*, GM, 1960-61
De or GDAMI	*The Geographical Dictionary of Ancient and Mediaeval India*, N. L. De, Oriental Reprint, Delhi, 1971
Dh. S.	*Dharma Sūtra* (preceded by the author's name such as Gautama)
ERE	*Encyclopaedia of Religion and Ethics* by Hastings
GP	*Garuḍa Purāṇa*, ed. R. S. Bhattacharya, Chowkhamba, Varanasi, 1964

GS	*Gṛhya Sūtra* (preceded by the name of the author such as Āpastamba)
HD	*History of Dharma Śāstra*, P. V. Kane, G. O. S.
IA	*The Indian Antiquary*
IHQ	*The Indian Historical Quarterly*
JP	*Purāṇa* (Journal of the Kashiraj Trust), Varanasi
KA	*Kauṭilya Arthaśāstra*
KP	*Kūrma Purāṇa*, Veṅkaṭeśvara Press Edn., Bombay; also Kashiraj Trust Edn., Varanasi, 1971
LP	*Liṅga Purāṇa*, GM, 1960; also MLBD, Delhi, 1981
Manu.	*Manusmṛti*
Mbh.	*Mahābhārata*, Gītā Press, Gorakhpur, VS 2014
MkP	*Mārkaṇḍeya Purāṇa*
MN	*Mahābhārata Nāmānukramaṇī*, Gītā Press, Gorakhpur, VS 2016
MtP	*Matsya Purāṇa*, GM, 1954
MW	Monier Williams' *Sanskrit-English Dictionary*, MLBD, Delhi, 1976
NP	*Nāradīya* or *Nārada Purāṇa*, Veṅkaṭeśvara Press, Bombay
PCK	*Bhāratavarṣīya Prācīna Caritrakośa*, Siddheshwar Shastri, Poona, 1968
Pd.P.	*Padma Purāṇa*, GM, 1957-59
PE	*Purāṇic Encyclopaedia*, V. Mani, English version, MLBD, Delhi, 1975
PR or PRHRC	*Puranic Records on Hindu Rites and Customs*, R. C. Hazra, Calcutta, 1948
ṚV	*Ṛg-Veda*, Svādhyāya Mandal, Aundh
Śat.Br.	*Śatapatha Brāhmaṇa*
SC or SMC	*Smṛti Candrikā* by Devanna Bhaṭṭa
SEP	*Studies in Epics and Purāṇas*, A.D. Pusalkar, Bharatiya Vidya Bhavan (BVB), Bombay

INTRODUCTION

In the introduction to the first part of this translation, the origin of the *Purāṇas*, the definition of the term and the five topics that the *Purāṇas* were expected to cover, the number and sequence of the *Purāṇas*, their date of composition and classification into different groups were explained in detail.

The *Purāṇas* themselves and the modern scholars as well have made attempts to classify the *Purāṇas* into different groups on the basis of their subject matter.[1] On account of the varied nature of their contents, the *Garuḍapurāṇa*, the *Agnipurāṇa* and the *Nāradapurāṇa* were classified as *Purāṇas* of an encylopaedic nature.

The traditional list of the *Purāṇas* found in the *Viṣṇupurāṇa*, places the *Agnipurāṇa* as the eighth in order. The text printed by the Venkatesvara Steam Press, Bombay has 383 chapters whereas the text printed by others has 382 chapters. This is because the former contains an additional chapter numbered 135 dealing with *Saṅgrāmavidyā*.

This *Purāṇa* as it is available to us now has been shown[2] to be a spurious one composed between 700 and 1000 A.D. on the basis of the materials on *dharma* incorporated therein. The *alaṅkāra* section also indicates the influence of various schools of *alaṅkāraśāstra* upto Bhoja's times and may be deemed to have been included around 9th century, and the genuine *Āgneyapurāṇa* with the name of *Vahnipurāṇa* is counted as an *Upapurāṇa*. Yet it is an invaluable piece of document throwing light on the culture of that period. Although the text itself gives the number of verses as 12000 (ch. 272, vv. 10-11), Bhāgavata, BV. & Padma as 15400, Skanda and Matsya as 11600, the text as in the

---

1. See Dr. N. Gangadharan, *Liṅgapurāṇa – A Study*, pp. 49-50.
2. R. C. Hazra, *PRHRC*, pp. 134-40.

present translation has about 9650 verses[1] besides some collection of tantric syllables not put in the metrical form.

Besides the five topics that a *Purāṇa* should deal with, according to the definition, this *Purāṇa* contains many other topics, some legitimately following from the five topics and others of varied nature. The subject matter coming under these topics reflect the cream of the culture of the particular period and serves as a guide to understand the same. This *Purāṇa* deals with varied topics such as (a brief description of) the manifestations of Viṣṇu (and) summary of the epics, *smṛti* material, *mantra* and *tantra*, physiognomy, political expediency, medicine, equinology, veterinary science, science relating to elephants, metrics, poetics, grammar, lexicography, archery and lapidary science.

As only a brief indication of these topics is given in the Introduction to the 'First Part a detailed survey is made now pointing out the sources wherever possible.

The Pañcalakṣaṇa (five topics)[2]

It was pointed out[3] in the Introduction to the First Part that this Purāṇa satisfies very meagrely the five-topics definition made applicable to a *Purāṇa*.

We find a theistic Sāṅkhya theory of evolution adopted by this Purāṇa. Though the theory of evolution of the universe from Prakṛti and Puruṣa is adopted, Lord Viṣṇu is described as the main force behind all creation. The creation is described as the sport of lord Viṣṇu as in the Vedānta. Viṣṇu enters Prakṛti and Puruṣa and agitates them. *Avyaktu* precedes the principle of *mahat*. *Ahaṅkāra* comes forth from *mahat*. Then come into being the *vaikārikas*, the *taijasa* and *tāmasa*. Ether, the sound-principle, wind, the principle of touch, fire, the colour-principle, water, the taste-principle and earth, the smell-principle came into being from the *rājasa ahaṅkāra*. The five *tanmātras*—sound, touch, light, taste and smell evolved from the *tāmasa ahaṅkāra*.

---

1. The number given on p. xxii in the Introduction to Part I may be corrected.
2. See pp. xvi-xviii, Introduction to Part I.
3. *Ibid.*

The organs of sense came into being from the *taijasa ahaṅkāra*. The ten celestials and mind came forth from the *vaikārika ahaṅkāra*. Then the self-born Brahmā became desirous of creating different beings. He first created water. Hence water is referred to as *nārāḥ*. Since the Lord had His abode in the water, He was designated as Nārāyaṇa.

The seed deposited by Brahmā in the water developed as the golden egg. Brahmā was born of his own accord from that. After living a year in that, Brahmā divided that egg into two—heaven and earth, and the Lord created the sky between them. The ten quarters supported the earth floating on the waters. Being desirous of creation, the Lord of beings created time, mind, speech, desire, anger, attachment and other counterparts. From lightning he created thunder and clouds, rainbow and birds. After creating Indra, he created the Vedic hymns. The higher and lower beings were created from the arms. He then created Sanatkumāra and Rudra from anger. He then created the seven sages, Marīci, Atri, Aṅgiras, Pulastya, Pulaha, Kratu and Vasiṣṭha. Having divided his body into two, he became a male with one half and a female with the other (known as Śatarūpā).

The different stages of creation : After having given an account of creation, the *Purāṇa* furnishes some details relating to the various stages of creation. The primary creation consists of the creation of *mahat*, *tanmātras*, the *vaikārikas*, namely, the *mukhya-sarga*, the *tiryaksrotas*, the *ūrdhvasrotas*, the *arvāksrotas*, the *anugraha* and the *Kaumāra*.

Intellect is the first creation of Brahmā. The subtle principles are then created. They are known as the elements. The evolutes known as sense-organs are then created. These are known as the primary creation. The fourth is the creation of the immobile things known as the main. The creation of the lower order refers to the creation of animals, birds etc. Then proceeds the sixth creation—higher orders, the celestials. Man is described as the seventh creation, referred to as the middle order. The eighth is the creation of compassionate divinities. These latter five are said to be subject to transformation. The ninth is the creation of Sanatkumāra and others. These are the nine creations of Brahmā which are the main constituents of the universe.

Mythological aspect of creation : In keeping with the Purāṇic tradition of describing the secondary creation, the Purāṇa describes the mythological aspect of creation. These accounts fall under four heads : (i) Svāyambhuva Manu and his progeny, (ii) Dakṣa and his progeny, (iii) Kaśyapa and his progeny, and (iv) the overlordship of different regions. These are described in chs. 18 & 19.

The female half known as Śatarūpā of ascetic disposition had two sons Priyavrata and Uttānapāda and a beautiful daughter[1] from Svāyambhuva Manu. Uttānapāda had two wives Suruci and Sunīti. Uttama was born as his son through Suruci and Dhruva through Sunīti. Dhruva practised austerities for gaining fame and attained an excellent position. Dhruva had two sons Śiṣṭi and Bhavya through his wife Śambhu. Śiṣṭi had five sons through Succhāyā. Ripu, the eldest among them had Cākṣuṣa through his wife Bṛhatī. Cākṣuṣa begot Manu through Puṣkariṇī (also known as Vīriṇī) (daughter of Vīraṇa Prajāpati). Manu had ten excellent sons through Naḍvalā. Ūru, the eldest among them got through Āgneyī six sons, Aṅga and others. Aṅga through Sunīthā got Vena. As Vena was cruel, he was killed by the sages. They churned his right hand and Pṛthu was born from it. He was the most important king who brought peace and prosperity for his subjects. Hence the earth was known as Pṛthvī. Then in line of succession were born Antardhāna and Prācīnabarhis. To Prācīnabarhis were born ten sons known as Pracetas through Savarṇā. They were proficient in archery. They did severe penance, remaining in the waters of the ocean for ten thousand years. Having gained the status of a progenitor and pleased Viṣṇu, they came out of the waters. They found the earth and sky overspread with trees. They burnt them down. Beholding that, Soma, the king of the plants approached them and requested them to renounce their anger, offering the excellent maiden Māriṣā born to the nymph Pramlocā and the ascetic Kaṇḍu and nourished by him. The Pracetas married her and Dakṣa was born to them.

1. The Purāṇa does not give her name. She is referred to as Devahūti in Bh. P.

Dakṣa created mentally the immovable and movable objects, bipeds, quadrupeds, and then the sixty maidens of whom he gave ten to Dharma, thirteen to Kaśypa, twenty-seven to Soma, four to Ariṣṭanemi, two to Bahuputra and two to Aṅgiras. Different beings were born from them. Among these, the two wives of Kaśyapa were Aditi and Diti. The twelve Ādityas—Viṣṇu, Śakra etc. were born through Aditi and the two demons Hiraṇyākṣa and Hiraṇyakaśipu and the demoness Siṁhikā were born through Diti. Among the sons of Hiraṇyakaśipu, Prahrāda was a great devotee of Lord Viṣṇu. Virocana was born from Prahrāda and Bali was born from Virocana. Bāṇa was the eldest among the hundred sons of Bali. He propitiated Lord Śiva and gained a boon.

Tāmrā, one of the wives of Kaśyapa, had six daughters, viz. Kākī, Śyenī, Bhāsī, Gṛdhrikā, Śuci and Sugrīvā. Different birds and animals were born from them. From other wives of Kaśyapa were born other kinds of birds and animals. Innumerable are their offsprings. Diti, who had lost her offspring, propitiated Kaśyapa, desirous of getting a son capable of destroying Indra. When she had gained her desire, Indra waiting for an opportunity when she was impure; destroyed the embryo. They became celestials known as Maruts, fiftyone in number.

Overlordship of different regions

After having installed Pṛthu as the ruler (of the earth), Lord Viṣṇu set apart different regions for others such as the Moon, Varuṇa, Vaiśravaṇa, Viṣṇu, Pāvaka, Vāsava, Dakṣa, Prahlāda, Yama, Hara, Himavat, Citraratha, Vāsuki, Takṣaka, Garuḍa, Airāvata, bull, tiger, Plakṣa, Uccaiḥśravas, Sudhanvan, Śaṅkhapād, Ketumat and Hiraṇyaromaka. This we find in ch. 19, verses 22 to 28. Then it describes the progeny of Bhṛgu, Marīci and others through Khyāti, Sambhūti and others.

Dissolution

This *Purāṇa* devotes two chapters (368 and 369) to describe the process of dissolution. Dissolution is said to be of four kinds—*nitya*, *naimittika*, *prākṛta* and *ātyantika* (continuous dissolution taking place daily, the dissolution that occurs at the end of a *kalpa* period, the dissolution of everything being burnt by fire, and the absolute dissolution).

The *naimittika* dissolution is first described. Hardly any life remains on the earth. For a hundred years it does not rain. The seven rays of the sun cause evaporation of all waters. All animals perish for want of food and drink. Viṣṇu takes his abode in the seven rays of the sun and drinks the water of the oceans as well as the water inside the earth and the nether region. The seven rays finally grow in intensity and get transformed into seven suns. Then the three worlds together with the nether regions are reduced to ashes. The surface of the earth also gets changed and appears like the back of a tortoise. After all things have been burnt, clouds gather from the breath of Viṣṇu. They pour down perpetual showers of rain and the fire that has been raging for a hundred years is put out. When the water rises to the level of the region of the seven sages (Great Bear), the final storm arises from the breath of Lord Hari and the clouds get dispersed by the storm. God Hari lies down on the surface of the water and is praised by the sages and the realised souls.

The *prākṛta* dissolution takes place as follows: The different modifications of *mahat* get dissolved one after the other. First the earth with its attribute *gandha* gets dissolved into water, water with *rasa*, into light and then fire alone persists in the universe. In its turn wind destroys the suns with their attributes of colour and light. Wind togther with its attribute touch gets destroyed by *ākāśa* (ether). *Ākāśa* gets merged in the universal space together with the material principles. *Mahat* consumes the universal space together with its attribute of egoism. Puruṣa, the pure consciousness and Prakṛti get finally merged in the Supreme Soul.

The *ātyantika* dissolution means the merger of the individual souls with the absolute Brahman. This is gained by knowledge and renunciation of the world. Agony is two-fold: (1) pertaining to body, and (2) pertaining to mind. The first one is manifold. After the death of a person, the individual soul discards the dead body and assumes the *ātivāhika* body that is taken to a region to suffer for his deeds. The god of death prescribes the nature of punishment or rebirth. Then the text describes heaven and hell and the nature of suffering of the soul which cannot be brought under the head of spiritual dissolution.

Genealogical lists in the Agnipurāṇa

The genealogical lists in the *Agnipurāṇa* are late compilations, just like those in the *Garuḍapurāṇa* and the *Bhāgavatapurāṇa.* They do not reproduce any of the old verses of *Vāyupurāṇa, Brahmāṇḍapurāṇa* etc. The genealogies are restated in fresh verses. The narration here gives mere pedigree without any allusions- The *Agnipurāṇa* follows the tradition set by the *Matsyapurāṇa* regarding the Aikṣvākus and the common tradition for other dynasties. Following the general Purāṇic view Manu is described as the originator of the two ancient dynasties—Solar and Lunar. He is given as fifth in descent from Lord Viṣṇu. The *Agnipurāṇa* gives the number of the sons of Manu as eight whereas the *Brahmapurāṇa* gives it as nine and the *Viṣṇupurāṇa, Matsyapurāṇa* and the *Padmapurāṇa* give it as ten by splitting the name Nābhāgodiṣṭa as Nābhāga and Diṣṭa in the *Viṣṇupurāṇa* and adding *Iṭa* as the eldest in the *Matsya-* and *Padma-purāṇas.*

The *Agnipurāṇa* speaks of Ilā as the daughter of Manu and summarises the episode relating to her metamorphosis without going into the details. Beginning with the description of the Solar race in ch. 273, it describes the Lunar race, the dynasty of Yadu, the lineages of Aṅga and Puru in the succeeding chapters concluding in ch. 278. The *Purāṇas* refer to two branches of the Solar dynasty—(1) the line of Ikṣvāku and (2) the line of Śaryāti (sons of Manu). The lineage of Ikṣvāku, the eldest son of Manu, is briefly narrated in the *Agnipurāṇa* (ch. 273, verses 18-39). The list of descendents of *Purūravas* representing the Lunar race is given in ch. 274, verses 12 to 23. The genealogy of the Yādavas beginning with Yadu is given in ch. 275 proceeding upto the progeny of Bālarāma and Kṛṣṇa. The account in the *Agnipurāṇa* does not speak about the kings of the period after the Bhārata war, which we commonly find in the other *Purāṇas* as the kings of the future.

The Manu-periods

This *Purāṇa* devotes only one chapter (ch. 150) to describe the fourteen Manu periods, the sons of Manus and the respective gods, sages and Indras during their period. While this subject has been dealt with in detail in the *Purāṇas* like Vāyu, the narration here is brief. Svāyambhuva Manu is the first Manu. For the sake of humanity, laws were codified by him. The names of other Manus are Svārociṣa, Uttama, Tāmasa, Raivata, Cākṣuṣa, Vaivasvata (the present Manu), Sāvarṇi, Dakṣasāvarṇi, Brahmasāvarṇi, Dharmasāvarṇi, Rudrasāvarṇi, Raucya and Bhautya.

Bhuvanakośa

Chs. 107 and 108 describe the different worlds, the earth and continents. The greatness of sacred spots such as the river Gaṅgā, Prayāga, Vārāṇasī, the river Narmadā and Gayā are described in chs. 109—14, followed by a detailed account of the mode of making a pilgrimate to Gayā in chs. 115 and 116 and the performance of ancestral rites in ch. 117. Then follows a description of Bhārata (country), the different continents and the extent of the universe in chs. 118-20. A list of the different hells and the nature of torments therein is given in ch. 371.

Material on dharma

In conformity with the contents of most of the *Purāṇas*, a considerable space has been devoted to matters relating to *dharma*. This material we find in chs. 151–212, 227, 252—72. We find here description of the duties laid down for different castes, the duties of men belonging to different stages of life, rules relating to marriage, codes of conduct, pollution and purification, the merits of offering libation and the performance of good deeds, propitiation of the planets, different kinds of major sins and expiations for them, the vows to be practised on the different lunar days, on week days, in different asterisms, in different months and seasons and rules and regulations relating to vows and gifts of varied nature.

In this section we also get a reference to the names of the twenty writers on *dharma* such as Manu, Viṣṇu, Yājñavalkya, Hārīta, Atri, Yama, Aṅgiras, Vasiṣṭha, Dakṣa, Saṁvarta, Śātātapa, Parāśara, Āpastamba, Uśanas, Vyāsa, Kātyāyana,

Bṛhaspati, Gotama, Śaṅkha and Likhita. In the above matter the *Agnipurāṇa* has based the account of the four stages of life on the *Manusmṛti*, even borrowing verses at times. Besides the above the *Purāṇa* also mentions the forty-eight *saṁskāras* such as *Garbhādhāna*, *Puṁsavana* etc. Chs. 253-58 describing the administration of justice, debts and their repayments, rules relating to disputes, different kinds of ordeals, procedure for division of properties, settlement of disputes relating to the boundaries of fields and punishment for making defamatory speeches and committing other offences are mostly based on the *Yājñavalkyasmṛti*.

The subsequent chs. 259—72 describe the application of the mantras of the different *Vedas* and different kinds of worship to ward off bad effects of portents etc. and they are narrated by Puṣkara.

Other philosophical concepts

Although all the schools of philosophy were developed by the time the *Agnipurāṇa* was compiled, we find here a gist of only a few systems, such as Yoga and Vedānta. Besides the meagre Sāṅkhya account of evolution which we have already noticed, these philosophical ideas are dealt with in chs. 372-382. Beginning with an exposition of the eight constituents of *Yoga* such as *yama*, *niyama* (and the like), the text explains knowledge relating to Brahman, summarises the *Bhagavadgitā* and concludes with a *Yamagitā* spoken by Yama to Naciketas. Although the exposition on principles of *Yoga* is a summary of those given in the sūtras of Patañjali, we find here an orientation of the same to establish the unity of the individual soul and Brahman.

Though there is no direct reference to the Vedānta system as such, it deals at length with the fundamental doctrine of identity of the individual soul and the supreme soul avoiding all sorts of discussions relating to technical matters. The *Advaita* viewpoint is illustrated by means of two episodes in ch. 380.

Gitā material in the Purāṇa : Bhagavadgitā

The knowledge and utilisation of the *Bhagavadgitā* by the

Purāṇas goes without saying. Dr. Raghavan has made[1] a comprehensive survey of the *Gītā* thought and expression as found in other parts of the *Mahābhārata*, the *Purāṇa* and *Upapurāṇa* literature. The *Agnipurāṇa* epitomises the *Bhagavadgītā* in 58 verses in ch. 381 and describes the *Yamagītā* in 37 verses in ch. 382. The following table shows how the *Agnipurāṇa* has ustilised the *Bhagavadgītā* material:

Bhagavadgītā Ch.	Verse	Agnipurāṇa Ch. 381 Verse
II	11a, 62, 63, 69	2a, 3, 4a, 5b, 6a
III	17b, 18a, 28	6b, 7a, 7b, 8a
V	10	9b, 10a
VI	29	10b, 11a
	41b	11b
	40b	12a
VII	14	12b, 13a
	16, 17a	13b, 14a
VIII	3-6	14b, 17a
	10b	17b
	13a	18a
XIII	1, 2b	20a, 20b
	5-17	21-33
	24, 25	34, 35
XIV	17	36
	23b	37a
	25	37b
XV	1	38
XVI	6a	39a
	2-3	39b
	7b, 21	40
XVII	7b, 8, 9, 10, 11b, 12, 14, 16	41-46
	20-22	47
	23a	48a
XVIII	5	48b
	12, 14	49, 51
	20-25	52-53a
	26-28, 30-35, 46	53b, 54-57a

1. See *Journal of Oriental Research*, Madras, II, pp. 86-122. See also Intro. to Part I, p. xxi of the translation of Agnip.

Besides the above, ch. 19 is an imitation of the Vibhūtiyoga chapter (number 10) of the Bhagavagdītā.

Yamagitā

The *Yamagitā* (ch. 382) mentioned as having been expounded by Yama to Naciketas contains also the doctrines of teachers such as Kapila, Pañcaśikha, Gaṅgāvisṇu, Janaka, Jaigīṣavya and others. Here we find references to the merits of devotion to Viṣṇu which confer the earthly benefits as well as release from this mundane existence. Lord Viṣṇu is regarded as the chief force behind all creation. The expositions of the teachers lay stress on the following: Self-realisation is much more beneficial than gratifying one's senses. Equanimity towards all the beings and shedding all desires is the greatest good. True knowledge consists of having the correct perspective of birth, youth and old age. One gets the ultimate good by discharging the duties as laid down in the Vedas. The renunciation of all desires leads one to Brahman.

The manifestations of Viṣṇu and the narration of the epics

After the introductory first chapter, the *Purāṇa* describes the ten manifestations of Lord Viṣṇu in chs. 2 to 16. Giving a brief account of His manifestations as a Fish, Tortoise, Boar, Man-lion and Dwarf, it elaborates the story of Rāma in chs. 5—11 and that of Kṛṣṇa in ch. 12 and describes the origin of the Kauravas and Pāṇḍavas in ch. 13. The story of the Mahābhārata is narrated in chs. 14 and 15. Then the *Purāṇa* describes the manifestations as Buddha and Kalki in ch. 16. Later in ch. 49 we find a description of the characteristic features of the images representing the ten manifestations of Lord Viṣṇu while dealing with those of the images of different gods. We have a description of the different manifestations of Lord Viṣṇu again in ch. 276. Here there is a reference to these manifestations as upholding dharma in the battles of the celestials against the demons. There were twelve such battles which resulted in events like the churning of the ocean, the destruction of Andhaka, the killing of the demon Vṛtra, the conquering of the deadly poison *hālāhala* etc.

Political expediency

Political expediency is described in chs. 220 to 242 preceded by two chapters describing the mode of performing the coronation of a king and the sacred syllables for the coronation. These occur in two versions here, the first one as expounded by Puṣkara and the second one as by Rāma. While the first version is a summary of the *Matsyapurāṇa* chs. 215—227, the second version is an adaptation from the *Nitisāra* of Kāmandaka. Sometimes even verses or lines are reproduced *verbatim*. The version by Puṣkara deals with the coronation ceremony, the requisites of those in the service of a king, the code of conduct for the servants, the building of a fort with the residence of the king within, the steps to be taken for providing security to the king as well as women, the duties of a king in general and towards women in the harem, the means of conciliation, the code of criminal laws, military expedition indicating the propitious periods for the same, good and bad auguries, the political expedients used by a king, the daily duties of a king, the rites preceding the march of a king and a hymn in praise of goddess Śrī (Lakṣmī) for the sake of success in battles and general welfare.

The version narrated by Rāma contains the general ethics, the seven constituents of a kingdom, viz. king, ministry, kingdom, fort, treasury, army and allies – helpful to one another, the duties of a king, priest and servants, the six expedients to be employed by a king, the importance of having a good counsel, four kinds of upāyas and the statesmanship of a king while making a military expedition explaining some of the different arrays of the army. An array is said to have seven parts such as chest, sides, wings, centre, back (hip), rear and the edge. It describes arrays such as *guru*, *bhoga* and *daṇḍa* and their modifications. Certain religious rites relating to a king's expedition and consecration of the umbrella and other royal insignia are described in chs. 268 and 269.

Physiognomy and characteristic features of royal fan, bow, sword etc.

In continuation of the previous section the *Purāṇa* describes the good and bad effects of the characteristic features of men and women in chs. 243 and 244. The next chapter deals with the characteristics of royal fan, bow and sword. The handle of a royal fan should be made of gold. A royal umbrella should be made of the feathers of particular birds only. It should be circular and white. The seat of a king should be made by using the wood of *kṣira* tree. Then the text describes in detail the characteristic features of different parts of a bow. The arrows may be made of iron, bamboo or reeds.

The science of archery, the use of other weapons, riding horses and elephants and thirty-two kinds of military art are dealt with in chs. 249 to 252. In the first two chapters here we find details about the different postures adopted in archery and practical hints for striking a target. The next chapter describes the method of making a noose and its use. The subsequent chapter opens with an enumeration of thirty-two kinds of employment of a sword, eleven ways of manipulating a noose and explains the use of weapons such as *tomara*, *gadā* and the like for specific purposes.

Ch. 246 gives the names of different kinds of gems and points out the characteristic features of an auspicious diamond for being worn by a king. It then describes briefly the excellent varieties of other gems also.

Alaṅkāraśāstra

The various elements constituting a *kāvya* such as characteristics of a *kāvya*, the sentiments, the literary diction, the embellishments of words and sense, and the literary merits and blemishes have been dealt with in chs. 337, 339-40, 343-47. The *Purāṇa* has taken this material from the *Nāṭyaśāstra* of Bharata and *Kāvyādarśa* of Daṇḍin.

After defining *kāvya*, the text gives the classification of *kāvya* as *gadya*, *padya* and *miśra* with their further divisions. The poetic embellishments are divided into those of words, of sense and mixed, with their further sub-divisions. The embellishments of sense are divided into eight categories : *Svarūpa* (natural state), *Sādṛśya* (similitude), *Utprekṣā* (poetic fancy), *Atiśaya* (exaggeration), *Vibhāvanā* (effect taking place without the cause), *Virodha* (contradiction), *Hetu* (reason) and *Sama* (evenness of description). Following Daṇḍin *Upamā* (simile) is divided into sixteen varieties. The embellishments of words are the following nine: *Chāyā*, *Mudrā*, *Ukti*, *Yukti*, *Gumphanā*, *Vākovākya*, *Anuprāsa*, *Citra* and *Duṣkara*. Among these the first six varieties are in fact different modes of expressions and cannot be termed as *alaṅkāras*. That is why only the last three are normally referred to as embellishments of words in rhetorics. Most probably the purāṇic text represents a different tradition. The *Purāṇa* treats *Yamaka* as a variety of *Anuprāsa*. The *Purāṇa* refers to the number of varieties of *Yamaka* as ten, but actually names only eight. *Anuprāsa* is said to be of five kinds. *Citra* is divided into seven varieties and *Duṣkara* into three. After defining the mixed variety of embellishments, the *Purāṇa* gives six sub-divisions which are actually treated as *Guṇas* by writers on rhetorics like Daṇḍin and Vāmana.

Guṇas (merits) are classified as *Sāmānya* and *Viśeṣa* and described as enhancing the beauty and sweetness of a description, imparting lustre to its theme. *Doṣas* (blemishes) are treated elaborately. They are said to be seven as associated with *vaktā*, *vācaka* and *vācya*. These are again subdivided. *Rītis* (style) are divided into four: *Pāñcālī*, *Gauḍī*, *Vaidarbhī* and *Lāṭī*, adding the last one to the three given by Vāmana in his *Kāvyālaṅkārasūtravṛtti*. These *rītis* have probably got these names from their use in a particular region. The *Purāṇa* makes a passing reference to the four *Vṛttis* used in dramatic compositions and discusses only the first two. They are mainly dependent on the action of drama and not upon the words or style thereof and are thus distinguished from *Rītis*.

Sentiments (*Rasas*)

Rasa is traced to the Supreme Reality, the very embodiment of *Ānanda*. *Ahaṅkāra* and *Abhimāna* proceed from that. The latter gives rise to *Rati*. The other sentiments arise from *Rati*. *Rāga*, *Taikṣṇa*, *Avaṣṭambha* and *Saṅkoca* are produced from that giving rise to the four sentiments *Śṛṅgāra*, *Raudra*, *Vīra* and *Bībhatsa*. Each one of these sentiments gives rise to *Hāsya*, *Karuṇa*, *Adbhuta* and *Bhayānaka* respectively. Although the theory of *Rasa* propounded by the *Purāṇa* agrees with the view of Bhoja, there is this difference that according to the latter *Śṛṅgāra* is the only sentiment and others proceed from it.

Concept of Dhvani

Though the principle of *dhvani* as envisaged by Ānandavardhana is not recorded in the *Agnipurāṇa*, we can say that the concept is not entirely unknown to it. The constituents of literature are *dhvani* (sound), *vāṇi* (import), *pada* (word) and *vākya* (sentence). The *Purāṇa* (ch. 345) includes *Abhivyakti* among the embellishments of words. While explaining this term, the text has discussed the different powers of words to indicate different senses. In that context, all expressions are divided into *Śruti* and *Ākṣepa*. *Abhidhā* and *Lakṣaṇā* are brought under the first category and *Dhvani* is included in the second. *Dhvani* is defined as the flashing of the sense not got by mere hearing. The word and sense make their own import secondary, giving primary importance to that got by means of *Dhvani*. Thus the definition here is not very much different from that given in *Dhvanyāloka*. But the *Purāṇa* treats this as an embellishment and includes it in *Ākṣepa*, *Samāsokti*, *Apahnuti* and *Paryāyokta* (ch. 345, v. 18).

Dramaturgy in the Agnipurāṇa

The topics relating to dramaturgy are : the characteristics of a hero and heroine, the movement of limbs at the commencement of a dance and exposition of acting (chs. 338 and 341-42). The subject is not dealt with in detail and the other important topics are merely summed up. They are: the purpose of drama, namely, the attainment of the three-fold objective of human existence, twentyseven types of drama without making any distinction such as *Rūpaka* and *Uparūpaka*, the plot together with the two movements (*Sāmānya* and *Viśeṣa*) associated with it, thirty-two kinds of introductories such as *Nāndi* etc., the prologue giving information about the poet's ancestry divided into three classes based on how the stage-director introduces the play, sources of the plot—old treatises or poet's creative genius, and mere listing of the five elements (*artha-prakṛti*) such as *bija* etc., five motions (*ceṣṭā*) such as *prārambha* etc. and five junctures (*sandhi*) such as *mukha* etc., the time and place of action of a drama, blemishes such as disclosing a thing at an improper time and inclusion of absurdities in the plot, the characteristics of hero and heroine etc. and the actions and movements of various parts in dancing and acting.

The last item in the above is described in two chapters (chs. 341-42). The *Purāṇa* does not discuss all the points and it merely refers to different technical terms, explaining some of them. This material has been drawn from the *Nāṭyaśāstra* of Bharata. Thus this *Purāṇa* has assimilated divergent views relating to different schools of *Alaṅkāraśāstra* from the originator Bharata down to Bhoja. Hence it is appropriate to assign a post-9th century date to this section of the *Purāṇa*.

Medical science including equinology etc.

The *Agnipurāṇa* in chs. 279-86 deals with various topics relating to the science of medicine such as medicines, diseases and properties of medicinal preparations most probably borrowed from the works of Suśruta, Caraka and other early writers on medicine. The text begins with a desire of the Fire-god to describe the science of medicine as expounded by Dhanvantari to Suśruta. The *Purāṇa* groups together diseases under four heads, viz. organic, mental, extraneous and functional. Fever and leprosy fall under the first head of ailments. Anger, envy etc. are classified as mental derangements. The third variety denotes the diseases owing their origin to some extraneous cause. The last variety consists of items such as thirst, inflamatory fever etc. It is explained how the three humours in the body—wind, phlegm and bile—get deranged on account of the food eaten by us and give rise to various diseases. Hence one should take care to eat food appropriate to the season and that too with moderation. One should take a drug which has an opposite action to nullify the effects of excessive production of a particular humour.

Drugs are divided into two classes, stimulating and soothing. The *Purāṇa* describes (ch. 281) the preparation of herbal extracts. In order to have a healthy life, a man should have the three physical functions—eating, sleeping and coition—

without abstaining from or indulging excessively in anyone of them. The remedial measures fall under five heads, viz. juice, cakes of poultices, distilled extracts, cold juice and fresh extracts (decoction). The text also explains the principle and benefits of massaging and doing physical exercises in the proper way.

The next chapter (ch. 282) describes horticulture dealing with the planting of different kinds of trees, rules of watering them and methods to get good fruits and flowers. Chs. 285-6 describe different kinds of recipes for various ailments as well as for longevity.

Elephant lore and equinology

The *Purāṇa* describes through the mouth of Pālakāpya the treatment of the diseases of elephants in ch. 287. It begins with the narration of the good and bad features of elephants and then deals with the treatment of their diseases. This ch. is an adaptation from the work of Pālakāpya. Ch. 291 describes the propitiatory rites for curing the ailments of elephants. Equinology is dealt with in chs. 288 to 290, Dhanvantari and Śālihotra being the interlocutors. Beginning with a description of the diseases of horses and the management of horses, it explains the remedial measures and the propitiatory rites for curing their ailments. The chapters relating to their diseases and treatment are obviously based on the work of Śālihotra. The *Purāṇa* (ch. 292) explains the greatness of cows and the need for attending to their welfare. The merits of cow's urine, feces, milk and *rocanā* are explained. The *Purāṇa* suggests a feed for making the cows yield profuse milk.

Prosody

The *Purāṇa* describes prosody that was expounded by Piṅgala and makes a summary of the eight chapters of *Chandassūtra* of Piṅgala in chs. 328-335. The first chapter here in three verses explains the *gaṇas* (formed by permutation of long and short vowels). The second and third chapters explain the Vedic metres briefly. This is continued in the next chapter also. Then the secular metres are described. Ten varieties of *Āryā*, six varieties of *Vaitālīya*, five varieties of *Mātrāsamaka*, two varieties of *Śikhā* and *Tūlikā* are described. Metres in Sanskrit are divided into three groups, viz. *Sama* (all the quarters having the same characteristics), *Ardhasama* (two halves similar in all respects) and *Viṣama* (two halves not equal). Ch. 332 summarises part of a chapter of *Piṅgalasūtra* dealing with the third category. The second and first categories are dealt with in order in the subsequent two chapters. The last chapter has very briefly summarised the *prastāra* method dealt with by Piṅgala. On the whole the *sūtras* of Piṅgala have been put in metrical form with the readings being incorrect sometimes and at times some metres having been omitted. In the translation the incorrect readings have been corrected as far as possible on the basis of Piṅgala's work.

Phonetics

This topic is dealt with in ch. 336 in 21 verses. Although there is no mention that this is a summary of *Śikṣā* ascribed to Pāṇini, most of the verses here agree with the text of Pāṇini. The total number of letters is given as either sixty-three or sixty-four. They are classified into twenty-one vowels, twenty-five consonants, eight semivowels, four twin sounds such as the nasal, *anusvāra*, *visarga*, *ka*, *pa* and *la*. The origin of sound is explained. The letters are divided differently into five classes on the basis of the places of articulation. The text lays emphasis on correct pronunciation of letters to avoid incurring sin.

Grammar

We find this topic described in this *Purāṇa* in chs. 349-59, having Skanda as the interlocutor for the first eight chs., and Kumāra for the rest. This is obviously a summary of the *Kaumāra Vyākaraṇa* or *Kātantra* of Sarvavarman. The topics dealt with are: the *Pratyāhāras* and their formation, rules of combination of vowels and consonants, finished forms of inflections in nouns, substantives in the feminine and neuter gender, the relation between a noun and a verb in a sentence (*kāraka*), different kinds of compounds, the formation of secondary nominal bases (*taddhitas*), the formation of primary nominal bases (*uṇādis*), verbal terminations and formation by adding primary affixes (*kṛts*) to verbs. Thus this summary covers all the important topics relating to grammar and it helps to understand a system of grammar different from Pāṇini. Whereas the text gives only the completed euphonic combinations, I have given (under ch. 350) in the translation the individual words which have been combined. Similarly under compounds also (ch. (355) I have given the individual words which have been compounded.

Lexicography

This section in *Agnipurāṇa* comprising chs. 360 to 367 does not mention the name of Amarasiṁha or his work *Nāmaliṅgānuśāsana* (*Amarakośa*). But it is a summary of the different sections of the lexicographical work of Amarasiṁha giving words pertaining to the celestial region and nether world, indeclinables, words having many meanings, words denoting earth, city, forest and herbs, words denoting men and their four classes, words relating to the class of brahmin and other castes and words dependent on substantives for their genders. The summary is very unsystematic. After giving a summary of the first *kāṇḍa* of *Amarakośa*, the *Purāṇa* jumps to the middle of the second *kāṇḍa* and after giving extracts from *kāṇḍa* three returns to the second *kāṇḍa* again.

Tāntric material

The *Purāṇa* has much material relating to *Tantra* such as description of various *maṇḍalas*, *cakras* and *mantras* relating to different gods and goddesses, Kubjikā, incantations of different kinds to remove evil effects of diseases and to destroy enemies. Besides the chapters bearing the influence of the Tāntric practices, there are many other chapters dealing with the worship of various deities bearing a tinge of Tāntricism. The mystic syllables like *haṁ*, *hrīṁ* etc. are profusely used. The preparation of the altar, *mantras*, *mudrās*, *dikṣā* of various types, mystic *maṇḍalas*, investiture of images with sacred threads, consecration of temples, making the images of different gods etc. bear the stamp of the tāntric practices. A perusal of this translation will show that chs. 21 to 106, 140 to 149 and 300 to 326 have enough material relating to the tāntric practices. This shows that this *Purāṇa* was influenced much by the Tāntric practices.

Jyotiṣa

The effect of the asterisms on human undertakings, the almanac setting forth the calculation involved in reckoning time, the circles such as the *Svarodayacakra*, *Śanicakra*, *Kūrmacakra*, *Koṭacakra* and *Rāhucakra* for subduing enemies etc., the essence of astrology as propounded in the science of victory in battles, combinations of good and bad asterisms to secure success etc., the auspicious and inauspicious periods of the day, guidelines for storing and selling grains, different circles and diagrams such as *Ghātakacakra*, *Naracakra* and *Jayacakra* indicating success or failure in battle, *Sevācakra* which indicates loss or gain and indications from planets about the traits of the newly born are described in chs. 121 to 133. Then ch. 139 gives the names of sixty years of the Hindu almanac indicating the good or bad results which they augur.

Architecture and Sculpture

This subject lies scattered in chs. 38-39, 42, 44-46, 49-57, 67 and 104-6. Beginning with a description of the benefits of constructing a temple and preparing the ground for constructing a temple, it proceeds to describe the construction of a temple. The characteristics of the images of Vāsudeva and other gods, the characteristics of pedestals and the physiological features of images, the characteristics of different *śālagrāma* stones representing different forms of Viṣṇu, iconographical representations of the manifestations of Viṣṇu and other forms of Viṣṇu, representations of images of different goddesses and the planets, the characteristics of the *liṅga*, the characteristics of the pedestals of images, the installation of images, renovation of old and damaged images and the general characteristics of a divine edifice are explained. In ch. 104 we get the names of five classes of temples, viz. *Vairāja*, *Puṣpaka*, *Kailāsa*, *Maṇika* and *Triviṣṭapa* characterised by structures of different shapes such as square, rectangle, circular, oval and octagonal. Each

CHAPTER THREE HUNDRED AND TWELVE

The occasions for the use of the Tvaritā-mantra and the benefits

Fire-god said:

1-3. I shall describe the application of the (Tvaritā) Vidyā that would bring about success in matters pertaining to *dharma* and fulfil worldly desires. One who knows the *mantra* divided and spread over nine squares in the regular and reverse order as a whole and divided in combination with *karṇā-vikarṇa*(?) and then by their parts combined in the different triangular forms together with the image of the Goddess would know the *mantras* that confer success as well as the manifold external applications.

4-10. The mantras are manifold in different scriptures. It is difficult to find (the description of) their application therein. The first would be long. It is not described in the early hours of the morning. (The *mantras*) having a single letter, two letters and three letters would be applied. (The mystic diagram) should be divided by four lines each drawn horizontally and vertically. Thus there would be nine chambers. These (letters) should be established in the central region clockwise and then the order is split. One who finds the order by means of combination of the order that votary would have all the desired things in his folded hands. The three worlds would be at his feet. He would get the earth consisting of nine sections. The votary should write the principle of Śiva all around on the skull or on a rag (got) from the cremation ground after he has come out. The name should then be written on it at the centre or on the pericarp. It should then be fumigated with the burning charcoal of *khādira* (tree). Then a piece of birch-bark should be held under the feet. (By this process) one would be able to bring under his control the entire universe together with the movable and immovable things in seven days.

11-12. (Otherwise) the name (of the enemy) should be written inside a thunderbolt (shaped) diagram drawn inside (a circle having) twelve spokes sanctified with (the principle of) Sadāśiva ('always auspicious'). (Alternatively) (the name should be written) on a wall, or a plank or a stone slab with turmeric. There would be paralysis of the face, the arrest of movement and the arrest (of the movement) of the army.

13-17. A wiseman should write (the name of the adversary) with poison and blood inside a diagram of a club in the middle of a hexagon on a skull in the cremation ground and add (the principle of) the Goddess. This would kill the enemy struck in the cremation ground in no time. It will also ruin the kingdom. The name of the enemy should be written on a disc. The Goddess should be invoked on the blades of the disc. The enemy would be destroyed by means of his name. A person should write the principal letter (of the *mantra*) of Tārkṣya in the middle part of the sword. Then the name of the enemy should be written with the ashes (collected) from the cremation ground. One would be able to win a country. One should strike with the ashes of a dead person. (The *mantra* of) Śiva should be used in creating dessension, division and death. The *Tāraka* and *Netra* (*mantras*) should be employed in propitiatory and nourishing (rites).

18-21. This is the application (known as) *dahanādi* (capable of) captivating even Śākinī (an attendant of Goddess Durgā). (The diagram) having the Vāruṇī (*mantra*) at the centre and endowed with Vakratuṇḍa (bent tusk) would no doubt destroy the diseases such as leprosy and the like. Repeating the Karālī (*mantra*) set up (as spreading) from the middle and ending with the northern direction would guard one's own amulet. The same should be coupled with the principle of Śiva and directed against the opponent. Then it should be located in (the directions) beginning with the west. This would destroy sufferings due to fever. (If the location is done) commencing with the north and ending with the middle, it would cause heaviness in the body. (If it is done) beginning with the east and ending with the middle, it would make (the body) light in a moment.

22-25. After having written this on the *bhūrja* leaf (with resin) endowed with the marks of thunderbolt, one should add the principal letters of the *mantra*. This would offer protection to the bodies etc. If it is encircled by engraved gold, this amulet would annihilate death. The same worn (on the body) would (remove) obstacles, sins and subdue enemies. (It) would (also) confer good fortune and longevity. No doubt, it would give victory in gambling and battle even if the army of Indra (is to be fought against). This amulet is one like the (gem) *cintāmaṇi* and would confer progeny on barren women. One would be able to conquer other kingdoms, (recover one's own) kingdom and gain sovereignty over the earth. By repeating (the syllables) *phaṭ, strīṁ, kṣe, hūṁ* a lakh (number of times), one would gain control over the *yakṣas* (semi-divine beings) and others.

CHAPTER THREE HUNDRED AND THIRTEEN

The mantras relating to the worship of different gods

Fire-god said:

1-2. I shall describe the mode of worshipping (lord) Vināyaka (the lord of obstacles). One should first worship the energy of the pedestal. One should worship the eight (things) such as the virtue and the like on the stem. The pericarp, filaments etc. (of a lotus) and a lotus representing the three qualities (should be worshipped). Then (the Goddesses) Jvālinī, Nandā, Suyaśā, Ugrā, Tejovatī and Vindhyavāsinī should be worshipped.

3-6. (The different) forms of Gaṇapati should then be worshipped (as follows): "Victory to *gaṇa*" would be for the heart. (Obeisance) to one having single tusk that is strong (is) for the head. (Obeisance) to the one having immovable ears (is) for the tuft. (Obeisance) to the elephant-faced (is) for the armour. The assignment should end with '*hūṁ phaṭ*'. (Then the following) eight (forms of Gaṇapati should be worshipped): Mahodara (big-bellied), Daṇḍahasta (one that holds the club in the hand), Jaya (victorious), Gaṇādhipa (lord of the Gaṇas), Gaṇanāyaka (leader of the Gaṇas), Gaṇeśvara (lord of the Gaṇas), Vakratuṇḍa (one having bent trunk) and Ekadanta (one having single tusk) should be worshipped in the east (and other directions); one that is fierce, Lambodara (big-bellied), Gajavaktra (having elephant face), Vikaṭanāmā (known as dreadful) and Vighnanāśana (the destroyer of obstacles) should be worshipped in the east (adding the syllable) *hūṁ*. Dhūmravarṇa (grey-coloured), Mahendra and others (should be worshipped) outside (the diagram). This is the mode of worshipping the lord of obstacles.

7-12. I shall describe the mode of worshipping (Goddess) Tripurā. (One should worship first) Asitāṅga (black-coloured one), Ruru, Caṇḍa (wrathful), Krodha (angry one), Unmatta (intoxicated), Kapālī (one wielding the human skull), Bhīṣaṇa (the dreadful one), Saṁhāra (the destroyer) and Bhairava (the terrible one) in order. (The Goddesses) Brāhmī, Hrasvā, Bhairavā, Brahmāṇī, Ṣaṇmukhā and Dīrghā (should be worshipped). The four celebates—Samayaputra, Yoginīputra, Siddhaputra and Kulaputra should be worshipped in (the angular points such as) the south-east and others. Hetuka, Kṣetrapāla, Tripurānta, Dvitīyaka, Agnivetāla, Agnijihva, Karālī, Kāmalocana, Ekapāda and Bhīmākṣa should be meditated as the seat of the pretas and worshipped with (the (*mantras*) *aiṁ* and *kṣeṁ*. Goddess Tripurā, seated on a lotus seat, holding a book and offering protection (with the right hand) and a garland and conferring boons with the left hand (should be worshipped with) the two (*mantras*) *aiṁ*, and *oṁ*. The location in the heart etc. is also done with the principal (*mantra*). It is a perfect net (that yields) the desired (result).

13-16. The name (of the enemy) should be written at the centre of (a diagram of) an eight-petalled (lotus drawn) on the ground. (Or it should be written) on a piece of cloth at the cremation ground with a charcoal from the cremation ground. Or an image (of the enemy) should be made with charcoal of the funeral pyre ground well. After contemplation (the incantation) should be placed inside the stomach (of the image) and it should be bound with blue thread. Then there would be the magic incantation. *Oṁ*, obeisance ! O Fortunate One ! Jvālāmālinī (one having the flames as a garland) ! One surrounded by flocks of eagles ! Oblations. A person who goes to the battle after repeating (this) *mantra* would become victorious. *Oṁ*, *śrīṁ hrīṁ*, *klīṁ* obeisance to Śrī. One has to worship Goddess Ghṛṇinī belonging to the sun on a square (drawn) in (the directions) commencing with the north. (Goddesses) Ādityā, Prabhāvatī, Hemādri, Madhurā and Śrī (should be propitiated). *Oṁ, hrīṁ* obeisance to Gaurī. This *mantra* of (Goddess) Gaurī would yield all things when (it is used) for doing oblation, meditation, repetition and worship.

17-20. A person who prays to the Goddess of red complexion, having four arms and holding a noose and conferring boons with the right hand and holding a goad and offering protection (with the left hand), after contemplation of Her form, would live for a hundred years. He would be a wiseman. There would not be fear due to thieves and enemies. An angry person would become graceful by drinking the water charmed with the *mantra* in the battle. A collyrium or mark (made with the same) would make one get poesy at the tip of his tongue. The repetition of that (*mantra*) at the time of coition would captivate (the concerned person). (One would captivate a person) by looking at the genital organ after the repetition of the (*mantra*). (A person would be captivated) by the touch (after the repetition of the same). One would accomplish all things by doing oblation with sesamum. A person who eats food that has been charmed seven times (with the above) would always (get) fortune.

21-22. This (*mantra*) is a form of Ardhanārīśa (hermaphrodite form of lord Śiva), as well as (Goddess) Lakṣmī, (lord) Viṣṇu and others. One has to repeat (the *mantras* of Goddesses) Anaṅgarūpā, Madanāturā, Pavanavegā, Bhuvanapālā, Sarvasiddhidā, Anaṅgamadanā and Anaṅgamekhalā for (gaining) fortune.

23-24. (The syllable) *hrīṁ*, the vowels and (the letters) *ka* etc. should be written at the centre and on the petals of a lotus or on a hexagon or on a pot. (A person that looks at women after doing thus) would captivate the women. *Oṁ, hrīṁ, chūṁ*, O Nityaklinnā (ever moist)! O Madadravā (one who exudes intoxicating fluid)! *Oṁ, Oṁ*. This principal *mantra* after location on the six limbs (the two shanks, two arms, head and middle) (and then written) on red-coloured triangle (and worn on the body) would have great power to melt (the heart), make happy and agitate.

25-26. (Goddess) Nityā (should be worshipped) at the centre as well as (the angular points such as) the north-east together with the noose, goad, skull, the wish-yielding tree, lute and red-coloured (?). (Goddesses) Nityā, Abhayā, Maṅgalā, Navavīrā, Maṅgalā(?), Durbhagā, Manonmanī and Drāvā should be worshipped in the (directions) commencing with the east.

27-28. *Oṁ, hrīṁ* obeisance to Anaṅga[1] (without a body). *Oṁ, hrīṁ, hrīṁ,* obeisance to Smara (one that makes one to remember), (obeisance) to Manmatha (one that agitates the mind), to Māra and to Kāma. The five (forms of God of love) should be contemplated as holding a noose, goad, bow and arrows and as in the union of Rati (Goddess of love) (and her companions) Virati (non-attachment), Prīti (pleasure), Viprīti (displeasure), Mati (thought), Dhṛti (firmness), Vidhṛti (fickle-mindedness), and Puṣṭi (nourishment). *Oṁ, chaṁ,* O Nityaklinnā (ever moist) ! Madadravā (exuding intoxicating liquid) ! *Oṁ, Oṁ, a, ā, i, ī, u, ū, ṛ, ṝ, ḷ, ḹ, e, ai, o, au, aṁ, aḥ, ka, kha, ga, gha, ṅa, ca, cha, ja, jha, ña, ṭa, ṭha, ḍ, ḍha, ṇa, ta, tha, da, dha, na, pa, pha, ba, bha, ma, ya, ra, la, va, śa, ṣa, sa, ha, kṣa. Oṁ, chaṁ* oblations to Nityaklinnā and Madadravā, The energy of support and the lotus (should be worshipped) on the lion and the Goddess in the heart and other (limbs). *Oṁ, hrīṁ,* Gaurī (white coloured) ! The consort of Rudra (Śiva) ! Yogeśvarī (mistress of faculties) ! *Hūṁ, phaṭ* oblations.

CHAPTER THREE HUNDRED AND FOURTEEN

Mantras relating to the worship of Goddess Tvaritā

Fire-god said :

1-3. *Oṁ, hrīṁ, hrūṁ, khe, che, kṣaḥ, strīm, hrūṁ, kṣe, hrīṁ, phaṭ* obeisance to (Goddess) Tvaritā. After doing the *nyāsa* (location of the *mantra*) (Goddess) Tvaritā possessing two or eight arms should be worshipped. The energy of support and lotus (should be worshipped) in (a diagram of) a lion and the Goddess and the heart etc. (should also be worshipped). Gāyatrī (per-

1. This and the following four names denote the God of love.

sonification of the *mantra*) should be worshipped in a circle in the east (and other directions) (showing) the *praṇitā* (*mudrā*). (The Goddesses) Huṁkārā, Khecarī, Caṇḍā, Chedanī and Kṣepaṇī (should also be worshipped). Hūṁkārā, Kṣemakārī and Phaṭkārī should be worshipped at the centre. Jayā and Vijayā (should be worshipped) at the entrance. The servant (should be worshipped) in front of them.

4-10. (One should do) oblations with sesamum with (the repetition of) the *vyāhṛtis* in order to get all things. Obeisance to Ananta[1] ! Oblations. Obeisance to Kalikā ! Svadhā. Oblations to King Vāsuki. Vauṣaṭ to Śaṅkhapāla. Vaṣaṭ to Takṣaka always. Obeisance to Mahāpadma. Oblations to Karkoṭanāga *phaṭ*. Obeisance to Padma. (The diagram of) *nigrahacakra* (the magic circle that causes obstruction) should be drawn on one's clothes, or a piece of cloth or on the body, or the birch-bark (leaf) or on a slab or on staffs. The name of the *sādhya* (the object to be accomplished, namely, the enemy) (should be written) in the middle chamber and (the syllables) *oṁ, hrīṁ, kṣūṁ* on the chambers on the east and other (directions). The thorns and Kālarātrikā (should be written) in the north-east, west etc. and (lord) Yama (the lord of death) outside. (The following mystic couplet should be written on the other chambers):

Kālīnārāvamālī kālīnāmākṣamālinī
māmodetat tadomomā rakṣata sva sva bhakṣa vā
yamapāṭaṭayāmaya maṭamo ṭaṭamo ṭamā
vāmo bhūrivabhūmeyā ṭaṭarīśvaśvarī ṭaṭa.

(The syllable) *vaṁ* (should be located) outside the chamber of lord Yama and (the syllable) *taṁ* that has the potency to kill.

11-12. (The above verse should be written) with crow's quill at the cremation ground or the junction of four roads with a mixture of lamp soot, the resin of neem, marrow, blood, poison, charcoal, and piṅgaladhārā (?) and placed under a pitcher. Otherwise it should be placed in an ant-hill. The spell (placed) under a *bibhītaka* tree is capable of destroying all the enemies.

13-16. The *anugrahacakra* (a circular figure that confers

1. This and the following are the names of different serpents.

grace) should be written on a white leaf or on the *bhūrja* (bark) with shellac or saffron or red sandal. The name (of the enemy) should be written in the central chamber on the earth and the wall. (The *mantra*) *Oṁ haṁsa* and the *paṭṭiśa* (a kind of spear) should be written in the region of the west. The charm of (Goddess) Lakṣmī and Śiva and others should be written in the north-west etc. in order. (The mystic verse is):

śrīḥ sāmamomā sā śrīḥ sānau yājñe jñeyā nausā
māthā līlā lālī vāmā yājñe jñeyā nausā māyā

Śīghrā (should be worshipped) outside where the six '*līlā*' (is placed). The pitcher is also (placed) outside. Śīghrā is outside where *jñeyā* is placed. (The syllable) *raṁ* is in the different direction. The pitcher would be outside.

17. The wheel of lotus on a lotus (figure) would conquer death, convey (a person) to heaven and (give) firmness. It is the foremost appeasing rite among such rites. It confers fortune etc.

18-22. (In the wheel known as) Rudra, there should be chambers of the number of Rudras (i.e. eleven). That (*mantra*) should be written therein beginning with the syllable *oṁ* and ending with *hrūṁ phaṭ*, the first letters of the *vidyā* being written at the end. This is known as the *pratyaṅgirā* which accomplishes all the desired objects. In (a circle having) eighty-one chambers, the first letters (of the *vidyā*) (should be located) such that they would be from the beginning to the end and the name (of the enemy should be added) ending with *vaṣaṭ*. This is (known as) a different *pratyaṅgirā* (*vidyā*) which would accomplish all tasks. The *nigraha* and *anugraha* (obstruction and grace) circles should be drawn to have sixty-four chambers. This is (known as) *amṛti vidyā* (reviving). (The syllables) *krīṁ saḥ hūṁ* with the name (of the enemy) at the centre and the syllable *phaṭ* at the beginning (written) on a leaf should be encircled by three syllables of *hrīṁ*. This (charm) worn with (a mark of) a pitcher will kill all enemies and yield all things. If (this *mantra*) is repeated in the ear letter by letter or as a *daṇḍaka* (a group of letters), it would destroy poison.

CHAPTER THREE HUNDRED AND FIFTEEN

Narration of mantras relating to paralysing, captivating etc.

Fire-god said :

1. I shall describe to you (the *mantras* and acts) relating to paralysing, stupefying, captivating, ruining the enemy, neutralising the (effects of) poison and diseases and causing the death (of an enemy).

2-4. A twice-born should draw (the figure of) a tortoise of six inches (length) on a birch-bark by (the act of) *tāḍana* and then locate the *mantra* on the face and four feet. The syllable *krīṁ* should be written on the four feet, the syllable *hrīṁ* at the centre of the face, the *vidyā* (*mantras*) on the belly and (the name of) the person concerned on the back. After having encircled it with the *mālāmantras* (garland of letters), it should be placed over a brick. It should then be covered with the back of a tortoise and then charmed with the *karāla* (*mantra*).

5-8. After having worshipped the great tortoise (manifestation of Viṣṇu), (the votary) should sprinkle water on the feet (of that form). After having thought of the enemy, (the votary) should kick seven times (on the ground) with the left foot (of the toroise). It would cause paralysis to the enemy. One should assume a terrible form by having change in the complexion of the face and write the garland of *mantras*. *Oṁ* ! One who paralyses the face of the enemy ! An embodiment of desire ! One that stands with arm discharging an arrow ! *Hrīṁ pheṁ*, Phetkariṇī ! Paralyse (2[1]) the face of my enemies given by the gods ! Paralyse (2) the face of all my enemies ! *Oṁ*, *hūṁ*, *pheṁ*, Phetkāriṇī ! Oblations ! *Phaṭ* ! After having written the *mantra*, one would gain great strength at the end of its repetition. One should draw (the figure of) a tree and the trident on the right hand with the left hand. The *mantra* of lord Aghora (a form of Śiva) should then be written. One would paralyse the enemies in the battle. *Oṁ*, obeisance to the Fortunate One ! O Bhagamālinī ! Agitate (2) ! Throb ! O Nityaklinnā ! melt (2), *huṁ saḥ* ! Embodiment of the syllable *krīṁ* ! Oblations. One who wears a mask with the resin with (the repetition of) this (*mantra*) would stupefy the world.

1. The figure indicates repetition of the preceding word.

9-13a. *Oṁ, pheṁ, hūṁ, phaṭ Phetkāriṇi* ! *Hrīṁ*, burn (2), stupefy (2) the three worlds. O Guhyakālikā ! Oblations. One would captivate the king and others by making a (fore-head) mark with this (*mantra*). The dust (under the feet) of a donkey mixed with the *sūtaka*[1] fluid and the menstrual blood of a woman should be thrown on the bed (of a person) in the night. This would cause enmity. The hoof and horn of a cow, the hoof of a horse and the head of a serpent (charmed as before and) thrown into the house (of a person) would cause the ruin of the enemy. The root of the yellow *karavira* together with mustard (would be potent) to cause death. The blood of a serpent and a musk-rat together with *karavira* would also produce similar result. A lizard, bee, crab and scorpion are ground well and thrown into oil. One who anoints with that (oil) would get leprosy. *Oṁ* (obeisance) to the nine planets. Conquer (2) my enemies. Kill (2) (them). *Āṁ, soṁ, maṁ, buṁ, cuṁ, oṁ, śaṁ, vāṁ, keṁ, oṁ* oblations.

13b-14. After having worshipped (the planets) with hundreds of *arka* (flowers), this should be placed in a cremation ground. The planets should be drawn on a birch-bark or in an image for the ruin of the enemies. *Oṁ* Kuñjarī, Brahmāṇī! *Oṁ* Mañjarī, Māheśvarī ! *Oṁ* Vetālī, Kaumārī! *Oṁ* Kālī, Vaiṣṇavī ! *Oṁ* Aghorā, Vārāhī! *Oṁ* Vetālī, Indrāṇī, Urvaśī! *Oṁ* Vetālī, Caṇḍikā! *Oṁ* Jayānī, Yakṣiṇī! O Nine Mothers ! eh ! Seize (2) my foe. After having written the name of the enemy on a birch-bark, if it is worshipped in the cremation ground, (the foe) would die.

CHAPTER THREE HUNDRED AND SIXTEEN

Narration of different kinds of mantras

Fire-god said:

1-5. The syllable *hūṁ* is at the beginning. Then the letters *khe*, *ca*, *che*, and the *visarga* that is outside the group of conson-

1. The discharge at the time of the birth of a child.

ants (are added). It ends with *strīṁ, hūṁ, kṣepa* and *phaṭ*. This *vidyā* is known as subduing all things. It also destroys the poisons of serpents. *Oṁ, khe, che* should be practised to revive a person bitten by a deadly serpent. *Oṁ, hūṁ, ke, kṣaḥ* should be used to destroy poison and enemies. *Strīṁ, hūṁ, phaṭ* is (the *mantra*) to be used for conquering sins and diseases etc. *Khe, cha* is the application for removing evil obstacles. The application of *hūṁ, strīṁ, oṁ* would captivate women. The application of *khe, strīṁ, khe, cha* should be used for captivating and conquest. *Aiṁ, hrīṁ, śrīṁ, spheṁ, kaiṁ, kṣauṁ*, Bhagavatī! Ambikā! Kubjikā! *spheṁ, oṁ, bhaṁ, taṁ* subjugate. Obeisance to Aghora on the face! *Brāṁ, brāṁ, kili, kili, viccā, sphauṁ, heṁ, sphūṁ, śrauṁ, hrīṁ, aiṁ, śrīṁ*. This *vidyā* of Kubjikā is known to accomplish all the things. I shall describe to you again the *mantras* narrated by (lord) Īśa (Śiva) to (lord) Skanda.

CHAPTER THREE HUNDRED AND SEVENTEEN

The different kinds of mantras of Śiva

The Lord said:

1. (The *mantras*) of Śiva are divided into eight kinds, such as *sakala* (endowed with parts), *niṣkala* (without parts), *śūnya* (void), *kalāḍhya* (abounding in parts), *khamalaṅkṛta* (adorning the sky), *kṣapaṇa* (suppressing), *kṣaya* (destroying) and *śiva* (benevolent). The letters which lay inside and belong to (the regions of) the throat and lips (should be present in them).

2. O Guha (name of Kumāra, son of Śiva and Pārvatī)! There are eight kinds of the benevolent (*mantra*) known as *para* (supreme). The form of the word Sadāśiva is efficacious for accomplishing all things.

3-8a. (The forms) of the vowels are Amṛta, Aṁśumat, Indu, Īśvara, Ugra, Ūhaka, Ekapāda, Oja and Auṣadha. Aṁśumat (among these) is capable of subjugating. (The forms) of the letters *ka* to *kṣa* are: Kāmadeva, Śikhaṇḍī, Gaṇeśa, Kāla, Śaṅkara, Ekanetra, Dvinetra, Triśikha, Dīrghabāhuka, Ekapād, Arddhacandra, Balapa, Yoginīpriya, Śaktīśvara, Mahāgranthi, Tarpaka, Sthāṇu, Dantura, Nidhīśa, Nandī, Padma, Śākinīpriya, Mukhabimba, Bhīṣaṇa, Kṛtānta, Prāṇa, Tejasvī, Śakra, Udadhi, Śrīkaṇṭha, Siṁha, Śaśāṁka, Viśvarūpa and Narasiṁha (representing) *kṣa*.

8b-11a. (The syllable of) Viśvarūpa should be made to be pervaded by the syllables of Sūrya (Sun). After having coupled the syllable of Śaśi (Moon) with Aṁśumat, (the syllable of) Īśāna pervaded by (the syllable of) Ojas should first be raised up. (Among the above names), the third should be known as (Tat)Puruṣa, the fifth as Dakṣiṇa, the seventh as Vāmadeva, the next one as Sadyojāta and the ninth as coupled with the *rasa* (*bija*). This is known as the *brahmapañcaka* (the five brahmans).

11b-14. All the mantras begin with the syllable *oṁ* and end with (the name in) the fourth case and obeisance. (The first one is presided over by) Sadyojāta. The second one is the heart together with the subordinate one. The fourth should be known as the head known by the name Īśvara. Ūhaka should be known as the tuft endowed with Viśvarūpa. Its *mantra* is known to be the eighth. The eye is considered as the tenth. O Śikhidhvaja (Kumāra, having peacock as the banner)! The weapon is said to be the Moon known as Śiva. Obeisance, oblation, *vauṣaṭ*, *hūṁ* and *phaṭka* is the order.

15-17. I shall describe the *prāsāda mantra* (the benevolent one) relating to the heart etc. belonging to *phaṭka*. One should raise the (syllable) known as Rudra from Īśāna adorned with Aṁśu that remains above the group in the region of head pervaded by Auṣadha. It has half-crescent *nāda* (nasal sound) upwards having two dots in the middle. Viśvarūpa is at the end bent thrice. This is the *prāsāda mantra* capable of accomplishing all the things.

18-21a. After having raised the syllables of the tuft ending with the syllable *phaṭ* placed on the half crescent, it is known as Kāmadeva that flows (and is verily) the great Pāśupata weapon that destroys all evils. I have described the *prāśāda* (*mantra*) endowed with parts. I will describe (the *mantra*) without parts now. (This consists of) Auṣadha, Viśvarūpa, Rudra, orb of Sun, coupled with *nāda* of the form of half-moon, without designation and bent. The *niṣkala* (*mantra*) confers enjoyment and emancipation. It is always benevolent because it is endowed with five parts.

21b-31. (The *mantras*) that are void (consist of) Aṁśumat, Viśvarūpa and divested of Brahmāṅga (class of letters). Its form is the essence. It destroys obstacles when worshipped by boys and ignorant men. Aṁśumat coupled with Viśvarūpa and situated over the Ūhaka is the *mantra* known as *kalāḍhya* (fully endowed with parts). It is always used in the worship in the same way as the *mantra* with parts. The *khamalaṅkṛta* consists of Narasiṁha (*mantras*) situated in Kṛtānta pervading above the radiant life force, coupled with Aṁśumat and pervaded by Ūhaka above and below. It is composed of half-moon *nāda* adorned by Brahmā and Viṣṇu. The Udadhi (*mantras*) and Narasiṁha should be divided with the vowels of Sūrya. The other subsidiary rites should be done as before. The first letter is that which is known as Ojas, coupled with Aṁśumat that is to be raised. The foremost among the second letter is the Aṁśumat pervaded by Aṁśu. Similarly the Aṁśumat (pervading) the Īśvara is capable of conferring emancipation. The Ūhakas are pervaded by Aṁśu and (followed by) Varuṇa, Prāṇa and Taijasa (syllables). It is known as the fifth one. The next one is the Kṛtānta. The Aṁśumat (coupled with) Udaka and Prāṇa is raised as the seventh one. The Padma is pervaded by Indu. The Nandīśa is coupled with Ekapāda. The first one is added at the end. (That is known) as Kṣapaṇaka consisting of ten syllables. The third, fifth and seventh would number half of it. The Sadyojāta would be the ninth, the *hṛd* and other (*mantras*) (taken) from the second. The *mantras* consisting of the (above said) ten syllables should end with *phaṭ*. This *astra* (*mantra*) should be raised.

32-34. The subordinate *mantras* (in the above) should be coupled with obeisance. It is not done in any other way. From the second to the eighth are considered as the Vidyeśvaras (the lords of the *mantras*)—Ananteśa, Sūkṣma, Śivottama the third, Ekamūrti, Ekarūpa, Trimūrti the next one, Śrīkaṇṭha and Śikhaṇḍī are known to be the eight Vidyeśvaras. The ends of the *mantras* from that of Śikhaṇḍī to the end of Ananta are said to be the embodied form.

CHAPTER THREE HUNDRED AND EIGHTEEN

The mode of worshipping Gaṇapati, accomplishing all things

The Lord said :

1-2. The Viśvarūpa (syllable) should be raised and placed above the Tejas. Then the Narasiṁha and Kṛtānta are placed below one below the other. The *praṇava* (*oṁ*) should be placed below that and the Udaka below that. The Aṁśumat that remains in the Viśvamūrti, the letter of the throat and lip region and the *praṇava* (*oṁ*) (should be below that).

3. The first four letters should end with obeisance. It should then be coupled as before with the *aṅgamantras* adding also the syllables of Sūrya and Viśvarūpa, the cause.

4. The syllable *oṁ* should be raised first and the luminous form without a second one should be repeated. The Ghoraghoratara (terrible one) (should be repeated). That form should then be remembered.

5-6. After having made the *caṭa* sound twice, the (syllable) *oṁ* should be repeated. Then one has to repeat twice 'burn' and then twice '*vama*'. After having stated 'kill' twice, one should repeat *hūṁ phaṭ* at the end. This would be the *mantra* of the weapon for (lord) Aghora. I shall describe the *gāyatri* (*mantra*) (sacred to the same deity) now—"We know the true self of (lord) Maheśa. We meditate on the supreme god. May that auspicious god kindle our (mind) to that." This *gāyatri* (*mantra*) is capable of accomplishing all things.

7-14. One has to worship (lord) Gaṇa (Gaṇapati) when one sets on a journey or in battle etc. for prosperity. One has to draw (the figure of a lotus having three petals inside a triangle on a fourth part of a square place divided into twelve chambers. On its back (back of the lotus) steps and pathway (should be drawn) having (the mark of) a horse on (each) petal. There should be silken cloth for footrest together with eight lotuses having three petals. The platform should be made above that measuring a fourth part. (The figure) should have a door containing (a figure of) a lotus. The side door from the chamber should be made pale. The circle drawn with doors and side-doors would destroy obstacles. The central lotus should be red. The lotuses outside that should (also be red). The pathway should be made white. The doors (should be coloured) as one wishes. The pericarp as well as the filaments would be yellow in colour. This circle is known as destroying obstacles. (Lord) Gaṇapati should be worshipped. The first name would be that of (lord) Śiva together with Indra and others. The head is struck with Tatpuruṣa. *Oṁ* is the first (syllable) with obeisance at the end.

15. (The gods) Gaja (elephant), Gajaśīrṣa (elephant-headed), Gāṅgeya (son of Gaṅgā), Gaṇanāyaka (lord of the Gaṇas), Trirāvartta (turned round thrice), Gaganaga (one who travels in the sky), Gopati (a leader) (should be worshipped) in the first row.

16-22. Vicitrāṁśa (one possessing strange characteristics), Mahākāya (one having a big body), Lamboṣṭa (having a hanging lip), Lambakarṇaka (one having drooping ears), Lambodara (big-bellied), Mahābhāga (very fortunate one), Vikṛta (having strange appearance), Pārvatī-priya (one who is dear to Pārvatī), Bhayāvaha (frightening), Bhadra (auspicious), Bhagaṇa (the cluster of asterisms), Bhayasūdana (one that destroys fear) are the twelve (to be worshipped) on the ten rows. Devatrāsa (frightening the celestials) (should be worshipped) on the west. Mahānāda (one having a great sound), Bhāsvara (one having lustre), Vighnarāja (lord of obstacles), Gaṇādhipa (lord of the Gaṇas), Udbhaṭa (the pre-eminent one), Svanābha (self-originating), Caṇḍa (wrathful), Mahāśuṇḍa (one having a big trunk), Bhīmaka (the terrible), Manmatha (captivating the mind), Madhusūda (the destroyer of Madhu), Sundara (beautiful one), and Bhāvapuṣṭaka (one that nourishes one's thoughts) (should be worshipped). (Lord) Brahmeśvara (lord of Brahmā), Brāhma, Manovṛtti (mental attitude), Saṁlaya (well-absorbed), Laya (absorption), Dūtyapriya (fond of being a messenger), Laulya (extremely desirous), Vikarṇa (having a strange ear), Vatsala (affectionate), Kṛtānta (the destroyer) and Kāladaṇḍa (death) (should be worshipped) on the north. A sacrificial pitcher should be worshipped as before. The *mantra* should be repeated ten thousand times. Oblation should be done one tenth of that number. When the other (*mantras*) are repeated oblations should be made ten times.

After having performed the final oblation, one should do the consecration. One would accomplish everything. A person should honour the preceptor by (giving) land, cows, horse, elephant, clothes and other articles.

CHAPTER THREE HUNDRED AND NINETEEN

Mode of worshipping Vāgiśvari (Goddess of speech)

The Lord said :

1. I shall describe the worship of (Goddess) Vāgīśvarī (Goddess of speech) in a circle. The *mantra* (made up of syllable of) Ūhaka together with (that of) Kāla added with the letters (would be the *mantra* for the Goddess).

2-4. O Niṣāda (hunter) (denotes Kumāra) ! The *mantra* (for Goddess Vāgīśvarī) should be used like that of the Moon and Sun. No letter need be assigned. One should contemplate (the Goddess) as having the complexion of jasmine and moon, embodying the fifty letters[1] (of the alphabet), adorned with garlands of pearls and flowers, (holding the postures of hand) offering boons and protection and holding books and possessing three eyes. One should repeat the garland of letters from 'a' to 'kṣa' remembering as pervading (the body of the Goddess) upto the tip of the head and the ends of the shoulders.

5-10. The preceptor should make a circle for the sake of initiating (the disciple) in a *mantra*. A lotus (figure) that is good (for the worship of the Goddess) should have twelve tips divided into two parts. One should make ready the pathway and steps. There should be eight lotuses on the cross-road. The pathway and steps should be provided outside also. There should be doors in two squares. Similarly the side-doors, the construction of angular points and two strips of cloth should be done. The nine lotuses (should be) white. The pericarp of the lotus (should have) the hue of gold. The filaments should be variegat-

1. The letters *a* to *kṣa* of the Sanskrit language.

ed. The angular points should be filled with red (-coloured substance). The inner space between the lines of the sky (should be painted) black. The doors should be of the measure of the elephant of Indra. (Goddess) Sarasvatī (should be contemplated) at the centre of the (above) lotus. (Goddess) Vāgīśī (should be contemplated) on the eastern lotus. (Goddesses) Hṛllekhā, Citravāgīśī, Gāyatrī, Viśvarūpā, Śāṅkarī, Rati and Dhṛti (should also be worshipped). (The syllable) *hrīṁ* and the respective syllables (should be worshipped) in the east and other (directions). (The Goddess) should be contemplated as (Goddess) Sarasvatī. Oblations (should be done) with clarified butter from the milk of a tawny cow. One would then become a Saṁskṛta and Prākṛta poet and one who is well-versed in the science of poesy and other things.

CHAPTER THREE HUNDRED AND TWENTY

The different mystic diagrams

The Lord said :

1-5a. O Guha[1] ! I shall describe to you the Sarvatobhadraka[2] (that which confers good from all sides). A wiseman should worship the favourite Goddess of energy on the east at (the time of) the equinox. Then he should hold the thread east-west having the middle point between (the asterisms) Citrā and Svāti and mark at its centre after causing it to move gently. Two points on the north and south should be marked from its middle point. The two points should be brought in line with the middle point after having moved (the string) gently north-south. The junctions of angular points should be marked such that one would have one hundred and fifty divisions. Thus a quadrangle would be formed by causing the four lines to move gently. The auspicious Bhadra diagram should be drawn in that.

---

1. denotes Kumāra, son of Śiva and Pārvati.
2. a kind of mystical diagram.

5b-8a. (The quadrangle) should be divided into eight squares. The pathways and doorways should be made in two squares each. The cupola should be proportionate to the measure of the lotus. The excellent angular joints should be formed by turning round two squares. The lotus should be (painted) white, the pericarp yellow, the filaments variegated, the pathway red and the door having the hue of Lokeśa (Lord of the world). The angular point (should be) red. (This is the lotus to be drawn) in the case of a daily rite. Listen to me! (I shall describe the mode of drawing) a lotus for an occasional (rite).

8b-9. There are two varieties of lotus (diagrams), (the diagram) that does not touch and (the diagram) that touches, which confer enjoyment and emancipation. That which does not touch (is intended) for those who desire for release (from worldly existence). That which touches is of three (kinds)—young one, middle one and old. (These three) yield the fruits and perfection according to their respective names.

10-14. Lines should be drawn in the different directions as well as the directions in between in the place for the lotus. Five circles should be drawn (having dimensions) equal to that of the lotus. There should be nine lotuses around the pericarp in the first (circle). The second (circle) should have twentyfour pericarps. There should be a union of petals, the tip of the petal resembling the temple of an elephant. The fifth should be of the form of the sky. This is known as contiguous (type of) lotus. In the uncontinguous one, the tip of the petal should be divided into four from the bottom. After having discarded two parts, a petal should be set with one-eighth of the remaining. The petal should be anointed with the line at the union from the base. This would be *Vṛddha* class on the left and right.

15-17a. In the alternative one should whirl round from the middle of the union to form a semi-circle. The two unions and the foremost line (should be made into circles). This would form a young type of lotus. One should turn it from behind with half the measure of the union line. This lotus having pointed tip known as youthful class is capable of conferring enjoyment and emancipation. The *bāla* class of lotus is known as of two kinds—*mukta* and *vṛddha* useful in subjugating (one's enemy) etc.

from grief etc. Tear is known as the water from the eyes produced by sorrow, happiness etc. Loss of consciousness is the cessation of (the working) of the sense-organs due to fasting etc. The depression of the mind arising from indifference (to worldly things) is said to be despair. Debility (is) physical langour from mental suffering and the like from the body.

23. Indifference arises from dependence on doubt. Envy is jealousy. Intoxication (is) the infatuation of the mind arising from the use of wine etc.

24. Weariness (is) exhaustion arising from the inner body caused by excess of work. Aversion of the mind towards acts such as love etc. is said to be indolence.

25. Miserable state is due to deviation from goodness. Thought is contemplation of objects. Perplexion is said to be not finding the mode of doing (a thing).

26. Recollection would be the reflection of an enjoyed thing. Opinion (is) ascertainment of purpose brought about by knowledge of reality.

27. Bashfulness (is) certain shrinking of the mind arising from passion and the like. Fickleness would be unsteadiness. Joy is the pleasure of the mind.

28. Excitement is the distress of the soul caused by the hope of remedy. The loss of intellect in those to be done is said to be stupidity.

29. Equanimity is the elevation in wealth on the attainment of the desired end. Pride is contempt for others and attitude of supremacy of the self.

30. Impediment caused by fate and the like in respect of the desired object is despondency. An unsteady condition caused by desire when the desired end has not been gained is longing.

31. Absent-mindedness (is) immobile condition causing benumbing of the senses and the mind. Terror (is) repeated surprise in the mind (caused) by opposition and the like in war.

32. Intolerance (is) non-pacification of anger. Awakening (is) the rise of consciousness. Dissimulation is the concealment coming under the range of gesture and appearance.

33. Harshness of vehement verbal attack arising from anger is known to be fierceness. Conjecture is examination

and determination. Disease (is) the impediment of the mind and body.

34. Madness (is) incoherent utterances and the like caused by passion and the like. Tranquility (is) the cessation of passion of the mind by means of the knowledge of reality and the like.

35-38. The emotions and sentiments should be employed by poets in poetry and the like in which (the emotions of) love and the like are developed. (The means) by which they are developed is known as excitant. It is of two kinds—supporting and enhancing. The supportive excitant is that on which the group of emotions such as love subsists. It is produced through (the medium of) the hero and the like. The hero is known to be of four types—brave and noble-minded, brave and haughty, brave and sportive and brave and tranquil. (The hero is also classified as) faithful, gallant, sly and saucy (on the basis of his relationship with one heroine or more).

39-40. Comrade (Pīṭhamarda), Companion (Viṭa) and Jester (Vidūṣaka) are the three minor heroes who help the hero in love as pleasure companions. The comrade is without resource. The companion is beautiful and belongs to the same country. The jester is the provider of mirth. The heroes and heroines (are of) eight (types) (as described in verse 37).

41. According to Kauśika, (the heroine may be) one's own or belonging to another or remarried, and general but not remarried. Thus there are many types.

42. The enhancing excitants are those which excite the feelings in the subsisting excitants by (means of) different kinds of refinement.

43. The sixtyfour (fine) arts are divided into two according as they begin with action or music. Jugglery, memory, and perhaps jester and the aids to jester (are included) in these.

44-45. The ensuant is known to be only the exertion of the mind, speech, intellect and the body arising from recollection, desire, hatred and effort of the learned and caused by the excited and accomplished emotions of the supportive excitant. Moreover this is experienced and certainly arises (after love etc.) and hence defined here.

46. The exertion of mind is said to be characterised by the occupation of the mind. This is also known to be twofold as relating to men or women.

47. Those relating to men are eight—beauty, vivacity, grace, steadiness, equanimity, gallantry, magnanimity and dignity.

48. Beauty (prevails) in contempt for inferiors and emulation of superiors. (It is) heroism. (It is) the cause of dexterity and the like. Beauty occurs in mental virtue in the same way as a house becomes beautiful.

49-50. The excitants of women are said to be (of) twelve (kinds)—(primary indication of) emotion, its manifestation (a little), its decided manifestation, brilliance, loveliness, lustre, sweetness, heroism, boldness, generosity, firmness and gravity. The primary indication of emotion arises from a little of joy and the little manifestation is the sportive indication of emotion.

51-54. The exertion of speech would be the appropriateness of speech. It is indeed (of) twelve (kinds): conversation, excessive utterance, sorrowful speech, repeated speech, question and answer, evasion, sending a message, expounding, pointing out truth, description of something else, instruction and dissimulating (speech). This process is for the understanding. It is said to be the exertion of good intellect. It has three divisions, namely, diction, mode, and perseverence.

CHAPTER THREE HUNDRED AND FORTY

Description of diction and mode

Fire-god said:

1. Diction (is essential) for a good knowledge of speech. It is of four kinds—Pāñcālī, Gauḍadeśīyā, Vaidarbhī and Lāṭaja (respectively belonging to the regions Pāñcāla, Gauḍa, Vidarbha and Lāṭa).

2-4. The Pāñcālī is endowed with metaphorical expression. (It is) soft (and has) shorter compounds. The Gauḍīyā is a loose composition having long compounds and not having many metaphorical expressions. The Vaidarbhī is not a very soft composition. It is devoid of metaphorical expressions and is free from compounds. The Lāṭīyā (is) a clear composition not having too many compounds. This is also devoid of much metaphorical expressions.

5. The mode is uneven in the actions (of a drama). It has been established as fourfold—Bhāratī, Ārabhaṭī, Kauśikī and Sātvatī.

6. The diction Bhāratī is said to be known so because it was formulated by Bharata. It is predominantly verbal, (consists) generally (of actions) of men but also of women and has expressions in Prākṛta.

7-9. Bhāratī has four components: Vīthī, Prahasana and Prastāvanā of the drama and the like. The sub-divisions of Vīthī are thirteen: Udghātaka, Lapita[1], the second, Asatpralāpa, Vākśreṇī[2], Nālikā, Vipaṇa, Vyāhāra, Trimata, Chala, Avaskandita[3], Gaṇḍa, Mṛdava and Añcita[4], the thirteenth.

10. Prahasana is the speech ridiculing the ascetics and the like. Ārabhaṭī is known to be abounding in trickery, witchcraft, war and the like. (It is of the varieties) Saṅkṣiptaka, Avapāta and Vastūtthāpana.

CHAPTER THREE HUNDRED AND FORTYONE

Description of the actions and movements of the limbs

Fire-god said:

1. The exertion of the body is regarded as the particular gesture relating to the limbs and subordinate limbs and as their action. The former generally relates to women.

---

1. The amended reading is Avalagita.
2. The amended reading is Vāgveṇī.
3. The amended reading is Avasyandita.
4. The printed text wrongly reads ucita.

2-5a. It is (divided) into twelve[1]—sportiveness, playful gesture, cessation (of care in dress etc.), amorous play or movement, amorous agitation consisting of laughter, weeping, etc., involuntary expression of affection towards the lover, repulse of lover's caresses, indifference towards a beloved object (*bibboka*), that which arises from tenderness (*lalita*), affected by passion or emotion, pleasure-giving pastime and amorous sport. Sportiveness (is) the imitation of the gesture of the beloved person in a hidden abode. Playful gesture is said by good people as exhibiting some peculiarities a little. *Kilakiñcita* is the combination of laughter, weeping and the like. *Bibboka* is some kind of perturbation. *Lalita* arises from tenderness.

5b-6a. The head, hand, chest, side, loin and foot (are) successively (known) as the limbs and the creeper-like (tender) eyebrows and the like as the minor limbs.

6b-7a. (There cannot be) the use of the limbs and minor limbs without the exertion born of effort. It is straight and indirect sometimes.

7b-9a. The head is known (to move) in thirteen ways—trembling, shaking, gentle shaking (*dhūta*), violent shaking (*vidhūta*), excessive movement (*parivāhita*), agitated, tossed, graceful, contracted, turned round, raised upwards, bent downwards and rolling.

9b. The movement of the eyebrow should be known as sevenfold (such as) lowering, knitting etc.

10. The glance (is said) to be threefold as being related to the sentiment, the permanent (feeling) and the transitory (feeling). It is divided into thirtysix kinds, among which eight arise from sentiments.

11. The function of the pupil is ninefold—moving, rolling and the like. (The actions of) the nose are known to be six. (Those of) respiration are said to be nine.

12. The actions of the lower lip are of six kinds. The actions of the chin are of seven kinds. Those of the face beginning with perturbation are of six kinds. (The actions of) the neck are known as of nine kinds.

---

1. The text explains only five among these.

13-19a. The hand is employed as unfolded and folded by the character. One banner, three banners, scissor-edge, half-moon, opening up, parrot-beak, fist, pinnacle, wood-apple, club-edged (?), needle-pointed, lotus bud, snake-hood, deer-head, *kāṅgulaka*, *alapadma*, round pillow, bee, swan-mouth, swan-wing, pincers, blossom, spider and cock are the twentyfour of the unfolded hands. Those of the folded hands are thirteen—slightly folded or open pigeon, crab, *svastika*. *kaṭakavardhamāna*[1], *asaṅga*[2], *niṣadha*, swing, flower-casket, crocodile, elephant tusk, *bahistambha*[3] and *vardhamāna*.

19b-20. The chest may be of five kinds, such as a little curved and straight[4] etc. The belly is threefold—not very slender, slender[5] and full. The actions of the sides are five. The actions of the shank are also five. The action of the feet in dance and the like in a drama is known to be manifold.

CHAPTER THREE HUNDRED AND FORTYTWO

Definition of dramatic representation

Fire-god said:

1-2. Dramatic representation should be known by learned men as carrying forward the sense (of the drama). It arises in four ways resting on internal feeling, speech, limbs and bringing out (the feeling). Stupor and the like are the internal (feeling). The speech is the beginning of speech. That relating to the limbs is the exertion of the body. The internal feeling is the operation of the exertion of the intellect.

3. The employment of sentiment and the like arising from

1. The text reads *kaṭaka* and *vardhamāna*. *Cf. NS* IX. 8-10 reading these two as one.
2. *utsaṅga* (lap). *Cf. NS* IX.
3. *Cf. NS* IX. given as *avahittha* (dissemination of internal feeling).
4. The text wrongly reads *nartana*. *Cf. NS* IX.
5. The text reads *khaṇḍa* for *khalla* in *NS* X.

conceit are being described now. Independence of all kinds (of gesticulation) is meaningless without this.

4. The erotic (sentiment) is said to be twofold, namely, love in union and love in separation. Both these are again twofold, namely, concealed and manifest.

5. The erotic (sentiment) known as love in separation is fourfold—incipient love, jealous anger, sojourn abroad and pathos.

6. The other kind is different from these in four ways and has the characteristic of increased enjoyment. But it does not surpass the former.

7. It arises in men and women. Love accomplishes it. All internal emotions except the change of colour and loss of consciousness (are) in it.

8-9a. The erotic (sentiment) thrives (aided) by piety, wealth, pleasure and emancipation on particular supportive (excitants) and (becomes) uninterrupted by their peculiarities. The erotic (sentiment) should be known as twofold consisting (of the mode) of speech and the act of decoration.

9b-11a. The comic (sentiment) is said to be fourfold[1]—*smita*, smile in which the teeth are not visible, *hasita*, in which the tips of the teeth are slightly visible and the eyes are dilated, *vihasita*, that is sonorous, *upahasita*, that is crooked[2], *apahasita*[3], that is with sound and *atihasita*, that is without sound.

11b-12. The sentiment known as pathos is of three kinds—arising from violation of virtue and originating from loss of wealth. While sorrow is the permanent (emotion), pleasure is considered the dominant (emotion) of the former two (sentiments of erotic and comic).

13. The sentiment of wrath is threefold—by means of limbs, dress and speech. Its accomplishing factors are anger, perspiration, horripilation and trembling.

14. The heroic (sentiment) is threefold—heroic in libera-

1. The *purāṇa* mentions only four divisions but defines six as in *NS* VI. 51-52.

2. The *purāṇa* wrongly reads *jihva* instead of *jihma*.

3. Wrongly printed as *pāpahasita*.

lity, heroic in virtue and heroic in battle. Enthusiasm is said to be the cause of its accomplishment.

15. The sentiment called terror which arises at the commencement (of an action), follows the heroic (sentiment) only. Fear is its accomplishing factor.

16-17a. (The sentiment of) disgust is said to be twofold—agitating and distressing. The agitating (type) would arise on account of stink[1] and the like and the distressing (type) by means of blood and the like. Aversion gives rise to it and the *sāttvika* element recedes in it.

17b-19a. The elements which add beauty to poetic compositions are said to be the embellishments. These embellishments are threefold—(tending to embellish) word, meaning and both. Rhetoricians declare those which are capable of embellishing word by means of proficiency and the like as embellisments of word.

19b-21. The nine, namely, *chāyā*, *mudrā*, *ukti*, *yukti*, *gumphanā*, *vākovākya*, *anuprāsa*, *citra* and *duṣkara* should be known as the embellishments of words because of the absence of commixture. There, *chāyā* (reflection) is the imitation of the utterance of others. It is again fourfold—imitation of popular saying, clever speech, childish utterance and intoxicated raving[2] (*matta*).

22. The proverb (*ābhāṇaka*) is a popular saying and they are common to all. That which follows the proverb is said to be the *lokokticchāyā* by the wisemen.

23. The clever are the cultured. Expert knowledge of fine arts is culture. That which delineates it is said to be the *Chekoktichāyā* by poets.

24. All understand childish speech as the utterance of the ignorant. The imitation of the childish speech hence merely imitates this kind of speech.

25. The vulgar speech of the intoxicated is similarly (composed of) confused letters. That which is similar to this is called *mattoktichāyā* which even surpasses the intoxicated speech.

26. That which exhibits the power of the poet in its particular purpose (is called) *mudrā* because it affords pleasure. This is also (known as) repose in our opinion.

1. Text wrongly reads *pluti* instead of *pūti*.
2. The textual reading is wrong.

27. That is said to be *ukti* (expression) in which some reasonable sense pleases the heart of good people because of some precept relating to the affairs of the world.

28. *Ukti* (expression) is sixfold—injunction and prohibition, restricted and unrestricted, and alternative and exclusive.

29-30. Combination is termed so by the wisemen because of its being made for connecting the two, word and sense, which are mutually unconnected. It is sixfold—inflected word, meaning of inflected word, sentence, meaning of sentence, context and amplification.

31. Stringing is the practice of composition within the scope of a word, meaning and their order. It is threefold based on imitation of word, succession of meaning and regular arrangement.

32-33. *Vākovākya* is a sentence containing question and answer. It is twofold on the basis of the classification as straight speech and crooked speech. The first of these is natural speech. It would be of two kinds according as it is preceded by a question or not. But, crooked speech is intonation or occurs by indirect speech. Hence it is twofold.

CHAPTER THREE HUNDRED AND FORTYTHREE

Definition of the embellishment of words

Fire-god said:

1-2. Alliteration is the repetition of letters in (inflected) word and sentence. The class of letters of repetition is twofold—single letter and many letters. Five kinds of mode are produced from the repetition of a single letter—sweet, soft, mature, graceful and harsh.

3-4. The consonant letters of the sweet (*madhurāvṛtti*) should occur below the last letters of the (respective) consonant classes: the letters *ra* and *ṇa* should be separated by short vowels, coupled with letter *na* and should be joined with hard aspirates and sibilants. The varga-varṇas (letters *ka*, *ca*, *ṭa*, *ta* and *pa*) should not be repeated in more than five ways. They are not to be followed by short syllables.

5. The soft one abounds in (the use of) *ra*[1] and *la*. In the mature one, (the letters) *pa*, *ṇa* and (other) consonants are joined with (the letter) *ra* at the head. But neither the cerebral nor the fifth (letters of the consonants are joined).

6-10a. The remaining (letters) would be present in the graceful one. The harsh one is said to be that in which the sibilants are joined with the very same letters. There is abundant repetition of vowels excepting the letter *a*. The *anusvāra* and *vissarga* are also constant in harshness. The sibilants are combined with *ra*. (The letters) *a* and *ha* are also abundantly joined for harshness. (They are also joined with) the semi-vowels, *na* and *ma*[2]. Otherwise, if the conjunct is a hindrance, a hard consonant (is used) as the first letter for harshness. But the fifth one is not favoured. The harsh one is employed in censure and imitation of words.

10b-11a. *Karṇāṭi*, *Kauntali*, *Kaunti*, *Vāmanāsikā*[3], *Drāvaṇi*[4] and *Mādhavi*[5] (are) respectively (characterised) by the semivowels and sibilants.

11b-17. That which has repetition of many letters conveying different meanings is *yamaka*. It is of two kinds—contiguous and non-contiguous. The contiguous one (has the letters) in close succession. The non-continguous one (has the letters repeated) with intervals. These two become fourfold on account of two kinds of differences in the position (of the letters) and the (metrical) foot. (The first kind is) of seven varieties according (as *yamaka* occurs) in one, two and three at the beginning, beginning of the foot, in the middle and at the end (of the metrical feet). The other kind occurs in six ways when the commencement of one, two or three metrical feet is similar in each successive foot with reference to each preceding one. The third (variety)

1. The printed text reads *va*.
2. The reading *antasthābhinnamābhyāñca* in the printed text has been changed to *antasthābhirnamābhyāñca*.
3. The correct reading seems to be *Vānavāsikā*.
4. Obviously wrong reading for *Drāviḍī*.
5. Obviously wrong reading for *Māthurī*.

is threefold (according as *yamaka*) occurs at the beginning, in the middle and at the end of (the metrical) foot. Other *yamakas* are many. The prominent ten are : *pādāntayamaka*, *kāñciyamaka*, *saṁsargayamaka*[1], *vikrāntayamaka*, *pādādiyamaka*, *āmreḍita*, *caturvyavasita* and *mālāyamaka*.

18. The repetition of a word is twofold according as it is independent or dependent on others. Thus men know the repetition of words which have different purposes.

19. The compounded (repetition) arises from the compounding of two repeated words. The uncompounded (repetition) arises from the absence of compounding between the two words from dissolving the compounds in one part of the metrical foot.

20. The repetition of a sentence is said to be possible in this way. Alliteration is thus the foremost among the embellishments by virtue of its fitness though being short in the middle.

21. That alliteration, where the similarity of sound is enjoyed by means of any *vṛtti* (mode), having uninterrupted sequence of words, is charming.

22-23a. *Citra* (picturesque *Kāvya*) is said to be a composition of words exciting curiosity in a learned assembly. It is of seven different varieties—*Praśna*, *Prahelikā*, *Gupta*, *Cyuta*, *Datta*, *Cyuta* and *Datta* combined and *Samasyā* arising from union of different meanings.

23b-24. That is *Praśna* (query) in which a reply is given having similar arrangement of letters. It is twofold according to the difference of reply to the question asked by one or two. The query asked by one, again, is indeed twofold according as it is compounded or uncompounded.

25-26a. *Prahelikā* (riddle) consists of words having even two meanings concealed. It has two kinds—verbal and meaningful. The meaningful arises from the comprehension of meaning and the verbal from the knowledge of word. *Prahelikā* is said to be of six kinds.

26b-27a. That is *Gupta* (concealed) in which even a part of a sentence remains concealed and the resultant meaning for which there is expectancy by that part is not wholly true. It (is) also (called) *Gūḍha* (covert).

1. Obviously wrong reading for *samudgayamaka*.

27b-28. Where there is the appearance of a different sense by means of dropping a part of a sentence etc. and there is expectancy raised by that part, it is known as *Cyuta* (dropped). It is fourfold arising from the dropping of the vowel, consonant, *bindu* (*anusvāra*) and *visarga*.

29. That is said to be *Datta* (added) in which a second sense is suggested, even though a part of the sentence is given. Its varieties are considered to be the same as in the previous by means of vowels and the like.

30. It is said to be *Cyutadatta* (dropped and added) in which there arises a different sense even when another letter is inserted in the place of the removed syllable.

31. That is *Samasyā* (union) in which one verse involves good puns and is composed of various verse fragments. (It arises) from the blending of the composition of others and of one's own.

32-33a. *Duṣkara* (difficult) is that (which is) constructed with very great difficulty, indicating poet's ability and producing great delight in clever persons in spite of tastelessness. It is threefold from *niyama* (restraint), *vidarbha*[1] (variation) and *bandha* (structure).

33b-34a. *Niyama* (restraint) is considered to be the fulfilment of promise of the poet, who is delighted for his composition. It is threefold according as it (is regulated) by position, vowel and consonant.

34b-35a. *Vikalpa* (variation) is so called from the reverse and natural order (of letters). The reverse and natural order arises from word as well as sense.

35b-37a. The skillful composition (of different kinds) of the forms of various well-known objects by means of arrangement of letters repeated in many ways is said to be *bandha* (structure). It is (divided into) eight (varieties)—*Gomūtrikā*, *Ardhabhramaṇa*, *Sarvatobhadra*, *Ambuja*, *Cakra*, *Cakrābjaka*, *Daṇḍa* and *Muraja*.

37b-39a. (*Gomūtrikā*) would have similar alternate syllables in each metrical foot in each half (of a verse). *Gomū-*

1. Obviously *vikalpa*. See verse 34b.

trikā (zigzagging like the cow's urine) is twofold—the first kind is said to be *Aśvapada* (horse foot) by others. The last kind of *Gomūtrikā* is also called *Dhenu* (cow) and *Jālabandha* (net structure). An arrangement of these is made by two halves and by half metrical feet.

39b-47. That is indeed *Sarvatobhadra* (good in every direction) where (i) the letters (are arranged) one below the other in successive order, (ii) the letters are arranged one below the other up to the fourth feet, and (iii) (the letters are arranged) from the fourth foot onwards the half foot in the reverse order. It is threefold—*Sarasiruha* (lotus), *Catuṣpatra* (four-petalled) and *Vighna*, both of which are four-petalled. The uppermost (letters) of the first foot are the letters of the three feet. They occur indeed at the end of all feet. The last two letters of the preceding foot are at the beginning of the succeeding foot in the reverse order. The last two letters of the last foot (are in the same order) at the beginning of the first foot. This would be in (the lotus of) four petals. But there would be three letters in the lotus of eight petals. On the other hand, it is alternate, if it is a single letter, in (the lotus of) sixteen petals. A series of letters in the form of the petals should be drawn above the pericarp in the lotus of four petals and then made to enter the pericarp. One letter should be written in the pericarp and letters two at a time in the cardinal and intermediate (points) in the lotus of eight petals. The entrance and exit (of letters) should be made in the cardinal (points). The insertion of similar syllables (is done) in the middle of dissimilar letters occurring in the rows of petals on all sides in the lotus of sixteen petals.

48-52. *Cakra* (wheel) is twofold—consisting of four spokes and six spokes. The first one among these has the first and fifth letters in the quarter of the first half as similar. The fourth and eighth letters of the odd and even foot are in order in its northern, eastern, southern and western[1] spokes. The four halves of the (two) feet should be in the nave. Its first letter should be taken as far as the last spoke, the remaining two feet (being)

1. The text is wrong. It has been corrected as *tasyodakprāgavākpratyagareṣu*

in the circumference. It is said to be the *Bṛhat-cakra* (big wheel), if the third letter at the end of the fourth foot and the first two letters are similar, if the tenth letters of the three feet are similar, if there are six letters at its beginning and end and if (a letter) is separated by two letters in the last foot.

53-54. (The two) feet are written one by one gradually in the two front spokes. But the tenth letter should be drawn in the nave and the fourth foot in the circumference. The first, last and tenth letters of the verse are similar. The first and the last (letters) of the two even feet (are also similar). The first, fourth and fifth letters of the first and fourth feet are similar.

55-58. If the third (foot) is produced by reversing the second and the petals are arranged, it is the *Daṇḍa* (staff). (It is known as) *Cakrābjaka* (lotus-wheel), if the second and seventh (letters) are similar in the first petal of a composition, (if) the succeeding two petals are similar by the two second (letters in each), (if) the second, sixth, fourth and fifth letters are similar in the two halves, (if) the first and the last feet, the seventh letters of the extreme halves are also similar. Then one should arrange the fourth and fifth similar (letters) in order. Similarly the two fourth (similar letters) of the *krama* feet at the end of the petals should be arranged.[1]

59-61. The first and the last of the two halves are similar in *Muraja* (drum). The letter occurs in the half-foot according to the natural or reverse (order). *Muraja* (drum) shape is obtained thus. The last is set in such a way that the fourth becomes the first*

62. The second (variety of) *Cakra* (circle) is accomplished with *Śārdūlavikriḍita*.[2] The *Gomūtrikā* (*bandha*) (is composed) in all the metres. But other *bandhas* (are set) in *Anuṣṭubh*[3].

63. If the names of the poet and the poetic composition are not found in these, friends become delighted and enemies also do not feel depressed.

64-65. The arrow, bow, sky, sword, club, lance, meeting

---

1. This line is not intelligible.

*Verses 60-61 are cryptic and the idea conveyed is not clear.

2. Metre consisting of *ma, sa, ja, sa, ta, ta* (*gaṇas*) and *ga*.

3. Consisting of eight syllables.

place of two, three or four[1] roads, thunderbolt, mace, goad, chariotwheel, food of the elephant, pond and knife are (the different) *bandhas* (patterns in which verses are composed). Others (*bandhas*) should be known by the wisemen similarly.

CHAPTER THREE HUNDRED AND FORTYFOUR

Description of the embellishment of sense

Fire-god said :

1-2a. The embellishment of sense is said to be the beautifying of senses. Even the beauty of words is not charming without that. The goddess of speech is just like a widow without the embellishment of sense.

2b-3a. It is of eight kinds—*svarūpam* (natural form), *sādṛśyam* (similarity), *utprekṣā* (fancy), *atiśaya* (exaggeration), *vibhāvanā* (imagination), *virodha* (contradiction), *hetu* (cause) and *samam* (evenness).

3b-4. The very nature of things is said to be the natural form. It is said to be twofold such as, innate and adventitious. The innate (is) natural and the adventitious is occasional.

5. Similarity is (the presence of) common attributes. It is indeed fourfold : *Upamā* (simile), *Rūpakam* (metaphor), S*ahokti* (description of the common action of two different objects as coexisting) and *Arthāntaranyāsa* (corroboration).

6-9a. It is named as *Upamā* (simile), in which, there exists a standard of comparison and a subject of comparison. The course of affairs proceeds by taking even a slight identity and the separate entity exists although possessing internal similitude. It is of two kinds—by compounding or not compounding the counter-parts (of comparison). The compounded (arises) from the compounding of the correlated expression and the latter is otherwise. The compounded is threefold—by (the compound

1. The reading *dvicatuṣka* seems to have sense instead of *dvicaturtha* in the text.

ing of) the word indicative of simile, (of) the word (expressive) of the subject of comparison and (of) both of these. The last one is of three kinds.

9b. Eighteen kinds of simile are distinguished.

10. The *Dharma* (attribute) and *Vastu* (object) *-upamā* is that where the common attribute is expressed or implied, (depending) on the prominence of *dharma* (attribute) or *vastu* (object).

11-12. Where the two (objects) having the (common) attribute are compared reciprocally, it would be *Parasparopamā* (mutual simile). When their (comparison) is reversal of what is well known, it would be *Viparītopamā* (reversed simile). *Niyamopamā* (restrictive simile) is that in which (the resemblance) is restricted (to one excluding others). *Aniyamopamā* (unrestrictive simile) would be from (the resemblance found) in others as well.

13-14. *Samuccayopamā* (cumulative simile) consists of the mention of multitude of other attributes. When difference is indicated in spite of similarity of many attributes, it is (known as) *Vyatirekopamā* (simile of contrast), because distinction is spoken of. It is the *Bahūpamā* (multiple simile) in which there is comparison with many similar (objects).

15. When the attributes are different for each standard of comparison it is indeed *Mālopamā* (garland of simile). If comparison is made by modifying the standard of comparison, (it is known as) *Vikriyopamā* (simile of modification).

16. That is well known as the *Adbhutopamā* (hypothetical simile) in which comparison is made by the poet by superimposing something non-existent in all the three worlds on the standard of comparison.

17. It is *Mohopamā* (illusive simile) in which, the subject of comparison is declared as identical with the standard of comparison, after imposing the standard of comparison on the subject of comparison. (It has) a mistaken statement.

18. *Saṁśayopamā* (simile by doubt) (arises) from the uncertainty of the real nature of both the entities having common attributes. *Niścayopamā* (determinative simile) (arises) from determining the subject of comparison after having doubted it.

19. *Vākyārthopamā* (simile of the sense of the sentence) arises from a comparison of verily the meaning of the sentences. *Asādhāraṇopamā* (absolute simile), (which is) extraordinary, (occurs) when there is a comparison of a thing with itself.

20. When a subject of comparison is (a standard of comparison) of another it is considered as *Anyasyopamā* (simile of another). It is (known as) *Gamanopamā*[1] (simile of succession) when the subject of comparison of a thing becomes the standard of comparison of another in regular succession.

21. *Upamā* (simile) is again known to be of five kinds : praise, censure, fancied, similar and little similar.

22-23a. It is known by the name *Rūpaka* (metaphor), in which the subject of comparison is identified with the standard of comparison after the perception of the similarity of attributes. Or, *Rūpaka* is indeed *Upamā* itself in which the difference (between the standard and subject of comparison) is concealed.

23b. *Sahokti* (connected description) (arises) from the description (of objects) having similar attributes as being simultaneous.

24a. *Arthāntaranyāsa* (corroboration) arises when there is a posterior similarity (of a preceding statement to the succeeding one).

24b-25a. It is said to be *Utprekṣā* (poetic fancy) where the condition of a sentient being or otherwise, which occurs in one way, is conceived (as occurring) differently.

25b-26a. It is named as *Atiśayokti* (hyperbole) wherein the attribute of an object, that has passed beyond ordinary limits, is described. It is twofold on the basis of possibility and impossibility.

26b-27a. That is said to be *Viseṣokti* (special utterance) where the imperfection in the quality, genus, action and the like (of an object) are perceived just for the purpose of showing (its) speciality.

27b-28a. That is *Vibhāvanā* (presumption) where a different cause or naturalness is presumed excluding a well known cause.

1. The printed text wrongly reads *Gaganopamā*.

28b-29a. It is said to be *Virodha* (contradiction) where there is realisation, by adjustment, of congruity between two incongruous things, with a previous contradiction.

29b-32. *Hetu* (cause) is that which accomplishes the object desired to be accomplished. It is produced in two (ways) such as *kāraka* (efficient) and *jñāpaka* (indicative). The efficient cause occurs before and (the other) after the production of an effect. These two kinds known as the precedent and antecedent arise from the controlling relation of cause and effect or identity. There is difference in the indicative one such as the perception of a flooding river. The rule of inseparable connection arises from the perception of inseparable connection.

CHAPTER THREE HUNDRED AND FORTYFIVE

The embellishments of sound and sense

Fire-god said :

1. An embellishment of both sound and sense adorns the two simultaneously just as a necklace laid in one place (adorns both) the breast and neck of a woman.

2. Six varieties of it are explicitly in existence, namely, *Praśasti*, *Kānti*, *Aucitya*, *Saṅkṣepa*, *Yāvadarthatā* and *Abhivyakti*.

3-4a. *Praśaṣti* (eulogy) (is) skillful speech (employed) for the act of melting the subtle (heart) as if it is subservient. It is of two kinds on account of the distinction as *Premokti* and *Stuti*. A friendly speech and a panegyric are the synonyms of *Premokti* and *Stuti* (respectively).

4b-5a. *Kānti* (loveliness) (is) the fitness of the expressed (sense) and the expressive (word) agreeable to all the minds. (In that) the diction is befitting the theme and the mode to the sentiment.

5b. The propriety arises from strong and soft compositions.

6. *Saṅkṣepa* (brevity) (is) the comprehension of many meanings by means of few expressive words. *Yāvadarthatā*

(correspondence) is neither deficiency nor excess of the word and the theme respectively.

7-9a. *Abhivyakti* (manifestation) (is) explicitness. It has also two (sub) divisions, *Śruti* and *Ākṣepa*. *Śruti* (direct hearing) is the word that gives up its own meaning. It is of two kinds—*Naimittiki* (occasional) and *Pāribhāṣiki* (technical). Technicality is convention. Hence arises the Technical. (The two) are again each divided as *Mukhyā* (primary) and *Aupacāriki* (metaphorical).

9b-10a. That is Metaphorical by which a word whose function deviates from its own primary sense expresses, for certain reason, a sense which is not primary.

10b-12a. It is Indicatory and Qualitative by association with indication and qualities (respectively). Indication is said to be the apprehension (of a secondary sense) always associated with the expressed sense. Indication is regarded as fivefold arising from connection with the primary sense, proximity, cohesion, contrariety and association through action.

12b-13. The Qualitative (is) endless in view of the endlessness of qualities in accordance with the desire of the speaker. It is known here as *Samādhi* (transference) in which the attribute of one object is transferred to another by a person complying with worldly limits.

14-16. That is *Ākṣepa* (interdiction), on account of which the vital essence not available from direct hearing (of the word) becomes manifest. It is also (known as) *Dhvani* (suggestion), since it is implied by suggestion by means of word and sense, where the (suggested) sense (appears) by subordinating[1] its own (expressed sense). That is said to be *Ākṣepa* (interdiction) where there is an apparent denial of the desired sense in order to convey something special.[2] Again, this (is known as) *Aprastutastotra*[3] (indirect praise) where there is a praise of another object deviating from the object on hand.

17. Because of brevity of expression that is termed by the wise as *Samāsokti* (brevity of speech), where another object

1. The reading is taken as *upasarjanam* instead of *upārjanam*.
2. The reading should be *viśeṣa* instead of *viśeṣo*.
3. The textual reading *atra stutam stotram* is obviously incorrect.

having common characteristics is suggested, when one object is described.

18. *Apahnuti* (concealment) (consists of) conveying another sense by concealing something. That is *Paryāyokta* (periphrasis) which is stated in a different way. Hence *Dhvani* (suggestion) is, indeed, *the name* of any one of these.

CHAPTER THREE HUNDRED AND FORTYSIX

Investigation into poetic excellences

Fire-god said :

1. Peotry, even though embellished, does not produce pleasure, if it is devoid of *guṇas* (excellences). A necklace would only be burdensome to women, if their bodies are not beautiful.

2. It cannot be said that excellence would only be the absence of defect.[1] Excellences such as *Śleṣa* (coalescence) and the like and defects scuh as *Gūḍhārtha* (obscurity of sense) and the like have been distinguished from one another.

3. An excellence is that which confers great charm to poetry. It exists in two forms such as general and particular.

4. That which is common to all[2] is considered to be the general. The general (excellence) is threefold relating to word, sense and both.

5-6a. The excellence (of word) is that which relates to the word, the body of the poetry[3]. The excellences of the word are sevenfold, namely, *Śleṣa* (coalescence), *Lālitya* (smoothness), *Gāmbhirya* (depth), *Saukumārya* (softness), *Udāratā* (richness of expression), *Sati* (purity) and *Yaugiki* (derivative).

6b. That is said to be Coalescence in which there is a closely coalesced arrangement of words.

---

1. The reading *doṣo bhāva* has been corrected as *doṣābhāva*.
2. Probably the Ritis.
3. The reading *kāvyaśarīram* is better than *kāvyaṁ śarīraṁ*.

7. Smoothness is declared as that in which a letter that is already combined in the words by means of (substitution such as) *guṇa*, *ādeśa* and the like is never euphonically combined.

8. The wise name it as Depth which is a composition chiselled by special characteristics and which contains elevated words; others (name) the same as *Suśabdatā* (grammatical correctness).

9. Softness consists of words mostly of unharsh letters. Elevatedness consists of elevated words and is endowed with praiseworthy epithets.

10. Splendidness (*Ojas*) (is) abundance of compounds. It is the life of prose etc.[1] From the Highest Being to a clump of grass, manliness (comes) by *ojas* alone.

11-12. That is said to be the Excellence of Sense[2] which brings out the excellence of a described object by whichsoever word. There are six varieties of it, viz., *Mādhurya* (tranquility), *Saṁvidhāna* (contrivance), *Komalatvaṁ* (softness), *Udāratā* (elegance), *Prauḍhi* (maturity) and *Sāmayikatva* (being conventional).

13. The gravity of appearance even in anger (and) deep state of composure is Tranquility. Contrivance (consists of) the effort for the accomplishment of an expected object.

14. An arrangement of words free from rigidity appearing after setting aside laxity (of structure) is (known as) Softness.

15. The excessive gracefulness of intention which indicates the characteristic of the disposition of being aimed at explicitly is the Elegance of *Guṇa*.

16. That is declared Maturity in which there are mature reasonings impregnated with logical reasonings bringing about accomplishment of what is intended.

17. The apprehension of the sense in the demonstrated conclusion[3] of something independent or dependent (is known as) 'Being Conventional'.

---

1. The text wrongly reads as *padya*.
2. *arthaguṇa* seems to be better than the reading *artho guṇa*.
3. The reading *rāddhāntaḥ samayo mataḥ* seems to be better than *bāhyāntaḥ samayogataḥ* of the printed text.

18-19a. That which embellishes both word and sense is known by the name 'the Excellence of Both'. *Prasāda* (lucidity), *Saubhāgya* (loveliness), *Yathāsaṅkhya* (relative enumeration), *Praśastatā* (praiseworthiness), *Pāka* (ripeness) and *Rāga* (tint) are its six (varieties) divulged in their manifoldness by the wise.

19b-20. Lucidity is glorified as consisting of words possessing very well-known sense. That which, when expressed, suggests some eminent attribute, is declared by the wise as *Saubhāgya* (loveliness) or *Udāratva* (elegance).

21-22a. *Yathāsaṅkhya* (is) Relative Enumeration extended to similar things. Praiseworthiness is the description of even a terrible object by means of a word not terrible, when there is an occasion.

22b-23. A certain high maturity is said to be Ripeness. It is of four kinds, viz., as the ripeness of grape and that of coconut water etc. That is indeed the ripeness of grape in which there is sweetness both at the beginning and the end.

24-25. It is glorified as Tint which is a special characteristic for the purpose of poetic composition. It excels even the natural grace (when) put to constant practice. It is again of three varieties : yellow, saffron and indigo. That which is within the range of its own characteristics is to be recognised as the particular (Excellence).

CHAPTER THREE HUNDRED AND FORTYSEVEN

Investigation into poetic blemishes

Fire-god said:

1. Blemish causes distaste in the refined men. It is sevenfold as applied to one, two and three of the speaker, the denoter and the denoted.

2-3. The speaker is certainly the poet therein. He is also known to be fourfold: suspicious, insolent, ignorant and learned. The denoter is that which affects the meaning on the ground (for employment) and technicality. Its subdivisions are two: word and sentence. The characteristics of both have been stated.

4. Grammatical incorrectness and reconditeness are the only two defects of word. Wisemen know grammatical incorrectness as repugnance to the science of word.

5-6a. Reconditeness is said to be the non-employment by the well-versed. It is fivefold: *Chāndasatva* (Vedic usage), *Avispaṣṭatva* (lack of clarity), *Kaṣṭatva* (unpleasantness), *Asāmayikatva* (not being conventional) and *Grāmyatva* (vulgarity).

6b-9. *Chāndasatva* is that which is not found in the spoken language. Lack of clarity arises from lack of understanding. Obscurity of meaning, Perversion of meaning and Ambiguity are varieties of Lack of clarity. It is known as obscurity of meaning in which the sense is understood with difficulty. Perversion of meaning again is wrong perception of the meaning of a word other than that intended. Non-conformity to established meaning and Incapability (of expressing the intended meaning) approach this only. Ambiguity is said to be the doubtful nature of the expressed (meaning).

10-11a. Without causing distress to good people, faultiness attaches to unpleasantness which comprises difficult pronunciation. Not being conventional consists of deviation from convention. The sages named it *Neyā*.

11b-12. Vulgarity is the damaging apprehension of a low meaning. It is threefold: arising from the expression of an intended vulgar sense, recollection (of the same) and from close resemblance (of an expression) with the word expressive (of that sense).

13. Defect of meaning is twofold: general and particular. The blemish that relates to many is said to be the general.

14. The general (impurities) are five, namely, *Kriyābhraṁśa* (dropping of the verb), *Kārakabhraṁśa* (dropping of the case-endings), *Visandhi* (lack of euphonic combination), *Punaruktatā* (tautology) and *Vyastasambandhatā* (confused connection).

15. The dropping of the verb is the absence of the verb. Dropping of the case-endings again is the absence of cases begin-

ning with the subject. Lack of euphonic combination is the deficiency of the same.

16. It is twofold: deficient euphonic combination or repugnant. The repugnance of euphonic combination (arises) from difficulty in reading or from the appearance of a different sense.

17-18. The continued repetition of an expression is Tautology. It is also twofold: repetition of sense and repetition of word. The repetition of sense is also twofold: by making use of a chosen word and by means of a different word. In the repetition of a word, a word is repeated and not the sense.

19-21. The confused connection (is) improper connection that arises from the intervention (of a word). It is, indeed, threefold—arising from the implication of a different connection, from the occurrence of a different connection and in the absence of both of them, from internal intervention. Each one of these is, again, twofold by means of the intervention of a word or a sentence. Of the word and the sentence, the meaning[1] is what is expressed, because it is intended to be conveyed. The expressed is divided into two, viz. already-developed or yet-to-be-developed.

22-23. The incapability of the cause is the state of causing obstacle to the intended. (It occurs in the following forms): inconclusiveness, contrariety, absence of invariable concomitance, being liable for a valid opposite argument, union of untimely reason, non-existence in the subject, non-existence in similar instance and existence in contrary instance.

24. The eleven kinds of meaninglessness do not become painful to those who are competent in poetry. They do not become defects in difficult compositions.

25. Obscurity of meaning does not make the knowers of defects in difficult compositions feel distress. Vulgarity does not annoy by being admitted by people (in general) and in technical works.

26. There is no blemish in the dropping of the verb because (the ellipsis) of the verb could be supplied. The dropping of

1. The correct reading is *vācyamartho*.

the case (becomes possible) when the case is supplied by means of implication.

27. Non-occurrence of euphonic combination does not affect in the (case of a) *pragṛhya*[1] (vowel). Absence of disagreeable euphonic combination that arises from difficulty in reading does not become unpleasant in harsh utterances and the like.

28-29a. The repetition of a word and confused connection are good in alliteration. It is not a defect in understanding the sense. It is also not tarnished by (the defects) such as the inversion of order and the like of the case ending, number and gender. There is no distress for the wise in these.

29b. There is difference in number between the standard of comparison and the object of comparison there.

30-33. The right practice of the poets is glorified as the (poetic) convention, where there is (comparison) of many with one and many with many, which is good. It is twofold: general and particular, similar to excellence. That which is well known from the absence of dispute among famous knowers of established truth is considered as the general convention of poets. According as all the knowers of truth or only a few agree faultlessly, the general is twofold. The other (namely, the particular), arises from defective doctrine, such as the error of some people.

34-35a. Some sage has the knowledge of reasoning. Some (has) transitory (consciousness) of the created beings. Some (has) self-manifestation[2] of knowledge. Similarly, there is grossness of known objects and uncertainty of words for the Arhats (Jains).

35b-36a. The Śaivas (devotees of Śiva), Vaiṣṇavas (devotees of Viṣṇu), Sauras (devotees of Sun god), who know the established truth, opine that Brahman is the cause of the world. (The cause is associated) with Pradhāna (Primordial) for the Sāṅkhyas.[3]

36b-40. It is said to be the particular, in this world of speech, that people moving together and perceiving mutually,

1. That which is not governed by the rules of *sandhi* or euphony and is permitted to be written and pronounced separately.

2. The reading *svaprakāśatā* seems to be better.

3. The followers of the Sāṅkhya philosophy, promulgated by Sage Kapila.

fasten upon. This being divided, is also known as twofold, according as being accepted as unreal and being non-accepted as real. That which gets affected by the means of knowledge such as perception and the like, is known as the unreal. That is to be accepted by the poet as the manifestation of knowledge. That alone which accomplishes an action with purpose, is (taken to be) the highest truth, out of ignorance. Brahman alone is the real, the highest truth, from knowledge. (Lord) Viṣṇu is the cause of creation and the like. He is embodied of words and embellishments. Knowledge is Parā (superior) and Aparā (inferior). One is released from birth by knowing it.

CHAPTER THREE HUNDRED AND FORTYEIGHT

List of mono-syllabic words

Fire-god said:

1-2. I shall describe the mono-syllabic (words) ending with the letters (of the alphabet). (The letter) "*a*" (denotes) (lord) Viṣṇu and negation. '*Ā*' (means) Brahmā, a sentence as well as a boundary. '*Ā*', when used as an interjection would also be (an expression of) anger and affliction. '*I*' (signifies) (God of) love. '*Ī*' (denotes) Rati (the wife of God of love) and Lakṣmī (Goddess of wealth and consort of Lord Viṣṇu). '*U*' (signifies) (lord) Śiva (and) '*Ū*', the demons and others.

3. '*Ṛ*' (denotes) a word and '*ṝ*', (the deity) Aditi (the mother of Āditya). (The letters) *ḷ* and *ḹ* (respectively) (denote) Diti (the mother of the demons) and Guha (son of Śiva and Pārvatī). '*E*' (denotes) the goddess and '*ai*' would mean Yoginī (female attendant of the Goddess). '*O*' (signifies) Brahmā and '*au*', Maheśvara (Lord Śiva).

4-5. '*Aṁ*' (denotes) the God of love and '*aḥ*' a commendable thing. '*Ka*' (stands for) Brahmā and others (and) '*ku*' contemptible thing. (The letter) '*khaṁ*' signifies void, the senses and a sword. A Gandharva and (lord) Vināyaka (lord of obstacles) (are denoted by the letter) '*gaṁ*'. '*Go*' (signifies) a song and the singer. '*Gha*' stands for a bell, a small bell and the like and beating. (The letter) '*ṅa*' signifies desire and Bhairava (a terrible form of lord Śiva).

6. '*Ca*' (stands for) the wicked (and) stainless. '*Cha*' (indicates) division and '*ji*', conquering. '*Jaṁ*' (denotes) a song and '*jha*', commendable. (The letter) '*ña*' (signifies) strength and '*ṭaḥ*', singing.

7. '*Ṭha*' (denotes) the orb of Moon, (lord) Śiva and tying. '*Ḍa*' is regarded (as signifying) Rudra, sound and fear. '*Ḍha*' (denotes) a drum and sound.

8. '*Ṇa*' (means) extraction and ascertainment. '*Ta*' (signifies) a thief and the inside of the tail. '*Tha*' (denotes) eating, '*daḥ*', cutting, sustaining and ornamentation.

9. '*Dhaḥ*' (signifies) Brahmā and the *dhuttūra* (flower). '*Na*' (stands for) a collection and correct course of action. '*Pa*' is known (to denote) a garden. *Pha*' is regarded (as signifying) a squall.

10. '*Pha*' (stands for) *phūtkāra* (blowing with the mouth) and fruitlessness. '*Bi*' (denotes) a bird and '*bhaṁ*', the asterism. '*Mā*, would (mean) Goddess of wealth, measure and mother. '*Ya*' (stands for) a sacrifice, traveller and a brave person.

11. (The letter) '*raḥ*' (denotes) Fire (god), strength and Indra. (The letter) '*la*' is said (to denote) the creator. '*Vi*' (signifies) separation and '*Va*', Varuṇa. '*Śaḥ*' (means) lying down and '*śaṁ*', happiness.

12. '*Ṣaḥ*' (denotes) excellence and '*saḥ*', the past. '*Sā*' (means) Lakṣmī (the goddess of fortune) and '*saṁ*' is regarded (as representing) locks of hair. '*Ha*' (denotes) sustenance and Rudra (a form of Śiva). '*Kṣa*' (stands for) the warrior class and regarded as the alphabet (imperishable).

13. (The letter) *kṣo* (denotes) (lord) Nṛsiṁha, Hari and the guardians of the land (and entrance). A sacred formula of one syllable (should be deemed as) the deity (itself whom it represents) and it confers enjoyment and emancipation.

14. The formula (running as) '*kṣaum* obeisance to Hayaśiras[1]' confers all knowledge. The letter '*a*' and the other letters

1. The horse-headed form assumed by Lord Viṣṇu to rescue the *Vedas*.

(described above are also) formulae. (They are known as) *mātṛkāmantras* and are excellent.

15-16. These (deities of the *mātṛkāmantras*) and the nine Durgās—Bhagavatī, Kātyāyanī, Kauśikī, Caṇḍikā, Pracaṇḍā, Suranāyikā, Ugrā, Pārvatī and Durgā. *Oṁ*, we may know (the Goddess) Caṇḍikā, let us meditate on the goddess and may (Goddess) Durgā lead our mind to that. Then the worship should be done in the proper way together with the six accessories. The *gaṇa* should be an aspirate.

17-18. Then (the goddesses) Ajitā, Aparājitā, Jayā, Vijayā, Kātyāyanī, Bhadrakālī, Maṅgalā, Siddhi and Revatī and the accomplished (deities) Vaṭukas should be worshipped. The nine guardian deities Hetuka, Kāpālika, Ekapāda and Bhīmarūpa (should be worshipped) in the middle.

19-20. *Hrīṁ*! O Durgā ! (2) Protector! Oblations for the sake of perfection of the formula. Then (goddess) Gaurī, Dharma and others and the female energies (such as) Skanda should be worshipped. Prajñā, Jñānā, Kriyā, Vācā, Vāgīśī, Jvālinī, Kāminī, Kāmamālā, the energies of Indra and others should be worshipped.

21-23a. "*Oṁ gaṁ* oblations" (is) the basic formula. "*Gaṁ*, obeisance to Gaṇapati (lord of the *Gaṇas*)" (is) the accessory formula. The six accessory (worship should be done). They are Raktaśukla (red and white), Dantākṣa (having axis like tusk), Paraśūtkaṭa (powerful axe), Samodaka (having the sweet ball cake), Gandhādi (fragrance etc.), and Gandholkāya (to the person having a fragrant stick) in order. The elephant (god), the great lord of the Gaṇas (attendants) and having a magnificent incense stick should be worshipped. Oblation to Kūṣmāṇḍa, to the single-tusked one, to the destroyer of the three cities, to the black-teethed one, to one whose dreadful laughter startles (all), to one having elongated nose and face, to one having the lotus in the tusk, to Megholka, to Dhūmolka, to one having curved trunk, to the lord of obstacles, to the fierce and dreadful one, to one having the gait of the elephant of Indra, one having the serpent-lord (Vāsuki) as a necklace, to one bearing the crescent moon, and the lord of the Gaṇas (attendants). After having worshipped with these formulae ending with oblations and with (the performance of) the oblations with sesamum, one would get wealth.

23b-24a. The formulae may, in the alternative, consist of the letters beginning with *ka* and with the subtle syllable and ending with obeisance separately having two *ras* and two faces and two eyes.

24b. I shall describe now the grammar that was imparted by Skanda to Kātyāyana.

CHAPTER THREE HUNDRED AND FORTYNINE

The pratyāhāras and fundamental rules in grammar

Skanda said :

1. O Kātyāyana ! I shall describe the essence of grammar that is of the form of perfected words for imparting to the beginners.

2. *Pratyāhāras*[1] etc. are the notations facilitating the function of the treatise, *Aiuṇ ṛḷk, eoṅ, aiauc, hayavaraṭ, laṇ, ñamaṅaṇanam jhabhañ, ghaḍhadhaṣ, jabagaḍadaś, khaphachaṭhathacaṭatav, kapay, śaṣasar, hal* are (the fourteen) *pratyāhāras*. In the enumeration, the consonant at the end is indicatory. The vowel would be (read with) the nasal. The first letter being taking together with the indicative letter at the end, would become the denotative of the letters which occur in between such as *aṇ, eṅ, aṭ, yañ, chav, jhaṁ, bhaṣ, ak, ik, aṇ, iṇ, yaṇ,* with the letter *ṇa* coming afterwards. (Similarly we have) *aṁ, yaṁ, ñaṁ, ac, ic, aic, ay, may, jhay, khay, jav, jhav, khav, cav, śav, aś, hāś, vaś, jhaś, al, hal, val, ral, jhal* and *al* the *pratyāhāras*.

1. Several letters or affixes are comprehended as one syllable by means of combining the first letter of an aphorism with its final indicatory letter or if several aphorisms are comprehended, the final letter of the last member is combined with the first such as *aṇ* etc. denoting *aiuṇ* etc.

CHAPTER THREE HUNDRED AND FIFTY

The forms of completed euphonic combinations

Skanda said :

1-5. I shall describe the forms of finished combinations[1] (of vowels and consonants). First (I shall describe) the combination of vowels.

daṇḍa	+	agram	=	daṇḍāgram
sā	+	āgatā	=	sāgatā
dadhi	+	idaṁ	=	dadhīdaṁ
nadī	+	īhate	=	nadīhate
madhu	+	udakaṁ	=	madhūdakaṁ
pitṛ	+	ṛṣabha	=	pitṛṣabha

The letter 'ḷ' also becomes similar.

(hotṛ	+	ḷkāra	=	hotṛkāra)
tava	+	idaṁ	=	tavedaṁ
sakala	+	udakaṁ	=	sakalodakaṁ

The following is a half-vowel :

tava	+	lkāra	=	tavalkāra
sā	+	eṣā	=	saiṣā
sā	+	aindrī	=	saindrī
tava	+	odanaṁ	=	tavaudanaṁ
khaṭvā	+	oghaḥ	=	khaṭvaughaḥ are thus formed
vi	+	asudhiḥ	=	vyasudhīḥ
vasu	+	alaṅkṛtaṁ	=	vasvalaṅkṛtaṁ
pitṛ	+	artha	=	pitrartha
	+	upavana	=	pitrarthopavana
nai	+	aka	=	nāyaka
lo	+	aka	=	lāvaka
te	+	iha	=	ta iha, tayiha etc.
te	+	atra	=	te'tra
yaḥ	+	atra	=	yo'tra
jale	+	akajam	=	jale'kajam

1. The text gives only the combined forms. The individual words have also been given here for easy comprehension.

(The following do not undergo any change) :

aho	+	ehi	=	aho ehi
a	+	avehi	=	a avehi
i	+	indrakaṁ	=	i indrakam
u	+	uttiṣṭha	=	u uttiṣṭha
kavī	+	etau	=	kavī etau
vāyu	+	etau	=	vāyu etau
vane	+	ime	=	vane ime
amī	+	ete	=	amī ete
yajñabhūte	+	ehi	=	yajñabhūte ehi
deva	+	imannaya	=	deva imannaya

6-9. I shall describe now the conjunction of the consonants.

vāk	+	yataḥ	=	vagyataḥ
ac	+	ekamātṛkaḥ	=	ajekamātṛkaḥ
ṣaṭ	+	ete	=	ṣaḍete
tat	+	ime	=	tadime
vā	+	ādi	=	vādi (?)
vāk	+	nītiḥ	=	vāṅnītiḥ
ṣaṭ	+	mukha	=	ṣaṇmukha etc.
vāk	+	manasaṁ	=	vāṅmanasaṁ
vāk	+	bhāgādiḥ	=	vāgbhāgādiḥ
vāk	+	ślakṣṇaṁ	=	vākślakṣṇaṁ
tat	+	śarīrakaṁ	=	taccharīrakaṁ
tat	+	lunāti	=	tallunāti
tat	+	caret	=	taccaret
kun	+	āste	=	kuṅṅāste
sugan	+	iha	=	sugaṇṇiha
bhavān	+	caran	=	bhavāṁścaran
bhavān	+	chātro	=	bhavānśchātro
bhavān	+	ṭīkā	=	bhavāṁṣṭīkā
bhavān	+	ṭakaḥ	=	bhavāṁṣṭakaḥ
bhavān	+	tīrtha	=	bhavāṁstīrtha
bhavān	+	stheyān	=	bhavāṁstheyān
bhavān	+	lekhā	=	bhavāṁllekhā
bhavān	+	jayaḥ	=	bhavāñjayaḥ
bhavān	+	śete	=	bhavāṁśchete
bhavān	+	ca śete	=	bhavāñcaśete
bhavān	+	śete	=	bhavāñśete

bhavān + dīnaḥ = bhavāṇḍīnaḥ
tvaṁ + bhartā = tvaṁbhartā
tvaṁ + karisyasi = tvaṅkariṣyasi etc.

The conjunctions of *visarga* are known (as follows):

10-11. kaḥ + chindyāt = kaśchindyāt
kaḥ + caret = kaścaret
kaḥ + ṭaḥ = kaṣṭaḥ
kaḥ + sthaḥ = kaṣṭhaḥ
kaḥ + calet = kaścalet

(In the following cases the *visarga* becomes the *upadhmānīya*):

kaḥ + khanet = kaḥ≍khanet
kaḥ + karoti = kaḥ≍karoti sma
kaḥ + paṭhet = kaḥ≍paṭhet or
kaḥ + phaleta = kaḥ≍phaleta

(The following may occur in two forms) :

kaḥ + śvaśuraḥ = kaśśvaśuraḥ (or) kaḥ śvaśuraḥ
kaḥ + sāvaraḥ = kassāvaraḥ or kaḥ sāvaraḥ

(In the following cases there is no change). :

kaḥ + phaleta = kaḥ phaleta
kaḥ + śayitā = kaḥ śayitā

(The following is an instance of change) :

kaḥ + atra yodhaḥ = ko'tra yodhaḥ

(The *visarga* is dropped in the following cases) :

12-13. kaḥ + uttamaḥ = ka uttamaḥ
devāḥ + ete = devā ete
bhoḥ + iha = bho iha
sodarāḥ + yānti = sodarā yānti
bhago + vraja = bhago vraja

(In the following the *visarga* becomes *repha* (r) :

supūḥ+sudūḥ+rātriḥ = supūḥ sudūrātriḥ
vāyuḥ + yāti = vāyuryāti
punaḥ + nahi = punarnahi
punaḥ + eti = punareti

(The *visarga* is dropped in the following cases) :

saḥ	+	yāti+iha	=	sa yātīha
eṣaḥ	+	yāti	=	eṣa yāti
kaḥ	+	īśvaraḥ	=	ka īśvaraḥ
jyotiḥ	+	rūpaṁ	=	jyotīrūpam

(The following are examples of other kinds of union) :

tava	+	chatram	=	tavacchatram
mlecchadhīḥ+chidraṁ+ ā+chidat			=	mlecchadhīśchidramāc-chidat

CHAPTER THREE HUNDRED AND FIFTYONE

Perfected forms of inflection in the nouns

Skanda said :

1-3. O Kātyāyana ! I shall describe to you the finished forms of inflections. There are two kinds of inflections—*sup* (substantives) and *tiṅ* (verbs). The substantives have seven cases. (The inflections) *su, au, jas* (constitute) the first (case) (Nominative). *Aṁ, au, śas* (are the inflections of) the second (case) (Accusative). *Ṭā, bhyāṁ, bhis* (are the terminations of) the third (case) (Instrumental). *Ṅe, bhyāṁ, bhyas* (constitute) the fourth (case) (Dative). *Ṅasi, bhyāṁ, bhyas* are (the inflections of) the fifth (case) (Ablative). *Ṅas, os, ām* (are the terminations for) the sixth (case) (Genitive). *Ṅi, os, sup* (are for) the seventh (case). (Locative). These would be added after the uninflected substantives.

4. The substantives are twofold—ending in vowels and ending in consonants. Each one of this would again be threefold : masculine, feminine and neuter.

5-7. The models of these are given. Those which are not mentioned here (follow those) on account of their strength. (Those ending in vowels are to be declined as the following examples). Vṛkṣaḥ (tree)[1], Sarvaḥ (all), Pūrvaḥ (former), Prathamaḥ (first), Dvitīyakaḥ (second), Tṛtīyaḥ (third), Khaṇḍapā (protector of a group), Vahniḥ (fire), Sakhā (friend), Patiḥ (husband), Aharpatiḥ (Sun), Paṭuḥ (clever), Grāmaṇī (chief of the village), Indra (the lord of the celestials),

1. The text gives only the nominative singular forms of the substantives in this charpter.

Khalapūḥ (one who sweeps), Mitrabhūḥ (being a friend), Svabhūḥ (an epithet of Brahmā), Suśrīḥ (good fortune), Sudhīḥ (a wiseman), Pitā (father), Bhrātā (brother), Nā (a man), Kartā (doer), Kroṣṭu (a jackal), Naptṛ (grandson), Surā (intoxicating drink), Rā (Rai means wealth), Gauḥ (cow), Dyauḥ (heaven), Glauḥ (Moon) (are) examples for the masculine (nouns) ending in vowels.

8-12a. (Examples for substantives ending with the consonants) : Suvāk (good expression or speech), Tvak (skin), Pṛṣat (a drop of water or any other liquid), Samrāṭ (a paramount sovereign), Janmabhāk (one who has obtained birth), Surāṭ (a good sovereign), Āpaḥ (water), Marut (Wind), Bhavan (becoming), Dīpyan (shining), Bhavān (you) (polite form), Maghavān (Indra) (prosperous), Piban (drinking), Bhagavān (fortunate, hence denotes the lord), Aghavān (a sinner), Arvān (a horse), Vahnimat (possessing fire), Sarvavit (knower of all things), Supṛt (a good army), Susīmā (good boundary), Kuṇḍī (Kuṇḍin denotes Śiva, holding a bowl), Rājā (king), Śvā (horse), Yuvā (youth), Maghavā (Indra), Pūṣā (Sun), Sukarmā (doer of good deeds), Yajvā (sacrificer), Suvarmā (good armour), Sudharmaṇā (council of gods, court-hall of Indra), Aryamā (Sun), Vṛtrahā (Indra, killer of Vṛtra), Panthāḥ (path), Sukakud (good summit) etc. and Pañca (five), Praśān (one who is tranquil), Sutān (one who spreads well), Pañca (five) etc., Sugauḥ (good cow), Surāḥ (one who is wealthy) and Supūḥ (good city), Candramāḥ (Moon), Suvacāḥ (good speech), Śreyān (excellent), Vidvān (learned), and Uśanas (the preceptor of the demons), Pecivān (one who has cooked), Gauḥ (cow), Anaḍvān (an ox), Godhuṅ (one who milks a cow), Mitradruh (one who is treacherous to a friend), Śvaliṭ (one who licks like a dog).

12b-19. (Substantives) in the feminine (are): Jāyā (wife), Jarā (old age), Bālā (young girl), Eḍakā (a ewe), Vṛddhā (old woman), Kṣatriyā (a woman of the Kṣatriya class), Bahurājā (land having many rulers), Bahuḍāmā (having many garlands) and Bālikā (an young girl), Māyā (illusion), Kaumudagandhā (smelling like a lily), Sarvā (all), Pūrvā (the preceding one) and Anyā (someone else), Dvitīyā (second one), Tṛtīyā (third one), Buddhi (intellect), Strī (woman), Śrī (Lakṣmī, goddess of wealth), Nadī (river), Sudhīḥ (wise), Bhavantī (one who becomes), Dīvyantī (one who shines), Bhātī (one who appears), Bhāntī (one who shines), and Yāntī (one who goes), Śṛṅvatī (one who hears), Tudatī (tormenting), Kartrī (doer), Tudantī (tormenting), Kurvatī (one who is doing), Mahī (earth), Rudhantī (one who is obstructing), Krīḍatī (one who is playing), Dāntī (one who is restrained), Pālayantī (one who is protecting), and Surāṇī (a celestial woman), Gaurī (having white complexion, denotes consort of Śiva), Putravatī (one who is having a son), Nauḥ (ship or boat), Vadhūḥ (bride), Devatā (deity) and Bhūḥ (earth). Tisra (three) and Dve (two) (both denoting feminine), Kati (how many), Varṣābhūḥ (a female frog), Svasā (sister), Mātā (mother), Varā (excellent), Gauḥ (cow), Nauḥ (ship or boat), Vāk (speech), Tvak (skin), Prācī (east), Avācī (south), Tiraścī (the female of an animal or bird), Samīcī (a doe), Udīcī (north), Śarat (autumn), Vidyut (lightning), Sarit (river), Yoṣit (lady in separation), Agnivit (knower of fire), Sampat (wealth), Dṛṣat (stone), Yā (who), Eṣā (this), Vedavit (knower of the Veda), Saṁvit (knowledge), Bahvī (many), Rājñī (queen), Tvayā (by you), Mayā (be me), Sīmā (boundary), Pañca (five) etc., Rājī (line or row), Dhūḥ (shaking), Pūḥ (purifying), Diśā (direction), Girā (speech), Catasraḥ (four), Viduṣī (learned person), Kā (who), Iyaṁ (this), Dik (direction), Dṛk (look), Tādṛśī (that kind). These are chief among (the substantives belonging to) the feminine gender. (I shall describe) the chief among (the substantives belonging to) the neuter.

20-22a. Kuṇḍaṁ (a bowl or pit), Sarvaṁ (all), Somapaṁ Dadhi (curd), Vāri (water), Khalapū (that which sweeps), Madhu (honey), Trapu (tin), Bhartṛ, Atibhartṛ, Payaḥ (milk), Puraḥ (city), Prāk (east), Pratyak (?) (backwards), Tiryak (across), Udak (above or nothward), Jagat (world), Jāgrat (awakening state), Śakṛt (excrement), Susampat (good wealth), Sudaṇḍī (good stick), Ahaḥ (day), Kiṁ (what), Idaṁ (this), Ṣaṭ (six), Sarpiḥ (clarified butter), Śreyaḥ (fortune), Catvāri (four), Adaḥ (that thing). Others are similar to these.

22b-28a. (The inflections of) the first case (Nominative) etc. would come after these uninflected forms. A form of a word which is neither a verbal root (*dhātu*), nor an affix (*pratyaya*) is a nominal base (*prātipadika*). The first case from the nominal base is employed to denote the subject. The first case (is also employed) in addressing when the agent and the object are mentioned. That which is done (by the agent) is the object (*karma*). Second case (Accusative) is used in the object. That by which something is done is the instrument (*karaṇa*). One who does is the agent (*kartā*). When the object is not specified to be the agent through the verbal affix or suffixes of the kṛt and taddhita type, the third case (Instrumental) is used in (denoting) the instrument and the agent. The fourth case is employed in *sampradāna* (to be given). It is said to be *sampradāna* in which the desire to give is indicated. *Apādāna*, is that from which something moves away or taken away. The fifth case (Ablative) is used (to denote) *apādāna*. The sixth case (Genitive) (is used to denote) one's ownership. The term *adhikaraṇa* is used in the sense of the base (*ādhāra*). The seventh case (Locative) (is used) therein.

28b-29a. Singular is used to denote a single thing. Dual comes in the sense of two things. Plural would occur in the (sense of) many. I shall describe the finished forms (now).

29b-32a. (The following are examples for the Nominative): Vṛkṣaḥ (tree), Sūryaḥ (Sun), Ambuvāhaḥ (cloud), Arkaḥ (Sun). The following are the examples for (the Vocative): *He* Ravi (O Sun!), *He* Dvijātayas (O twiceborns!), Viprau (O Brahmins!). (Then the example for the Accusative): Gajān (the elephants). (Then the examples for the Instrumental): Mahendreṇa (by Mahendra, the lord of the celestials), Yamābhyām (by two Yamas—by the twins), Analaiḥ kṛtam (done by Anala, fire plural). Rāmāya (for Rāma), Munivaryābhyām (for the two excellent sages), Kebhyaḥ (for whom, plural) (are examples for the Dative). Dharmāt (from Dharma), Harau ratiḥ[1] (?), Śarābhyāṁ (from the two arrows), Pustakebhyaḥ (from the books) (are illustrations for the Ablative). Arthasya (of the sense), Īśvarayoh (of the two lords), Gatiḥ bālānāṁ (the fate of children) (are for the Genitive). Sajjane prītiḥ (pleased in good people), Haṁsayoḥ (in the two haṁsas), Kamaleṣu (in the lotuses) (are examples for the Locative). In the same way, the words

1. The reading is obviously wrong.

Kāma (God of love), Maheśa (the great lord) and other (words) should be known like (the word) Vṛkṣa (tree).

32b-36a. Sarve (all), Viśve (all or entire or whole), Sarvasmai (for all), Sarvasmāt (from all) and Katara (who or which of two) are regarded (as similar). Sarveṣām (of all), Svam (one's self), Viśvasmin (in the whole). The other forms are like (the word) Vṛkṣa (tree). Similarly Ubhaya (both), Katara (who or which of the two), Katama (who or which of many), Anyatara (one of two) etc. (should be known). Pūrve (all the former), Pūrvāḥ (all the former, feminine), Pūrvasmai (for the former), Pūrvasmāt (from the former), Pūrve (in the former), Pūrvasmin (in the former). The other forms are like that of Sarva. Para (superior), Avara (inferior) as well as Dakṣiṇa (south), Uttara (north), Antara (in between), Aparāḥ (others), Adharaḥ (below) (are to be known) in the same way. Nemāḥ (parts), Prathamāḥ (the first ones), Prathame (in the first one) are like the word Arka (Sun). In the same way (we whould have) Caramāḥ (last), Alpa (little), Ardha (half) and the Nema (part) and others.

36b-41a. Dvitīyasmai (or) Dvitīyāya (for the second), Dvitīyasmāt (or) Dvitīyakāt (from the second), Dvitīyasmin (or) Dvitīye (in the second) and Tṛtīya (third) like (the word) Arka (Sun). Somapāḥ (a drinker of Soma) and Somapau (two drinkers of Soma) should be known. Go to Somapāḥ (drinkers of Soma) (or) Somapāṁ (a drinker of Soma). Kīlālapau (two drinkers of a heavenly drink similar to nectar) and Somapaḥ (drinker of Soma), Somapāḥ (drinkers of Soma), Somape dada (give to a drinker of Soma), Somapābhyāṁ (to two drinkers of Soma), Somapābhyaḥ (to many drinkers of Soma), Somapaḥ (drinker of Soma), Somapau (two drinkers of Soma) (belong to) a group. (The words) such as Kīlālapāḥ (drinkers of a celestial drink) would be similar. Kaviḥ (poet), Agniḥ (fire) and Arayaḥ (enemies), He kave ! (O poet !), Kaviṁ (the poet, accusative), Agnī (two fires, accusative), Tān Harīn (those Hari-s), Sātyakinā hṛtaṁ (taken by Sātyaki), Ravibhyāṁ (by two Suns), Ravibhiḥ (by the Suns), Dehi vahnaye yaḥ samāgataḥ (Give to Fire who has come), Agneḥ (of fire), Agnyoḥ (of two fires), Agnīnāṁ (of many fires), Kavau (in the poet), Kavyoḥ (in the two poets) and Kaviṣu (in many poets) (are examples for words ending in '*i*'). Similarly Susṛtiḥ (good path), Abhrāntiḥ (not an error),

Sukīrtiḥ (good fame) and Sudhṛtiḥ (firmness) (are to be declined).

41b-43a. (Some more examples for words ending in 'i'): Sakhā (a friend), Sakhāyau (two friends), Sakhāyaḥ (many friends). 'He sakhe ! vraja satpatiṁ' (O Friend ! go to a good master), Sakhāyaṁ (the friend), Sakhāyau (the two friends), Sakhīn (the friends) (are accusative forms). Sakhyā gataḥ (gone with the friend). Dada sakhye (give to the friend). Sakhyuḥ (from a friend), Sakhyuḥ (of the friend), Sakhyoḥ (of the two friends). That rest (are formed like) the forms of Kavi (poet). Patyā (by the master), Patye (for the master), Patyuḥ (from the master), Patyuḥ (of the master), Patyoḥ (of the two masters) are like (the word) Agni (fire).

43b. Dvau (two), Dvau (the two), Dvābhyām (by the two), Dvābhyām (for the two), Dvayoḥ (from the two) and Dvayoḥ (of the two) are in the sense of dual.

44. Trayaḥ (three), Trīn (the three), Tribhiḥ (by the three), Tribhyaḥ (for the three), Trayāṇāṁ (of the three) and Triṣu (in the three) (are) in order. Kati (how many) and Katī (how many). The other plural forms are like Kavi (poet) (in the plural).

45. (The word Nī, leader is declined as follows): Nīḥ (a leader), Niyau (two leaders) and Niyaḥ (many leaders). He nīḥ (O leader !), Niyam (one leader), Niyau (two leaders), Niyaḥ (many leaders). Niyā (by a leader), Nībhyāṁ (by two leaders), Nibhiḥ (by many leaders). Niye (for a leader), Nībhyaḥ (for many leaders). Niyāṁ (of many leaders), Niyi (in a leader) and Niyoḥ (in two leaders).

46-48a. Suśrīḥ (good fortune), Sudhīḥ (good intellect) etc. Grāmaṇīḥ (a leader), pūjayeddhariṁ (should worship Hari). Grāmaṇyau (the two chiefs), Grāmaṇyaḥ (the many chiefs), Gramaṇyaṁ (the chief, accusative), Grāmaṇyā (by the chief), Grāmaṇibhiḥ (by many chiefs), Grāmaṇyaḥ (of a chief), Grāmaṇyāṁ (in a chief). Words beginning with Senānī (leader of an army) are similarly (declined). Subhūḥ (good land) and Sabhuvau (two good lands). Svayambhuvaḥ (self-born), Svayambhuvaṁ (self-born, accusative), Svayambhuvā (by the self-born), Svayambhuvi (in the self-born). Pratibhuvaḥ (bail or surety) etc. (should be formed) similarly.

48b-49. Khalapūḥ (that which sweeps), Khalapvau (the two which sweep), Śreṣṭhau (that are excellent), Khalapvaṁ (that which sweeps, accusative), and Khalapvi (in a sweeper). (The words) beginning with Śarapūḥ would be in the same way. Kroṣṭhā (a jackal) and Kroṣṭhāraḥ (many jackals), Kroṣṭhūn (the jackals, accusative plural), Kroṣṭhunā or Kroṣṭhrā (by a jackal), Kroṣṭhūnāṁ (of the jackals), Kroṣṭhari (in a jackal) are said to be (formed) thus.

50-52a. Pitā (father), Pitarau (two fathers), Pitaraḥ (many fathers), He pitaḥ (O Father!), Pitarau śubhau (O Auspicious fathers!), Pitṝn (the fathers, accusative), Pituḥ (from the father), Pituḥ (of the father), Pitroḥ (of the two fathers), Pitṝṇāṁ (of many fathers), Pitari (in the father) are formed) thus. In the same way Bhrātā (a brother), Jāmātṛ (son-in-law) and others (words) (are formed). Then Nṝṇāṁ or Nṛṇāṁ (of the men). Kartā (doer), Kartārau (two doers), Kartṝn (many doers, accusative), Kartṛṇāṁ (of many doers) and Kartari (in a doer) are thus (formed). Udgātā (a singer of Vehic hymn), Svasā (sister), Naptṛ (grandson) are known to be like (the word) Pitṛ (father).

52b. Surāḥ (good fortune), Surāyau (dual), Surāyaḥ (plural), Surāyaṁ (accusative), and Surāyi (locative).

53. Gauḥ (a cow), Gāvau (two cows), Gāṁ (accusative), Gāḥ (accusative, plural), Gavā (instrumental), Goḥ (genitive), Gavoḥ (genitive, dual), Gavāṁ (genitive, plural) and Gavi (in a cow). In the same way Dyauḥ (heaven) and Glauḥ (Moon)and the chief masculine words ending in vowels.

54-57a. Suvāk (good speech), Suvācī (nominative dual), Suvācā (instrumental), Suvāgbhyāṁ (instrumental, dual), Suvākṣu (locative, plural). Similarly the directions beginning with (east). Prāṅ (east), Prāñcī (nominative neuter dual), Prāñcaṁ (to the east) bho vraja (you go). Prāgbhyām (instrumental, dual), Prāgbhiḥ (instrumental, plural), Prācāṁ (genitive), Prācī (locative, singular), Prāṅsu and Prāṅkṣu (locative, plural). In the same way Udaṅ or Udīcī (north), Samyaṅ (well), Pratyak (western), Samīcī (a doe), Tiryaṅ (that which moves horizontally), Tiraśca[1], Sadhryaṅ (a companion, especially

1. Seems to be Tiraścī, denoting a female of any animal.

husband), Viṣvadryaṅ (all-pervading) are known to be like the former. Adadṛyāṅ, Adamuyaṅ, Amumuyaṅ (all meaning going to that) etc. are similar. Adadryoñc (one who has gone to that direction) and Amudrīcaḥ (one who has gone to that direction) and Adadryābhyāṁ are as before.

57b-59a. Tattvatṛṭ (desirous of truth) (nominative), Tattvatṛṣau (dual), Tattvatṛṅbhyāṁ (with men desirous of Truth) samāgataḥ (one has come together), Tattvatṛṣi (in one desirous of truth), Tattvatṛṭsu (among those desirous of truth). In the same way Kāṣṭha (wood), Taḍa (?) etc. (are formed). Bhiṣak (a physician), Bhiṣagbhyāṁ (by two physicians), Bhiṣaji (locative). (The words) such as Jannabhāk (are) then (similarly declined). Marut (wind), Marudbhyāṁ (by two winds), Maruti (in the wind). In the same way (we have) Śatrujit (conqueror of an enemy) etc.

59b-61. Bhavān (you, polite form), Bhavantau (dual), Bhavatāṁ (of you, plural), Bhavan (vocative), Bhavati (in you). Mahān (great), Mahāntau (dual), Mahatāṁ (of great people), Bhagavat (fortunate) etc. In the same way Maghavan (Indra), Maghavantau (dual). Agniçit (one who has kept the sacred fire), Agniciti (locative), Agnicitsu (locative, plural). In the same way Anyat (another), Vedavit (one who knows the scriptures), Tattvavit (knower of truth) etc. (We will have) Vedavidāṁ (in locative singular). In the same way Anyat (some other person). One who knows all is Sarvavit.

62-64. (The word Rājan is declined thus): Rājā (king), Rājānau (dual), Rājñaḥ (genitive), Rājñi or Rājani (locative), Rājan (vocative). Yajvā (a performer of a sacrifice), Yajvānaḥ (plural) are similar. Karī (an elephant), Daṇḍī (one who holds a stick), Daṇḍinau (dual), Panthāḥ (path), Panthānau (dual), Pathaḥ (plural), Paṭhibhyāṁ (instrumental, dual) and Pathi (locative) (will be) similar. Manthā (that which churns), Ṛbhukṣāḥ (nominative plural) (Ṛbhukṣaḥ means Indra) and Pathya (wholesome food) etc. (should be known). Pañca (five), Pañca (accusative), Pañcabhiḥ (instrumental). Pratān (one who spreads well), Pratānau (dual), Pratānbhyāṁ (instrumental, dual), He Pratān (vocative) and Suśarmaṇaḥ (vocative, those who are happy). (The following is always plural): Āpaḥ (water) (nominative), Apaḥ (accusative), Adbhiḥ (instrumental). In the same way Prasān (one who is tranquil) and Praśāni (locative) also.

65-67. Kaḥ (who), Kena (by whom) like Sarva (all). Keṣu (among whom), Ayaṁ (this), Ime (dual), Imān (accusative plural), Anena (by this), Ābhyāṁ (instrumental, dual), Ebhiḥ (instrumental, plural), Asmai (dative, singular), Ebhyaḥ (dative plural), Svaṁ (one's own), Asya (genitive), Anayoḥ (genitive, dual), Eṣāṁ (genitive, plural) and Eṣu (locative, plural) would be (formed). Catvāraḥ (four), Caturaḥ (accusative), Caturṇāṁ (genitive), Caturṣu (locative). Sugīḥ (good speech), Sugīrṣu (locative, plural), Sudyauḥ (good day), Sudivau (dual), Sudyubhyam (instrumental dual). Viṭ (merchant), Viśau (dual), Viṭsu (locative, plural). Yādṛśaḥ (ablative, singular, from which kind of a thing), Yādṛgbhyāṁ (ablative, dual) Viḍbhyāṁ (dual in the third, fourth and fifth cases). Ṣaṭ (six), Ṣaṭ (accusative) Ṣaṇṇāṁ (genitive plural), Ṣaṭsu (locative, plural).

68-70a. Ṣuvacāḥ (eloquent), Ṣuvacasā (instrumental), Suvacobhyāṁ (instrumental, dual), He Suvaco (vocative), He Uśanan (Uśanas denotes the preceptor of the demons) (vocative), Uśanā (instrumental), Uśanasi (locative), Purudaṅśā (a goose), Añchā (a stupid person), He Vidvan (O Learned man !), Vidvān (nominative) Viduṣe namaḥ (obeisance to the learned, dative), Vidvadbhyāṁ (instrumental, dative and ablative, dual), Vidvatsu (locative, plural). Babhūvivān (one that has become). (We have) in the same way, Pecivān (one that cooks), Śreyān (excellent), Śreyāṁsau (nominative, dual), Śreyasaḥ (accusative, plural).

70b-73. The following are the forms of Adas (that) : Asau, Amū, Amī (nominative, singular, dual and plural), Amum and Amūn (accusative singular and plural), Amunā, Amībhiḥ (instrumental singular and plural), Amuṣmai (dative), Amuṣmāt (ablative), Amuṣya, Amuyoḥ, Amīṣāṁ (genitive singular, dual and plural) and Amuṣmin (locative). Similarly (we have) (the forms of Godhuk, one who milks the cow): A person has come with one who milks the cow. Godhukṣu (locative plural). Thus (we have) other (forms). Mitradruhaḥ (one who is treacherous to a friend), Mitradrugbhyāṁ (dual instrumental), Mitradrugbhiḥ (plural) and Cittadruhaḥ (inimic to the mind) etc. Svaliṭ (one who licks himself), Svaliḍbhyāṁ (instrumental dual), Svalihi (locative). Anaḍvān (nominative of Anaḍuh, a bull), Anaḍutsu (locative plural). These are (the words) ending in the vowels and consonants in the masculine. I shall describe (now) those in the feminine.

CHAPTER THREE HUNDRED AND FIFTYTWO

Narration of the finished forms of the substantives in the feminine

Skanda said :

1-2. (The following are the forms of feminine nouns ending in *ā*) : Ramā (Lakṣmī, consort of Viṣṇu), Rame, Ramāḥ (the three forms in the nominative) are auspicious. Ramāṁ, Rame, Ramāḥ (the three forms in the accusative), Ramayā, Ramābhyāṁ, Ramābhiḥ (tht three forms in the instrumental) (by Ramā) it was made imperishable. Ramāyai, Ramābhyāṁ (are the singular, dual dative). Ramāyāḥ, Ramayoḥ, Ramāṇāṁ (are the three forms in the genitive). Ramāyāṁ and Ramāsu (are the singular and plural forms of the locative). Kalā (fine arts) is similar.

3-4. (The following are also feminine) : Jarā (old age), Jarasau or Jare, Jarasaḥ or Jarāḥ (are the forms in the nominative). Jarāṁ or Jarasaṁ (is the form in the accusative singular), Jarāsu (is the locative plural). Similarly (we have) Sarvā and Sarve (all) (in the nominative singular and dual). Sarvasyā (instrumental), give Sarvasyai (dative) (to all). Sarvasyāḥ (ablative), Sarvasyāḥ (and) Sarvayoḥ (genitive singular and dual). The other forms are like that of Rāma. (The following are always plural) : Dve (two in the nominative), Dve (in the accusative) and Tisraḥ (three in the nominative) and Tisṛṇāṁ (in the genitive).

5-8. (The following are examples of substantives of the feminine ending in '*i*') : Buddhiḥ (intellect) (nominative), Buddhyā (instrumental), Buddhaya (dative) and Buddheḥ (ablative and genitive). (The vocative form of Mati, mind, is) He mate. (The word Muni) will have (the forms) like that of Kavi (poet) : Munīnāṁ (genitive) (of the sages). (The following are the forms of the substantives of the feminine ending in *i*) : Nadiḥ, Nadyau (singular and dual in the nominative). Nadīṁ, Nadīḥ (are the singular and plural in the accusative). Nadyā, Nadībhiḥ (are the singular and plural in the instrumental). Nadyai (is dative singular). Ṅadyāṁ and Nadīṣu (are the locative singular and plural). Similarly (we have the forms of) Kumārī (a young girl), Jṛmbhaṇī (yawn) etc. Śrīḥ (fortune), Śriyau, Śriyaḥ (are the three forms in the nominative). Śriyā (instrumental), Śriyai and Śriye (dative) (are the other forms). The following are the forms of the word Strī (woman) : Strīṁ and Striyaṁ (in the nominative singular) and Strīḥ or Striyaḥ (in the plural), Striyā (instrumental), Striyai (dative), Striyāḥ and Strīṇāṁ (singular and plural in the genitive) and Striyām (locative singular). (Similarly) Grāmaṇyā (locative singular). (The forms of words ending in '*u*' are) : Dhenvā (by a cow) and Dhenave (dative). (The following are examples for those ending in *ū*) : Jambū (the rose apple), Jambvau (nominative singular and plural), Jambuḥ (accusative singular), Drink the fruits of the Jambu (genitive). Vàrṣābhvau (is the nominative dual of Varṣābhū, a female frog) and Punarbhavau (nominative dual of Punarbhū, a widow remarried). Mātṝḥ (is the accusative plural of Mātṛ, mother ending in *ṛ*). Gauḥ (cow), Nauḥ (boat) (are examples of words ending in *O*).

9-10. (Now we have examples for words ending in consonants) : Vāk (speech) (nominative), Vācā, Vāgbhiḥ (instrumental singular and plural) and Vākṣu (locative plural) and Sragbhyāṁ (instrumental dual) and Sraji, Srajoḥ (locative singular and dual) (for the word Srak (garland). (The forms of the word Vidvat, learned, are) Vidvadbhyāṁ (dual in the instrumental, dative and ablative) and Vidvatsu (locative plural). (The following words ending in *t* take *i*—ending) : Bhavatī (respect form), Bhavantī (one who is becoming), Dīvyantī (shining) Bhātī (shining), Bhāntī (appearing), Tudantī (inflicting pain), Tudatī, Rudatī (crying), Rundhatī (obstructing), the Goddess Gṛhyatī (who is seizing or holding) and Corayantī (one that is stealing).

11-12a. (The following are other examples of nouns ending in *t*) : Dṛṣat (stone), Dṛsadbhyāṁ (instrumental, dative and ablative dual), Dṛṣadi (locative) are the special models. Samit (twig), Samidbhyāṁ (instrumental, dative and ablative dual), Samidhi (locative) (are other examples). (The following are examples for words ending in *n*): Sīmā (boundary) (nominative), Sīmni or Sīmani (locative). Dāmanībhyāṁ (instrumental etc. from the word Dāman meaning a line or streak). Kakudbhyāṁ (from Kakud, summit). Kā (who) (is a pronoun), Iyaṁ (this) (demonstrative pronoun) and Āsu (locative plural, in them).

12b-13. (The forms of the word Gīḥ, speech, are as follows) : Gīrbhyāṁ (dual in instrumental, dative and ablative), Girā (instrumental) and Gīrṣu (locative plural). (The following are also feminine nouns) : Subhūḥ (good land), Supūḥ (good city), Purā (through a city), Purī (in a city). (The following are the forms of dyo, heaven) : Dyauḥ, Dyubhyāṁ (dual, instrumental etc.), Divi (locative), Dyuṣu (plural). Tādṛśyā (by that kind) (instrumental). That kind of direction etc. Yādṛśyāṁ (in which kind), Yādṛśī (which kind) are similar. Suvacobhyāṁ (with good words), Suvacaḥsu (locative). Asau (that, nominative), Amūṁ (accusative), Amūḥ (plural), Amūbhiḥ (instrumental plural), Amuyā (instrumental singular) and Amuyoḥ (genitive and locative dual) (are the forms of Adas in the feminine).

CHAPTER THREE HUNDRED AND FIFTYTHREE

The finished forms of substantives in the neuter

Skanda said :

1. (The forms) in the neuter (are as follows) : Kiṁ, Ke, Kāni (the three forms in nominative, meaning what). Kiṁ, Ke, Kāni (are the forms in the accusative). Then (the word) Jalaṁ (water). Sarvaṁ (all) (nominative), Sarve (nominative, dual), Pūrva and other (words), Sīmapaṁ (protecting the boundary) (accusative), Sīmapāni (accusative, plural).

2. (The words ending in '*i*' are as follows) : Grâmaṇi, Grâmaṇinī, Grâmaṇī and Grâmaṇīni (are the forms in the nominative of Grâmaṇi, leader). Vâri, Variṇī, Vārīṇi (in the nominative), Variṇāṁ[1] (in the genitive plural) and Vāriṇi (locative singular) are thus (the forms of Vāri, water).

3. (The word Śuci, pure, has two forms in the dative) : Śucaye and Śucine dehi (give). Similarly (the word Mṛdu, soft, has two forms in the instrumental) : Mṛdune and Mṛdave. (The word Trapu, tin has the forms) : Trapu (nominative), Trapuṇi (locative singular) and Trapūṇāṁ (genitive plural). Khalapūni (nominative plural) and Khalapvi (locative singular, (forms of Khalapū, a sweeper).

4. Kartrā (instrumental), Kartṛṇe or Kartre (dative) (are the forms of Kartṛ, doer). Atirī (nominative) and Atiriṇāṁ (genitive plural) (are the forms Atirīṅ, one who goes beyond). Abhini, Abhininī (are nominative forms of the word denoting performance). Suvacāṁsi (nominative plural) and Suvākṣu (locative plural) (are from Suvāk, good speech).

5. (The relative pronoun) Yad, yat (who), and pronoun Ime (that), Tat (that) (belong to neuter). Karmāṇi (is the plural of Karma, work). Idaṁ, Ime, Imāni (are the forms of Idam, this). Īdṛk (this kind), Adaḥ, Amuni, Amūni (in the nominative), Amunā (in the instrumental) and Amīṣu (in the locative plural) (are the forms of Adas, that).

6-9. (The forms of Asmad, I, are) : Ahaṁ, Āvāṁ, Vayaṁ (nominative), Māṁ, Āvāṁ, Asmān (accusative), Mayā, Āvābhyāṁ, Asmābhiḥ (instrumental) done. Mahyaṁ and Asmabhyam (dative singular and dual), Mat, Āvābhyāṁ, Asmat (ablative). Mama, Āvayoḥ and Asmākaṁ (genitive) ayaṁ putraḥ (This is my, our son). Asmāsu (locative plural). (The forms of Yuṣmad, you, are), : Tvaṁ, Yuvāṁ, Yūyaṁ (nominative) ījire (praise). Tvāṁ, Yuvāṁ, Yusmān (accuative), Tvayā and Yuṣmābhiḥ (instrumentral, singular and plural) are stated (to be the forms). Tubhyaṁ, Yuvābhyāṁ, Yuṣmabhyaṁ (dative), Tvat, Yuvābhyāṁ, Yuṣmat (ablative), Tava, Yuvayoḥ, Yuṣmākaṁ (genitive) and Tvayi, Yuṣmāsu (locative, singular and plural). These are the characteristics of the

1. Obviously a mistake for Vāriṇāṁ.

language. (The substantives) ending in vowels and consonants have been described.

CHAPTER THREE HUNDRED AND FIFTYFOUR

The relation between a noun and a verb in a sentence

Skanda said :

1. I shall describe the *kāraka* (the relation that exists between a noun and a verb) together with the significance of the inflection (of nouns). (There) is a village. O Great Arka (Sun) ! I salute (lord) Viṣṇu together with Śrī (His consort) here.

2-4. The agent is said to be fivefold : (1) The agent is independent. The composers of the sacred knowledge are respected. (2) The agent gets to that cause when the agent is the doer. The dull headed breaks up himself. The tree cuts itself. (3) The agent expressed is good. The agent not expressed is low. (An example) for the agent not expressed (is): The dharma is being expounded to the pupil. Listen to me ! (I shall describe) the seven kinds of objects.

5-8a. (The first one is) the desired object such as "An ascetic pays respect to (lord) Hari (Viṣṇu)". (The second one is) the object that is not desired, such as "A person jumps over a serpent repeatedly." "After drinking milk, eat dust" (is an example) for neither desired nor not desired (object of the third kind). (The fourth one consists of) not being told (such as) "The cowherd is milking the cow". (The next one is) the object of the agent such as "Let the preceptor send the disciple to the village". (An example for the sixth variety, namely), the object that is expressed, (is) "Worship is made to (lord) Hari for prosperity". "Make an eulogy to (lord) Hari that yields all (things)" (is an example) for the object that is not expressed, (the seventh variety of object).

8b-9a. The instrument is said to be two kinds—external and internal. A person perceives the form by means of the eye (in an example for the internal). May a person cut that with a sickle (is an instance of) external.

9b-10. The *sampradāna* (giving) is said to be threefold : (1) *preraka* (sending) a cow to a brahmin, (2) *anumantṛka* (with consent) (such as) "A person gives a servant for the king", (3) *anirākartṛka* (a thing that could not be refused) (such as) "A good person may give flowers to the master."

11. The *apādāna* (that which is being taken away) is said to be twofold : (1) *calaṁ* (moveable) : (A person) has fallen from a running horse and *acalaṁ* (immoveable) : That devotee of Viṣṇu comes from a village.

12-14a. The *adhikaraṇa* (the base) is fourfold : (1) *vyāpaka* (pervading) just as ghee in curd, (2) *aupaśleṣika* (juxtaposition) is said (to be the existence of) oil in sesamum for the sake of God, (3) *vaiṣayika* (pertaining to an object) is known (to be) like the monkey may remain on a house (or) a tree, (and) (4) *sāmīpyaka* (proximate) known (to be) like fish in the water and a lion in a forest. (A fifth variety) is known as *aupacārika* (metaphorical) such as the existence of a hamlet on the (river) Ganges.

14b-17. (Now I shall describe the use of different inflections indicating different senses.) The third or the sixth (case) is known (to be used) when (the intention is) not expressed. (Lord) Viṣṇu is worshipped by people, To be gone by him or of him (are examples). The first case (is used) when the agent is expressed. (Accusative is used to denote) object : May a person make obeisance to Hari. The third case (is used to denote) cause (of an action)[1] : May one live for the sake of another. The fourth case is expressive of the purpose for which anything is done[2] : The water (is) for the three. The fifth case (is indicated) by means of (the words) *pari*, *upa* and *āṅ* etc.[3] in combination. Outside the village this God was strong before. (Other examples)[4]. 'To the east of the village', 'without (lord) Viṣṇu (there is) no emancipation' and 'different from Hari'.

18. There would be either third of fifth case with (the

1. cf. *Pa.* II. 3.
2. See Kale, Higher Skt. Gr. 827.
3. It should be *pari*, *apa* and *āṅ*. See *Pa.* II. 3. 10.
4. See Kale, ib. 840

words) such as Pṛthak, Vinā etc.[1] : different from the village, without sport (with the word) *śri* (prosperity) (such as) śriyā (instrumental) and śriyaḥ (ablative).

19. There would be second case when combined with *karmapravacanīyas*.[2] The warriors are inferior to Arjuna (and) near the village are said (to be examples).

20. The fourth case is used with (the particles) *namaḥ* (obeisance), *svāhā* (ablations), *svadhā*, *svasti* (well-being) and *vaṣaṭ* etc.[3] : Obeisance to the lord and Farewell to thee. (The fourth case) of an abstract noun (formed from a root may be used) to express the sense of the infinitive (of the same root).[4]

21. (The object governed by an infinitive mood not actually used but implied is put in the fourth case such as) (He) goes for cooking (in order to cook) (*pākāya*). The third case (is used)when accompanied by (the word) *saha*. The third case (is also employed) to express the cause or motive[5] (or the object or purpose of an action), (to express) some defect in a limb[6] (of the body) or a characteristic attribute[7] (indicative of the existence of a particular state).

22-23a. (The following are illustrations for the use of the third case) : The father went with the son (*saha putreṇa*); blind of one eye (*kāṇo 'kṣṇā*); He is Hari (apparent) from his club (*gadayā*); The servant may stay on account of the wealth (*arthena*). The seventh case (is used (to denote) the time (of action) and becoming. (The following are the examples) : One would get release (from bondage) when (lord) Viṣṇu is propitiated(*viṣṇau nate*). (He) attained Hari in the spring.

23b-24. (We have the sixth or seventh case in the following instances) : Master of men (or) master among men, lord of men, lord of good people, witness of men (or) witness among

1. See *Pa* II. 3. 32
2. Prepositions used by themselves and governing nouns are known as *Karmapravacanīyas*. See *Pa*. II. 3.8.
3. See *Pa*. II. 3. 16.
4. See *Pa*. II. 3. 15.
5. See *Pa*. II. 3.
6. Cf. *Pa*. II. 3.20.
7. See *Pa*. II. 3. 21.

men, lord among the cows, born among the cows (or) born of the cows, a heir or son of kings.

25. (When the word *hetu*, cause or object is used in a sentence, that which is the object and the word *hetu* are put in the genitive)[1] : (A person) dwells for the sake of food. A word or object expressing remembrance (is put in the genitive) (such as): Remembers the mother (mātuḥ), the guardian always. (The genitive is used) in the sense of the subject or the object (of the action denoted by the primary nominal bases) : The splitter of water, your action. The genitive (is) not used with past participles (*niṣṭhā*)[2]

CHAPTER THREE HUNDRED AND FIFTYFIVE

Different kinds of compounds

Skanda said :

1. I shall describe the six kinds of compounds. They are again divided into twentyeight kinds. They are twofold being divided as eternal and non-eternal, those which drop (the suffixes) and those which do not drop.

2-3a. (The following are examples of) eternal (compounds): Kumbhakāraḥ (a potter), hemakāraḥ (goldsmith) etc. Rājñaḥ pumān or rājapumān (a person with royal authority). This also is an eternal compound. Kaṣṭaśritaḥ (kaṣṭena śritaḥ) (joined with difficulty) (is an example of) dropping (the suffix). Kaṇṭhekālaḥ etc. (kaṇṭhe+kālaḥ) (black-necked) (are examples) for not dropping (the suffix).

3b-7. Tatpuruṣa (Determinative compound) is of eight kinds. The first one is that where the words when compounded with substantives are placed first. This is the first (variety) of Tatpuruṣa. Pūrvaṁ Kāyasya when (the compound is) dissolved

1. Cf. *Pa*. II. 3. 27.
2. See *Pa*. II. 3. 69.

(becomes) purvakāyaḥ[1] (the upper part of the body), Aparakāyaḥ (lower part of the body), Adharottara-kāyakaḥ (the lower and higher part of the body). Ardhaṁ Kaṇāyāḥ (becomes) Ardhakaṇāḥ (half of a grain). Bhikṣātūryaṁ[2] (begging alms a fourth time)is also of this type(signifying the whole of which they are parts) (optionally placed first). Āpannajīvikaḥ[3] (āpanno jīvikāṁ) is similar (in the second case). Adharāśritaḥ(adharaṁ āśritaḥ—one who has resorted to a lower person). Varṣambhogyaḥ (or) Varṣabhogyaḥ (to be enjoyed for a year). (An instance of compounding) with (nouns in) the third case : Dhānyārthaḥ (Dhānyena arthaḥ) (wealth obtained by means grain). (The noun) would be in the fourth case (when compounded with the word *bali*) : Viṣṇubaliḥ (Viṣṇave baliḥ). Vṛkabhītiḥ[4] (Vṛkāt bhītiḥ, fear from a wolf) (is an example for compounding with a noun in) the fifth case. (An example for) sixth case (is) Rājñaḥ pumān (an officer of a king) (becoming) Rājapumān. Similarly (we have) Vṛkṣaphalaṁ (the fruit of a tree). The seventh case (is used in the following): This one (is) Akṣaśauṇḍa[5] (Akṣeṣu śauṇḍaḥ) (skilled in dice). Ahitaḥ (not beneficial) (is an example) for Negative Tatpuruṣa.

8-12. Karmadhāraya (appositioned compound) is sevenfold[6]. Nīlotpala (*Nīlaṁ ca tad utpalaṁ ca*) etc. are known (to be the examples) for compounding the adjective and the noun it qualifies). (1) The qualifying word is placed first or (2) the word that is qualified is placed afterwards. (Words expressive of the persons or things condemned are placed first) : Vaiyākaraṇakhasūciḥ (a bad grammarian) (an example for first kind). Śītoṣṇaṁ (cold and hot) and Dvipadaṁ (two words) (are examples for the second). (3) Expressive of standard of comparison placed as first member : Śaṅkhapāṇḍara (white as the conch) (*śaṅkhaḥ iva pāṇḍaraḥ*). (4) The standard of comparison

1. See *Pa.* II. 2. 1. They are not strictly Genitive Tatpuruṣa. But called by some as Prathamā Tatpuruṣa.
2. See *Pa.* II. 2.3.
3. See *Pa.* II. 1. 24.
4. See Vārttika under *Pa.* II. 1. 37.
5. *Pa.* II. 1. 40.
6. But it is actually six-fold.

placed as the second member : Puruṣavyāghraḥ (a man like a tiger) (puruṣo vyāghraḥ iva). (5) Words of respect placed first: Guṇavṛddhiḥ dissolved as *guṇaḥ iti vṛddhiḥ* (elongation). Suhṛd and Subandhu (are examples). (6) The word signifying prominence is placed as the first member (*pāda eva padmaṁ* = *pāda-padmaṁ*). Bahuvrīhi (attributive compound) is sevenfold. (The following are examples) for the Bahuvrīhi having two words : *ārūḍhabhavano naraḥ* (A man who has stepped into a house).

13. These brahmins are about ten (ie., nine or eleven). upadaśāḥ (= daśānāṁ samīpe ye santi te) is (an example of Bahuvrīhi having the) numeral as the second member. (Examples of Bahnvrīhi) having both (the members) as numerals are such as *dvitrā* (two or three), *dvyekatraya* (two or one or three) men.

14. The particle *saha* (may be compounded) when it becomes the first member. The tree has been pulled out together with its root (samūla) (is an example). Those having the characteristic of reciprocity : (a battle in which the warriors fight) seizing each other's hair, (keśākeśī) fighting one another with nail (nakhānakhī).

15. (A Bahuvrīhi compound may be formed) to denote a direction (in between two directions) : *dakṣiṇapūrvā* (the point of direction in between the south and east). A Dvigu (having a number as the first member in a compound) is said to be twofold. It becomes singular (when denoting an aggregate), 'having two peaks' 'having five roots'. It is possible in many ways.

16. A Dvandva (copulative compound) is twofold *itaretarayoga* and *samāhāra* (the members are treated separately, and an aggragete of the things enumerated constituing a complex (idea). (An example for the first is) Rudraviṣṇū (Rudra and Viṣṇu). (An example for the second is) Bherīpaṭaha. (It is always singular.)

17-18. Avyayībhāva (compound consisting of two members, the first of which is, mostly, an indeclinable) is said to be of two kinds. An example for one having a noun as the first member (is): *śākasya mātrā* (very little vegetable) = śākaprati. An example for one with the first member as an indecliable (is) : *upakumbhaṁ* (near a pot) and *uparathyaṁ* (near a chariot). The compounds are fourfold on account of the prominence (of one member)—that which has the second member prominent and Dvandva, where both (the members) are prominent. Avyayībhāva has the first member prominent and Bahuvrīhi (in which the importance lies) externally.

CHAPTER THREE HUNDRED AND FIFTYSIX

The rules governing the formation of taddhita (secondary nominal bases)

Skanda said :

1-4. I shall describe the three kinds of *taddhita*; the general type (will be formed) by using the following affixes)

lac (*la*)	—	aṁsalaḥ (having muscular shoulders); vatsalaḥ (compassionate).
ilac (*ila*)	—	phenila (foamy); picchila (slippery).
śe (*śa*)	—	lomaśaḥ (hairy, a monkey).
ne (*na*)	—	pāmanah (sulphur)
aṇ (a)	—	prājña (wise), ārcaka (relating to a worshipper).
urac (*ura*)	—	forms dantura (having projecting teeth) from danta (tooth).
ra	—	madhura (sweet); suṣira (for a long time).
		(by adding va) Keśava (having beautiful hair) (is formed) similarly.
ya	—	hiraṇyaṁ (gold)
va	—	Mālava (name of a country)
valaci (*vala*)	—	rajasvalā (menstruous woman)
ini	—	dhanī (rich); karī and hastī (elephant)
ṭikan (*ika*)	—	dhanika (rich)
vin	—	payasvī (milky); māyāvī (magician)
yuyuc (*yus*)	—	Ūrṇāyuḥ (woolen)
5-8. *min* (*mi*)	—	vāgmī (eloquent)
ālac (*āla*)	—	(vācāla)
and		

āṭac — vācāka (eloquent)
ina — phalinaḥ (fruitful) ; barhiṇaḥ (a peacock) ; kekī (a peacock)
kan — vṛndāraka (venerable or beautiful)
āluc — śītālu = śītaṁ na sahate (unable to endure cold) ; himālu = himaṁ na sahate (not able to bear snow)

We would have the form *vātula* from *vāta* (by adding) *ulac*. *an* (is used to denote) progeny (such as) Vāsiṣṭha, Kaurava.
so'sya vāsakaḥ—Pāñcālaḥ
tatra vāsaḥ —Māthuraḥ
vetti adhīte cāndravyākaraṇam—Cāndrakaḥ

9-12. *Khañ* (ka) priyaṅgūnāṁ kṣetram praiyaṅgavīnakam
iñ (*i*) — Dākṣiḥ (the son of Dakṣa) ; Dāśarathiḥ (the son of Daśaratha).
kac — Nāṛāyana
phañ — Āśvāyanaḥ
yac — Gārgyaḥ (son of Garga) ; Vātsyakaḥ (of the family of Vātsya)
ḍhak (*eya*) — Vainateya (son of Vinatā, ie., Garuḍa) etc.
crak — Cāṭakerah
ḍhak — Gandheraka
gha (*iya*) — kṣatriya (born in the race of a ruler)
kha (*īna*) — kulīnaḥ (born of a good family)
ṇya (*ya*) — Kauravya (a descendant of Kuru)
yat — mūrdhanya (being in or on the head) ; mukhya (chief) etc.
— sugandhiḥ (good fragrance)

13. *itac* (ita) (will be used) for Tāraka group[1] (of words) (in the sense of that is obtained or possessed by) such as 'the sky studded with stars'.
anaṁ (an) — kuṇḍodhnī (a cow with a full udder) ; puṣpadhanvan (the god of love) ; sudhanvan (having an excellent bow).

1. See Pa. V. 2. 36

14. *cuñcup* (*cuñcu*) — vittacuñcuḥ would be used in the sense of one having wealth.

caṇap (*caṇa*) — keśacaṇah (renowned for the hair)

rūpa — paṭarūpa (in the form of a cloth).

15-16 *iyas* — it would be paṭīyān (cleverer)

tarap (*tara*) — akṣatara (fairly proficient in dice); pacatitarāṁ[1] (cooking fairly well)

tamap (*tama*) — aṭatitamāṁ[2] (wandering excellently); mṛdvītamā (much soft).

kalpap (*kalpa*) — Indrakalpaḥ (equal to Indra); ardhakalpakaḥ (equal to half)

deśīya or *deśya* — rājadeśīyaḥ (almost a king)

17. *jātiya* — Paṭujātīya (belonging to an intelligent group)

mātrac (*mātra*) — jānumātraṁ (reaching as far as the knee)

dvayasac (*dvayasa*) — ūrudvayasa (reaching upto the thigh)

dadhnac (*dadhna*) — ūrudadhna (reaching upto the thigh)

18. *tayap* (*taya*) — pañcatayaḥ (fivefold)

ṭhak (*ika*) — dauvārikaḥ (door-keeper)

The general suffixes have been described. (I shall describe now) the secondary affixes known as indeclinables.

19-20. *tasil* (*tas*) — *yataḥ* is formed (in the sense of) from which.

tral is said (to form) *yatra* (where), *tatra* (there), *adhunā* (is used in the sense of) at that time, and *dān* (is used in) *idānīṁ* (now). *Dā* is used (to form) *sarvadā* (always) together with *sarva*. *hil* (hi) forms *tarhi* in the sense of that time and *karhi*, at which time. *Ha* (is used to form) *iha* (in the sense of) now.

21-24a. *thāl* (*thā*) — yathā (when);

tham (*tha*) — kathaṁ (how).

Let one gather in the eastern direction *astāt* (il) for pūrva (śabda).

May the leaders move in the front (purastāt). (The word) *sadya* is said (to be used) (in the sense of) same day. *Ut* (is used) for the previous year and *Parut* for (the year) preceding

1. See *Pa.* V. 4.11
2. See *ibid.*

that *Parāri* is also (used in the same sense). *Aiṣamo* (is used in the sense of) this year derived from the word *samas*). Edyavau and Paredyavi would (denote) the next day. Adya means today. Dye is used in combination as Pūrvedyuḥ and Edyuḥ (the previous day).

24b-27. Let one dwell in the southern direction. Dakṣiṇāt and Dakṣiṇādi (in the southern direction). May one dwell in the northern direction: Uttarāt and Uttarādi (in the northern direction). May one dwell above: Upariṣṭāt. Riṣṭati and Ūrdhvakāt (above) (have similar meaning). By adding suffix *āc* we have dakṣiṇā. By adding *āhi* we have *dakṣiṇāhi* (in the south) *vaset* (may one dwell). *Dha* in *dvidhā* denotes two ways. When *dhyamuñ* is added to eke it becomes ekadhyam (thinking in one form only), Likewise *dhamuñ* is added to *dvi* we have dvaidham (to forms)...[1]

28-30. The particles which are secondary suffixes have been described. (I shall describe) the secondary affixes which are abstract nouns. Paṭor bhāvaḥ = paṭutvaṁ (cleverness) (using) (suffix) *tva*. *Paṭutā* is said (to be by using) *tālic*. By adding *iman* to *pṛthu* (we have) *prathimā* (extension). Saukhyaṁ (happiness) is said to be from *sukha* (by adding) *ṣyañ*. *Steyam* (theft) (is fromed) (by adding) *yat* to *stena* (a thief). The state of being a monkey is *kāpeyaṁ*. *Sainya* (army) and *pathya* (beneficial) are said (to be formed by adding) *yak* (*ya*). *Āśvaṁ* (relating to a horse), *kaumārakaṁ* (relating to boyhood) and *yauvanaṁ* (relating to youth) (are from) *aṇ* (*ā*). *Ācāryakaṁ* relating to the preceptor) (is) from *kan*. The other secondary suffixes are said (to be formed) in the same way.

1. The next two words are not clear.

CHAPTER THREE HUNDRED AND FIFTYSEVEN

The formation of the primary nominal bases by adding primary affixes known as uṇādi, beginning with affix u

Kumāra said :

1-2a. The Uṇādis (a kind of primary nominal affixes) are spoken as *pratyayas* (suffixes) added to roots. (The word) *Kāru* (denoting) an artisan (is formed by adding the suffix) *uṇ*. (The other examples are) *jāyuḥ* (medicine or physician), *māyuḥ* (meaning) bile, *gomāyuḥ* (biles in the cow). These *uṇādis* are widely used in the Āyurveda (Indian system of medicine) terminology.

2b-4a. (The other examples are) *āyuḥ* (life), *svādu* (sweet), *hetu* (cause) etc. *Kiṁśāruḥ* (means) the beard of a corn. *Kṛkavāku* denotes a cock. *Guru* is the master. *Maru* is (a desert). *Śayu* is known as a big serpent. *Saru* is said to be a weapon (sword). *Svaru* (denotes) the thunderbolt. *Trapu* (means) *sisam*[1]. *Phalgu* is said (to mean) worthless thing.

4b-6. (The following words) are known (to be derived by adding the corresponding suffixes): *gṛdhraḥ* (vulture) (from) *kran, mandiram* (an abode) and *timiraṁ* (meaning) darkness (from) *kirac, salilaṁ* (meaning) water and *bhaṇḍila* (meaning) auspicious (from) *ilac. Budhaḥ* (meaning) a learned person (from) *kvasu.* (The word) *śibira* (denotes) a concealed position. *Otuḥ* (denotes) a cat (from the suffix) *tun.* (The words) *karṇaḥ* (ear), *kāmi* (a lustful person), *gṛhaṁ* (house), *bhūḥ* (earth), *vāstu* (the site of a house) and *jaivātṛkaḥ* (the moon) are known to be *uṇādis* because they denote (objects).

7. (The word) *anaḍvān* (a bull) is from (the root) *vaḥ* (to bear) with *ḍvan. Jiva* (life), *arṇava* (ocean) and *auṣadha* (herb) convey genus. (The word) *vahni* (fire) is (by adding the suffix) *ni, hariṇaḥ* (meaning) a deer (from *inan*) and *kāmi* (one who is lustful) (denotes) a fit person.

8. *Saṅghāta* (a collection); *varūḍa* (mixed caste), *saraṇḍa* (means) an animal, *eraṇḍa* (is a kind of) tree; *sāma* (chant). *nirbhara* (full).

1. But *trapu* denotes tin and *sisam*, lead.

9. (The word) *sphāraṁ* would mean (plenty)... (The words) *cira* (denoting) a bark garment belongs to the same category. (The word) *kātara* (means) timid. But *ugra* (means) fierce. *Javasa* (denotes) grass.

10. *Jagat* (signifies) the earth and *kṛśānu*, the lustre of the Sun. *Varvara* (means) curled and *dhūrta* (a wicked person). *Catvaraṁ* (denotes) a junction of four roads.

11. *Civara* (is) the dress of a mendicant. *Āditya* is said to be *Mitra* (the Sun). (The word) *putra* (stands for) a son and *pitā*, for father. (The words) *pṛdāku* (denotes) a tiger and a scorpion. *Garta* (denotes) a hole. *Bharata* (means) an actor. These are the other *uṇādis*.

CHAPTER THREE HUNDRED AND FIFTYEIGHT

The completed forms of the verbs after adding the conjugational signs etc.

Kumāra said:

1. I shall describe the terminations (which are added) to the verbs as well as the substitutes in brief. The verbs occur in three forms such as *bhāve* (impersonal), *karmaṇi* (passive) and *kartari* (active).

2. They are known to be transitive and intransitive in the two *padas* (Ātmanepada and Parasmaipada) in the Active. In the same way the substitutes in the transitive and intransitive.

3. *Laṭ* is the designation for the present tense. *Liṅ* is said to be in the sense of the potential (mood) etc. *Loṭ* (is) for benediction and conditional etc. *Laṅ* (is the designation) for the past not relating to the present day.

4. *Luṅ* (is the name) for the past (Aorist) and *liṭ* for remote past and *luṭ* for immediate (first) future. *Liṅ* (is used) for benediction and *lṛṭ* in the remaining senses. *Lṛṅ* would denote the (second) future.

5. (*Lṛṅ*, conditional) (is used in the sentences) in which the Potential may be used, when the non-performance of action is

implied. The latter nine (are) Ātmanepada (the result of the action accruing to one's self) and the former nine (are) Parasmaipada (the result of the action accruing to another person). *Tip*, *tas* and *anti* (are the terminations of) the *prathamapuruṣa*.[1]

6-7a. *Sip*, *thas* and *tha* (are the terminations of) the *madhyamapuruṣa*[2] and *mip*, *vas* and *mas* (for) the *uttamapuruṣa*[3]. *Ta*, *ātāṁ* and *anta* (are) the *prathamapuruṣa* (terminations) in the Ātmanepada, *thās*, *āthāṁ*, *dhvaṁ* in the *madhyama* and *i*, *vahi*, *mahi* in the *uttama* (in the imperfect). *Bhū* (to be) etc. are known to be the roots.

7b-10a. The following are the important roots belonging to the different conjugations[4]. (The roots) *bhū* (to be), *edh* (to prosper), *pac* (to cook), *nand* (to rejoice), *dhvaṁs* (to perish), *śaṁs* (to praise) (belong to the first conjugation). *Pad* (to go) (fourth), *ad* (to eat) (second), *śiṅ* (to lie down, second), *krīḍ* (to buy) (first), *juhoti* (*hū* to offer in a sacrifice) (third), *jahāti* (*hā* to abandon, third), *dadhāti* (*dhā* to bear, third), *divyati* (*di* to play or to shine, fourth), *svapiti* (*svap* to sleep, second), *nah* (to tie, fourth), *sunoti* (*su*, to press out juice, fifth), *vas* (to dwell), *tud* (to strike, wound, sixth), *mṛśati* (*mṛś* to touch, sixth), *muñcati* (*muñc* to lose, sixth), *rudh* (to hold up, seventh), *bhuj* (to enjoy, seventh), *tyaj* (to abandon, first), and *tan* (to spread, eighth). (The roots) *man* (to think), *karoti* (*kṛ*, to do), *krīḍati* (*krīḍ*, to play), *vṛṅ* (to choose), *grah* (to seize), *cur* (*cur*, to steal), *pā* (to drink and protect), *nī* (to carry) and *arc* (to worship) are the important in the *śap*[5] and other modifications.

10b-13a. In (the root) *bhū* (by adding *tiṅ*, we would have *saḥ bhavati* (he becomes), *tau bhavataḥ* (they two become) and *te bhavanti* (they all become). (Similarly we have) you become, you two become and you all become and I become, we two become and we all become. (Similarly in the Ātmanepada), the

1. corresponding to the third person.
2. corresponding to the second person.
3. corresponding to the first person.
4. The roots are divinded into ten conjugations known as *bhvādi*, *adādi*, *juhotyādi*, *divādi*, *svādi*, *tudādi*, *rudhādi*, *tanādi*, *kryādi* and *curādi*.
5. *śap* is the designation of the termination added to the first conjugation.

family prospers, two prosper and (many) prosper. You grow with intellect, (you two) prosper and you all prosper. We two grow with intellect. We all prosper with devotion to (lord) Hari. (He) cooks etc. are as before.

13b-15. One becomes and one enjoys (are examples) for the impersonal forms. The passive (is formed by adding) *yak*. The desiderative form (of root *bhū* is) *bubhūṣati*. Thus in the causal (one) meditates on the lord. In the frequentative (we have the form) *bobhūyate* (Ātmanepada) or *bobhoti* when *yoṅ* is dropped (is the form) in the Parasmaipada frequentative. *Putrīyati* (treats like a son) on account of desire for children and thus *paṭapaṭāyate* (utters the sound *paṭpaṭ*), *ghaṭayati* (brings about) (are examples) of the desiderative. He causes the figure to be adorned (*bubhūṣayati*) (is the form) in the causal.

16. Bhavet (may become), bhavetāṁ, bhaveyuḥ, bhaveḥ bhavetaṁ, bhaveta, bhaveyaṁ, bhaveva, bhavema are (the forms in the three persons in the singular, dual and plural) in the Potential (mood) (in the Parasmaipada).

17. Edheta, edheyātāṁ, edheran (grow or prosper) with the mind and prosperity, edhetāḥ, edheyāthāṁ, edhedhvaṁ, edheya, edhevahi, edhemahi (are the forms of the Potential moon in the Ātmanepada).

18-19a. Let it be. Bhavatāṁ, bhavantu, bhavatād or bhava, bhavataṁ, bhavata, bhavāni, bhavāva, bhavāma (are the forms) in the Imperative mood. Edhatāṁ (may one prosper), edhetāṁ, edhantāṁ (in the third person), edhai (in the first person singular) (are the forms of Ātmanepada Imperative). Pacāvahai, pacāmahai (are the forms of Ātmanepada Imperative dual and plural from *pac* to cook).

19b-20. Abhyanandat (felicitated), apacatāṁ (cooked), apacan (they cooked), apacaḥ (you cooked), abhavataṁ (you two became), abhavata (you all became), apacaṁ (I cooked), apacāva (we two cooked), apacāma (we all cooked) (are the examples for the past (imperfect) in the Parasmaipada). Aidhata, aidhetāṁ (third person singular and dual), aidhadhvaṁ (second person plural), aidhe, aidhāmahi (first person singular and plural) are said to be (the forms in the past tense, Ātmanepada).

21. Abhūt, abhūtāṁ, abhūvan, abhūḥ and abhūvaṁ (are the forms of the root *bhū* to be or become) in the Aorist. Aidhiṣṭa, Aidhiṣātāṁ (Men prospered), aidhiṣṭhāḥ, aidhiṣī (are) thus (the forms of the Aorist Ātmanepada).

22. (The root *bhū* becomes) babhūva, babhūvatuḥ, babhūvuḥ, babhūvitha, babhūvathuḥ, babhūva, (babhūva), babhūviva and babhūvima (are the forms) in the Perfect tense (in the Parasmaipada).

23. Pece, pecāte, pecire (cooked) and edhāñcakṛṣe tvaṁ (you prospered), edhāñcakrāthe, pecidhve, pece, pecimahe (are the forms in the Perfect in the Ātmanepada and Periphrastic perfect).

24-25. In the first future (the root *bhū* has the forms) bhavitā, bhavitārau, bhavitāraḥ (will become) Hara and others. Bhavitāsi, bhavitāsthaḥ; bhavitāsmaḥ vayam (we) (are the other forms). Paktā, paktārau, paktāraḥ (are the forms of the root *pac* in the first future third person). You will cook (paktāse) good food. Paktādhve, I will cook (paktāhe), paktāsmahe (we will cook) the porridge for lord Hari (are examples for some of the forms of the root *pac* in the first future Ātmanepada).

26-30. In the benedictive: May there be (bhūyāt) happiness, Hari and Saṅkara bhūyāstām (be benevolent), bhūyāsuḥ they, you bhūyāḥ, you two gods bhūyāstaṁ, you all bhūyāsta, ahaṁ bhūyāsaṁ (May I be), bhūyāsma (we all may be) always (happy). Yakṣīṣṭa, edhiṣīyāstāṁ, yakṣīran, edhiṣīya, yakṣīvahi, edhiṣīmahi (are some of the forms of the roots *yaj*, to sacrifice and *edh* to prosper in the Ātmanepada) in the Benedictive. Ayakṣyata, ayakṣeyātāṁ, ayakṣyanta, ayakṣye, ayakṣyethāṁ you two, ayakṣyadhvaṁ, aidhiṣyāvahi, aidhiṣyāmahi we all (are the forms) in the Conditional mood in the Parasmaipada, Ātmanepada. *Bhaviṣyati* would be (the form) in the second future. Edhiṣyāmahe is similar. In the same way vibhāvayiṣyanti, bobhaviṣyati (frequentative second future) (will become again and again). Ghaṭayet, paṭayet, putrīyati, kāmyati (are other forms of nominal verbs and frequentatives).

CHAPTER THREE HUNDRED AND FIFTYNINE

The finished forms after adding the kṛt affixes (primary affixes added to verbs)

Kumāra said:

1-3. The *kṛts* are to be known in all the three forms (such as) the impersonal, passive and active. *Ac, lyuṭ* (to form neuter abstract nouns by adding *na*), *ktin* (*ti*) (to form feminine abstract nouns), *ghañ* (added to roots ending in consonants), and *yuc* in the impersonal (are the affixes). (Their examples are) in the *ac*: *vinaya* (modesty), *utkaraḥ* (heap, multitude), *prakaraḥ* (collection, heap), *devaḥ* (lord), *bhadraḥ* (good), *śrikaraḥ* (conferer of prosperity). The form in *lyuṭ* (is) *śobhanaṁ* (auspicious), in *ktin* (*ti*) (the forms are) *vṛddhi* (increase), *stuti* (praise) and *mati* (intellect). (The form) in *ghañ* is *bhāva* (feeling or state), in *yuñ*—*kāraṇā* (doing action), *bhāvanā* (bringing into existence) etc. and in the syllable *a*—(represented) by *cikitsā* (remedy).

4. Then (the affixes) *tavya* and *aniya* (forming the words) *kartavyaṁ, karaṇiyakaṁ* (fit to be done), (the affix) *yat* (to form) *deyaṁ* (ought to be given) and *dhyeyaṁ* (ought to be meditated), in *ṇyat* (to form) *kāryaṁ* (a work or task) and *kṛtyakāḥ* (work to be done).

5. *Kta* and other (affixes) are to be known in the active, and some in the impersonal and passive. (A person) has gone to the village. The village has been reached. The preceptor has been embraced by you.

6. *Śatṛṅ* (present participle in the Parasmaipada) and *śānac* (present participle in the Ātmanepada) are *bhavan* (becoming) and *edhamāna* (being prosperous). *Ṇvuḥ* and *tṛc* (are) added to all the roots (to form agents such as) (*bhāvakaḥ* and *bhavitā* (feeling or manifestation and that which is about to become).

7. (An example) for ending in *kvip* (is) Svayambhūḥ (self-originated). *Kvas* (*vas*) and *Kānac* (*āna*) (are the affixes) (of the participles) of the perfect (Parasmaipada and Ātmanepada). *Babhūvivat* and *peçivat* (in the Parasmaipada) and *pecānaḥ* and *śraddadhānakaḥ* (in the Ātmanepada) (are the examples).

8. *Kumbhakāra* (a potter) etc. would be (formed by adding the affix) *aṇ*. The *uṇādis* are known to be in the past. *Vāyuḥ* (wind), *pāyuḥ* (the anus) and *kāru* (artisan) would be (formed from them). These are said to be widely used in the Vedas.

CHAPTER THREE HUNDRED AND SIXTY

*The synonyms of group of words denoting the celestial region and the nether world**

Fire-god said:

1. I shall describe to you (the synonyms) of heaven etc. of which lord Hari is the indication. Svaḥ, svargaḥ, nākaḥ, tridivaḥ, dyauḥ, triviṣṭapa are synonyms (denoting heaven).

2-3a. Devas, Vṛndārakas and Lekhas (are the names for the celestials). Rudra and others (are) the chief of group of gods. Vidyādharas, Apsaras, Yakṣas, Rakṣas, Gandharvas, Kinnaras, Piśācas, Guhyakas, Siddhas and Bhūtas had celestial origin.

3b. The enemies of the Devas, Asuras and Daityas (born of Diti) (are the names of the demons). Sugataḥ and Tathāgataḥ (denote Buddha).[1]

4. Brahmā, Ātmabhūḥ (self-born), Surajyeṣṭha (chief of the Devas) (are the synonyms of Brahmā). Viṣṇu, Nārāyaṇa and Hari (are the names of Viṣṇu). Revatīśa (husband of Revatī), Halīrāma (Rāma with with plough) (are the words denoting Balarāma) (elder brother of Kṛṣṇa). Kāma, Pañcaśara (having five shafts) and Smara (are the names of God of love).

5. Lakṣmī, Padmālayā (having the lotus as abode), and Padmā (are the names of Goddess Lakṣmī). Sarva (all things), Sarveśvara (lord of all beings), and Śiva (auspicious) (are the

*The Purāṇa summarises the Amarakośa in eight chapters. This chapter is an abridgement of the Kāṇḍa I, Svargavarga 6-79 verses and Pātālavarga 239-347 verses.

1. The founder of Buddhism.

names of Śiva). Kaparda is his matted hair. Pināka is the bow (of lord Śiva) also known as Ajagava.

6. His attendants are (known as) Pramathas. Mṛḍānī (compassionate), Caṇḍikā (fierce) and Ambikā (mother) (are the names of Goddess Pārvatī). Dvaimātura[1] (having two mothers) and Gajāsya (having an elephant face) (are the names of lord Gaṇeśa). Senānī (leader of an army), Agnibhū (fire-born) and Guha (reared in a secret place) (are the names of Skanda).

7. Ākhaṇḍala (breaker), Sunāsīra (favourable for the growth of grain), Sūtrāman (guarding well) and Divaspati (lord of the heaven) (are the names of Indra). Pulomajā (duaghter of Puloman, a demon), Śacī (powerful) and Indrāṇī are the names of wife (of Indra).

8. His (Indra's) mansion (is known as) Vaijayanta. Jayanta (victorious) (is the name of) Pākaśāsani (son of Pākaśāsana, Indra). Airāvata, Abhramātaṅga (elephantine cloud), Airāvaṇa and Abhramuvallabha (mate of the female elephant of the east) (are the names of the elephant of Indra).

9. Hlādinī (that which delights), Vajra, that it not a feminine (word), Kuliśa, Bhidura (neuter words) and Pavi (masculine) (are the words denoting Indra's club). Indra's chariot is called) Vyomayāna and Vimāna (the vehicle of the sky). (The latter word is) not feminine. Pīyūṣa, Amṛta and Sudhā (denote ambrosia).

10. Sudharmā is the council of gods. Svargaṅgā and Suradīrghikā (denote the celestial Ganges). The celestial women such as Urvaśī and others (are denoted by the words) Svarveśyā and Apsarasaḥ. (Here the latter word is always) feminine and plural.

11-12. Hāhā and Hūhū (are the names of) Gandharvas (semi-divine beings). Agni, Vahni, Dhanañjaya (conqueror of wealth), Jātavedas (knower of all things), Kṛṣṇavartman (whose way is black), Āśrayāśa (consuming everything with which it comes into contact), Pāvaka (purifier), Hiraṇyaretas (having golden seed), Saptārcis (having seven rays), Śukra (white). Āśuśukṣaṇi (shining forth), Śuci (pure) and Appittam (bile of

1. having a natural mother and a step-mother.

water) (are the words denoting fire). Aurva, Vāḍava and Vaḍavānala (denote the submarine fire).

13-14. Among the words denoting the flames of fire, Jvāla and Kīla (are masculine and feminine), Arcis (feminine and neuter) and Heti and Śikhā (are) feminine. Sphuliṅga and Agnikaṇa (denote a spark of fire). (These words are used) in all the three (genders). Dharmarāja (lord of virtue), Paretarāṭ (master of the dead), Kāla (the Time), Antaka (Destroyer), Daṇḍadhara (Wielder of a staff) and Srāddhadeva (lord of the ancestral rite) (are the synonymns of God of Death). Rākṣasa, Kauṇapa (coming from a corpse), Asrapa (blood drinker), Kravyāda (flesh eater), Yātudhāna and Nairṛti (are the words denoting a demon).

15. Pracetas, Varuṇa and Pāśī (having a noose) (denote Varuṇa, the upholder of moral laws). Śvasana (who breathes), Sparśana (who touches), Anila, Sadāgati (always moving), Mātariśvan, Prāṇa (life breath), Marut and Samīraṇa (denote wind).

16. *Java*, *raṁha* and *tara* (denote speed). *Laghu*, *kṣipram*, *aram*, *drutam*, *satvaram*, *capalam*, *tūrṇam*, *avilambitam* and *āśu* (denote haste).

17-18. *Satatam*, *anāratam*, *aśrāntam*, *santatam*, *aviratam*, *aniśam*, *nityam*, *anavaratam* and *ajasram* (mean eternally). *Atiśaya*, *bhara*, *ativelam*, *bhṛśam*, *atyartham*, *atimātram*, *udgāḍham*, *nirbharam*, *tivram*, *ekāntam*, *nitāntam*, *gāḍham*, *bāḍham*, and *dṛḍham* (denote excess).

19. Guhyakeśa, Yakṣarāja (chief of Yakṣas), Rājaraja and Dhanādhipa (lord of riches) (denote Kubera). Kinnara, Kimpuruṣa, Turaṅgavadana (horse-faced) and Mayu (denote the Kinnaras, a class of semidivine beings).

20. *Nidhi* and *śevadhi* (mean treasure). (Both the words are) masculine. *Vyoma*, *abhram*, *puṣkaram*, *ambaram*, *dyo*, *divam*, *antarikṣam* and *kham* (denote the sky).

21-22a. *Kāṣṭhā*, *āśā* and *kakubha* (denote) the direction. *Abhyantara* and *antarāla* mean the interspace (between the heaven and earth). *Cakravāla* and *maṇḍala* (mean a range or orb of things). *Taḍitvān* (having lightning), *vārida* (giver of water), *megha*, *stanayitnu* (that which makes sound) and *balāhaka* (stand for cloud). *Kādambinī* and *meghamālā* (denote a row of clouds). *Stanita* and *garjita* (mean the rumbling of thunder clouds).

22b-23. *Śampā, Śatahradā, hrādinī, airāvatī, kṣaṇaprabhā, taḍit, saudāminī, vidyut, cañcalā* and *capalā* (denote lightning).

23b-24. *Sphūrjathuḥ* and *vajranirghoṣa* (mean the peel of thunder). The cessation of rain (is denoted by the word) *avagraha*. *Dhārāsampāta* and *āsāra* (denote incessant rain). *Śīkara* (is known to be) drops of water (carried by wind). *Varṣopala* and *karakāḥ* (are the first rain drops falling like a stone). A cloudy day (is known as) *durdinam* (a bad day).

25. *Antardhā, vyavadhā* (feminine), *antardhi* (masculine), *apavāraṇam, apidhānam, tirodhānam, pidhānam,* and *ācchādanam* (mean concealing or covering).

26-27. (The words) *Abja, Jaivātṛka, Soma, Glauḥ, Mṛgāṅka, Kalānidhi, Vidhu* and *Kumudabandhu* (denote the Moon). *Bimba* and *maṇḍala* (are the words denoting the orb of the moon, the former is) feminine (and the latter is used in) all (the genders). A sixteenth digit (of the moon) is *kalā*. *Bhitta, śakala* and *khaṇḍaka* (denote a part). *Candrikā, kaumudī* and *jyotsnā* (denote the lustre of the moon). *Prasāda* and *prasannatā* (denote clear lustre).

28-29a. *Lakṣaṇam, lakṣmakam* and *cihnam* (stand for a mark). *Śobhā. kānti, dyuti* and *chavī* (denote lustre). *Suṣamā* (denotes) exquisite lustre. *Tuṣāra, tuhinam, himam, avaśyāya, nihāra, prāleyam, śiśira* and *himam* denote snow).

29b. *Nakṣatram, ṛkṣam, bham, tārā, tārakā* and *uḍu* (denote an asterism). There the last word may also be feminine.

30. *Guru, Jīva* and *Āṅgirasa* (are the words standing for Jupiter). *Uśanas, Bhārgava* and *Kavi* (denote Venus). *Vidhuntuda* (afflicting Moon) and *Tama* (denote) Rāhu. The rise of the constellations is known to be *lagna*.

31. Sages such as Marīci, Atri and others[1] are the seven sages. (They are known collectively as) *Citraśikhaṇḍins*. *Haridaśva, Bradhna, Pūṣā, Dyumaṇi, Mihira* and *Ravi* (denote the Sun).

32-34a. (The halo around the Sun is known as) *pariveṣa, paridhi, upasūryakam* and *maṇḍalam.* (The ray of the Sun is denoted by the words) *kiraṇa, usra, mayūkha, aṁśu, gabhasti, ghṛṇi, dhṛṣṇi*[2],

---

1. Aṅgiras, Pulastya, Pulaha, Kratu and Vasiṣṭha are the remaining five.

2. the Amara 210 reads *pṛśni*.

bhānu, *kara*, *marici*, and *didhiti* where *marici* is feminine and masculine (while) *dīdhiti* is feminine. (The lustre is denoted by the words) *prabhā*, *ruk*, *ruci*, *tviṭ*, *bhā*, *bhāḥ*, *chavi*, *dyuti*, *dipti*, *roci* and *śoci*, where the last two are neuter, (while the other words are feminine). (The lustre of the Sun is denoted by the words) *prakāśa*, *dyota* and *ātapa*.

34b-38a. (The words) *koṣṇam*, *kavoṣṇam*, *mandoṣṇam* and *kaduṣṇam* (denote little heat). They take neuter when referring to a quality and take all genders as attributes. Similarly (the words) *tigmam*,'*tīkṣṇam* and *kharam* (denoting excessive heat) take neuter or all the genders. (The words) *diṣṭa*, *anehā* and *kālaka* (denote time). (The words) *ghasra*, *dinam* and *ahas* (denote day). *Sāyam*, *sandhyā* and *pitṛprasūḥ* (denote the evening). *Pratyūṣas*, *aharmukham*, *kalyam*, *uṣas* and *pratyūṣas* (denote dawn). The three twilights (are known as) *prāhṇa* (morning), *aparāhṇa* (evening) are *madhyāhna* (midday). Night is denoted by the words) *śarvarī*, *yāmī* and *tamī*. (The night endowed with darkness is) *tamisrā* and (that with moonlight is) *jyotsnī*. The night together with the preceding and succeeding days (is known as) *pakṣiṇi*. The two (words) *ardharātri* and *niśitha* (denote) midnight. *Pradoṣa* and *rajanimukham* (is the period preceding the night).

38b-40. The intervening period between the pratipat (first lunar day) and the fifteenth (lunar day) is *parvan*. There are two fifteenth (days) at the end of each one of the fortnights. *Paurṇamāsi* and *pūrṇimā* (denote the last days of the bright lunar fortnight). (If that full moon) is a digit less (it is known as) *anumati*. If it is full, (it is) *rākā*. *Amāvāsyā*, is being near; *darśa* and *sūryendu-saṅgama* (union of Sun and Moon) (denote the last days of the dark lunar fortnight). If the moon is perceived (on the new moon day), (it is) *sinivāli* and if the same (is seen) a digit less, (it is) *kuhū*.

41-42a. *Saṁvarta*, *pralaya*, *kalpa*, *kṣaya* and *kalpānta* (denote deluge). (The words) *kaluṣam*, *vṛjinam*, *enaḥ*, *agham*, *aṁhaḥ*, *duritam* and *duṣkṛtam* (denote sin). (The words) *dharmam*, *puṇyam*, *śreyas*, *sukṛtam* and *vṛṣa* (denote good deeds). The word *dharmam* (is used) in the masculine and neuter.

42b-43a. (The words) *mut*, *priti*, *pramada*, *harṣa*, *pramoda*, *āmoda*, *sammada*, *ānandathuḥ*, *ānanda*, *śarma*, *sātam* and *sukham* (denote rejoice).

43b-44a. (The words) *śvaḥśreyasam*, *śivam*, *bhadram*, *kalyāṇam*, *maṅgalam*, *śubham*, *bhāvukam*, *bhavikam*, *bhavyam*, *kuśalam* and *kṣemam* (denote only welfare). (There) *kṣemam* is used in masculine and neuter.

44b. *Daivam*, *diṣṭam*, *bhāgadheyam*, *bhāgyam*, *niyati* and *vidhi* relate to (fruits of) previous birth. (The latter two) are feminine.

45a. *Kṣetrajña*, *ātman* and *puruṣa* relate to the soul in the body. *Pradhānam* and *prakṛti* (relate to the state in which the three qualities are in the same proportion). (The latter is used) in the feminine.

45b-46a. *Hetu*, *kāraṇam* and *bījam* (denote) cause. But *nidāna* is the primary cause. *Cittam*, *cetas*, *hṛdayam*, *svāntam*, *hṛt*, *mānasam* and *manas* (denote mind).

46b-47a. *Buddhi*, *manīṣā*, *dhiṣaṇā*, *dhīḥ*, *prajñā*, *śemuṣī*, *mati*, *prekṣā*, *upalabdhi*, *cit*, *saṁvit*, *pratipat*, *jñapti* and *cetanā* (denote intellect).

47b-48. The intellect (*dhī*) which possesses retentive power (is known as) *medhā*. *Saṅkalpa* (resolve) is an activity of mind. *Carcā* (discussion), *Saṅkhyā* (deliberation) and *vicāraṇā* (inquiry) (relate to examination of an object by means of knowledge). *Vicikitsā* and *saṁśaya* (relate to doubtful knowledge). *Adhyāhāra* (inference), *tarka* (logical reasoning) and *ūha* (conjecture) (relate to logic), *Nirṇaya* and *niścaya* mean conclusive knowledge.

49. (The words) *mithyādṛṣṭi* and *nāstikatā* (are used to denote knowledge arising from the argument that the other world does not exist). *Bhrānti*, *mithyāmati* and *bhrama* (mean false (knowledge). *Aṅgikāra*, *abhyupagama*, *pratiśraya* and *samāśraya* (denote acceptance).

50-51a. Knowledge relating to liberation from mundane existence (is) *jñānam*. (When it is used with reference to) architecture and scientific literature, (it is) *vijñānam*. *Mukti*, *kaivalyam*, *nirvāṇam*, *śreyas*, *niḥśreyasam*, *amṛtam*, *mokṣa* and *apavarga* (denote liberation from mundane existence). (The words) *ajñānam*, *avidyā* and *ahammati* (stand for ignorance). (Among these, the last two words are used) in the feminine.

51b-52a. (The word) *parimala* (is used to denote) fragrance arising from pounding or rubbing which attracts men. That which attracts very much (is known as) *āmoda*. (The words) *surabhi* and *ghrāṇatarpaṇa* (denote an object possessing good fragrance).

52b-53. (The words) *śukla, śubhra, śuci, śveta, viśada, śyeta, pāṇḍara, avadāta, sita, gaura, valakṣa, dhavala, arjuna, hariṇa, pāṇḍura* and *pāṇḍu* (denote white). That which is little white (is denoted by the word) *dhūsara*.

54. (The words) *nīla, asita, śyāma, kāla, syāmala* and *mecaka* (denote) black. (The words) *pīta, gaura* and *haridrābha* (denote yellow). (The words) *pālāśa, harita* and *harit* (mean) the green colour.

55. (The words) *rohita, lohita* and *rakta* (denote red colour). (The word) *śoṇa* (denotes) the colour resembling red lotus. Little redness (is denoted by the word) *aruṇa*. (The word) *pāṭala* (stands for) red mixed with white.

56-57a. *Śyāva* and *kapiśa* (denote whitish red). *Dhūmra* and *dhūmala* (denote) red and black mixed. *Kaḍāra. kapila, piṅga, piśaṅga, kadru* and *piṅgala* (denote reddish brown). *Citram, kirmira, kalmāṣa, sabala, eta* and and *karbura* (denote variegated colours).

57b. (The words) *vyāhāra, ukti* and *lapitam* (denote speech). *Apabhraṁśa* (means) a corrupted word.

58. A collection of *tiṅ* (verb) and *subanta* (noun) is a sentence. Or it may be an activity together with the case relation between a noun and a verb. *Itihāsa* is that which has happened in the past. *Purāṇa* has five characteristics.[1]

59. *Ākhyāyikā* is a narrative of a past event. *Prabandha* is an imaginary story. *Samāhāra* and *saṅgraha* (denote a collection of stories). *Pravahlikā* and *prahelikā* (are involving conjecture).

60. *Samasyā* is a puzzle that has to be completed. *Smṛti* is a collection of texts (composed for propagating) religious and moral duties. *Ākhyā, āhvā* and *abhidhāna* (denote name). *Vārtā* and *vṛttānta* are said (to denote) narration of worldly course of events.

61. (The words) *hūti, ākāraṇā* and *āhvānam* (denote calling). *Upanyāsa* and *vāṅmukha* (mean beginning of a speech). *Vivāda* and *vyavahāra* (are used in the sense of disputes relating debts,

---

1. These are: creation, secondary creation, royal genealogies, Manu periods and genealogy of gods and sages.

gifts etc.). (The words) *prativākyam* and *uttaram* (are used in the sense of reply).

62. *Upodghāta* and *udāhāra* (are used to denote the thought relating to accomplishment of a contextual object). *Mithyābhiśaṁsanam* and *abhiśāpa* (mean insult or abuse). (The words) *yaśas* and *kīrti* (denote fame). (The words) *praśna*, *pṛcchā* and *anuyogaka* (mean a query).

63. (The word) *āmreḍitam* (means) repetition two or three (times). (The words) *kutsā*, *nindā* and *garhaṇam* (denote censure). (The words) *ābhāṣaṇam* and *ālāpa* would (mean conversation preceded by mutual call). *Pralāpa* is meaningless utterance.

64. *Anulāpa* and *muhurbhāṣa* (mean repeated conversation). *Vilāpa* and *paridevana* denote speech preceded by weeping. *Vipralāpa* and *virodhokti* (denote mutually contradictory utterances). *Saṁlāpa* is conversation between one another.

65. *Supralāpa* and *suvacanam* (mean good utterance). *Apalāpa* and *nihnava* (mean veiled statement). *Ruśati*[1] means inauspicious utterance. *Saṅgatam* and *hṛdayaṅgamam* (would denote well-constructed sentence).

66. That which is exceedingly sweet is *sāntvam*. *Abaddham* and *anarthakam* would (mean absurd). *Niṣṭhuram*[2] and *paruṣam* (mean harsh utterance). *Aślīlam* and *grāmyam* (mean unrefined utterance). The statement which is pleasing and true (is) *sūnṛtam*.

67-69. *Satyam*, *tathyam*, *ṛtam* and *samyak* (would mean truth). (The words) *nāda*, *nisvāna*, *nisvana*, *ārava*, *ārāva*, *saṁrāva* and *virāva* (denote ordinary sound). *Marmara* (denotes) the sound made by cloth and leaves. (The sound made) by the ornaments (is) *śiñjitam*. *Nikvaṇa* and *kvāṇa* (denote the sound) of a lute. The sound made by birds (is) *vāśitam*. *Kolāhala* and *kalakala* (mean the clear sound made by many). The two (words) *gītam* and *gānam* mean the same (namely, a song). *Pratiśrut* and *pratidhvāna* (mean echo), where the former is feminine. (The sounds such as) *niṣāda* (and the like) arise from stringed instruments and throats (of singers).

---

1. The printed text wrongly reads *uṣatī*.
2. The Purāṇic text mixes this term and the next. This has been corrected on the basis of *Amara*.

70-71. A subtle (sound) is *kākali*. That which is sweet and not explicit is *kala*. *Mandara* is a lofty sound. *Tāra* is a very loud sound. Where there is a resonance and well blending of the (last) three sounds it is said to be *ekatāla*. *Viṇā*, *vallaki* and *vipañci* (denote lute). That which is known to have seven strings is *parivādini*.

72. *Viṇā* and other instruments are spread out. *Muraja* and the like are bound. *Vaṁśa* (flute) and others have holes. An instrument made of bell-metal and the like is *ghanam*.

73. Thus there are four kinds of musical instruments having the appellation *vāditram* and *ātodyam*. *Mṛdaṅga* and *Muraja* (are synonyms). *Aṅkyāḥ*, *āliṅgyaḥ* and *ūrdhvaka* are different kinds of *Mṛdaṅgas*.

74-75a. The drum that is sounded (at first) for the sake of fame (is known as) *Ḍhakkā*. *Bheri* and *Dundubhi* (are synonyms), the former is feminine and the latter masculine.[1] *Ānaka* and *Paṭaha* (are synonyms). *Jharjhari*, *Ḍiṇḍima*, *Mardala* and *Paṇava* (are different kinds of percussion instruments).[2] *Tāla* is the measure of time relating to the performance.

75b. *Laya* is the equal proportion of the performance and time (relating to music, dance etc.) *Tāṇḍavam*, *nāṭyam*, *lāsyam* and *nartanam* (are synonyms).

76. *Nṛtyam* (dance), *gitam* (singing) and *vādyam* (instrumental), the three (are known collectively as) *tauryatrikam*. The king is known as *Bhaṭṭāraka* and *Deva*. (The queen) who had been anointed is *Devi*.

77-81a. *Śṛṅgāra* (erotic), *vīra* (heroic), *karuṇa* (pathos), *adbhuta* (wonder), *hāsya* (mirth), *bhayānaka* (frightening), *bibhatsa* (disgust) and *raudra* (wrath) are the sentiments. The erotic (is also denoted by the words) *śuci* and *ujjvala*. The heroic sentiment (is also known as) *utsāhavardhana*. *Kāruṇyam*, *karuṇā*, *ghṛṇā*, *kṛpā*, *dayā*, *anukampā* and *anukrośa* (denote the sentiment of pathos). *Hasa*, *hāsa* and *hāsyam* (mean the same). *Bibhatsa* (is also known as) *vikṛta*. These two are masculine (when denoting the sentiment). *Vismaya*, *adbhutam*, *āścaryam* and *citram* (denote wonder). *Bhairavam*, *dāruṇam*, *bhiṣaṇam*, *bhiṣmam*, *ghoram*, *bhimam*, *bhayānakam*,

1. The textual reading is wrong.
2. The reading *tulye* in the text is not correct; *anye* would be better.

bhayaṅkaram and *pratibhayam* (denote frightening). *Raudra* is *ugra* (terrible). (These fourteen beginning with *adbhuta* are masculine relating to a sentiment.) (Otherwise they take) the three (genders). *Dara, trāsa, bhītiḥ, bhīḥ, sādhvasam* and *bhayam* (mean fear).

81b. The change relating to mind is *bhāva*. *Anubhāva* is the expression of the mental change.

82. (The words) *garva, abhimāna* and *ahaṁkāra* (denote pride). *Māna* is elevated thinking. *Anādara, paribhava, paribhāva* and *tiraskriyā* (mean disrespect).

83. (The words) *vrīḍā, lajjā, trapā* and *hrī* (would mean shyness). The desire for wealth (is) *abhidhyānam*[1]. (The words) *kautūhalam, kautukam, kutukam* and *kutūhalam* (denote curiosity).

84. (The words) *vilāsa, bibboka, vibhrama, lalitam, helā* and *līlā* denoting the behaviour of women are known as *hāva* produced from erotic state.

85. (The words) *drava, keli, parihāsa, krīḍā* and *līlā* (denote only erotic sport). *Kūrdanam* (means child's play). A burst of laughter with a motive (is) *ācchuritakam*. The same, if little, (is known as) *smitam*.

86. *Adhobhuvanam* and *pātālam* (denote the nether world). (The words) *chidram, śvabhram, vapā* and *śuṣi* (denote a hole in general). *Garta* and *avaṭa* (denote) a hole or pit in the earth. (The words) *tamisram, timiram* and *tama* (denote darkness).

87. (The words) *sarpa, pṛdākuḥ, bhujaga, dantaśūka* and *bileśaya* (denote a serpent). (The words) *viṣam, kṣveḍa* and *garalam* (mean poison). (The words) *niraya* and *durgati* (mean hell). The latter is feminine.

88. (The words) *payaḥ, kilālam, amṛtam, udakam, bhuvanam* and *vanam* (are used in the sense of water). *Bhaṅga, taraṅga* and *ūrmi* denote waves. *Kallola* and *ullola* (denote mighty waves).

89. (The words) *pṛṣanti, bindavaḥ* and *pṛṣataḥ* (stand for drops of water). (The words) *kūlam, rodhas* and *tīra(ka)m* (denote banks). That which rises from water is *pulinam* (sand). (The words) *jambāla, paṅka* and *kardama* (mean mire).

90-91. The overflow of floods is (denoted by the words)

---

1. Amara 409 reads '*abhidhyā*' meaning desire to covet another's property.

jalocchvāsāḥ and *parivāhāḥ*. (The words) *kūpakāḥ* and *vidārakāḥ* (are pits made in the dry bed of rivers). *Ātara* and *tarapaṇyam* (are used in the sense of ferry charges). The wooden water-carrier is *droṇi*. *Kaluṣa* and *āvila* are (used to mean) impure and *accha*, pure. (The word) *gabhīrakam* (denotes deep). *Agādham* (means very deep). (The words) *dāśa* and *kaivarta* (denote a fisherman). *Jambūkas* (bivalve shells) are oysters in the water.

92. *Saugandhika* and *kalhāra* (denote white lotus blossoming in the evening). *Indīvara* is a blue lotus. *Utpala* and *kuvalaya* denote blue lotus. *Kumuda* and *kairava* (are used to denote) white (lotus).

93. The root of these lotuses (is) *śālūka*. (The words) *padmam* and *tāmarasam* (denote a lotus). *Nīlotpalam* and *kuvalayam* (denote a lily). The red lotus is known as *kokanadam*.

94-95. *Karahāṭa* and *śiphākandam* (denote the root of a lotus). *Kiñjalka* and *kesara* mean the filament, not in feminine.[1] (The words) *khani* and *ākara* (denote the place from where the gems are produced). The former is feminine. *Pāda* and *pratyantaparvata* (denote) smaller hills. That which is still nearer to the hill, (is said to be) *upatyakā*. The earth above the hill (is known as) *adhityakā*. The groups of words belonging to the heaven and hell have been described. Listen to me ! I shall describe words having different meaning.

CHAPTER THREE HUNDRED AND SIXTYONE*

The indeclinables

Fire-god said :

1. (The indeclinable) *āṅ* is used in the (following) in the sense of a little, pervading, limit and in combination with verbs. (The particle) *ā* known as *pragṛhya* is used in sentences to denote remembrance. (The same with a *visarga*) (denotes) anger and affliction.

1. After summarising the first *Kāṇḍa* of *Amara*, the *Purāṇa* jumps to the middle of the second *Kāṇḍa*.

*The Purāṇa summarises in this chapter, from *Amara* III. paṅkti 2814.

2. (The particle) *ku* (is used) in the sense of sin, condemnation and little. *Dhik* (is used in the sense of) disgust and censure. *Ca* (is used) to connect with another, as a collection, union with one another, for connecting mutually independent words with a common word.

3. *Svasti* (is used in the sense of) benediction, well-being and meritorious act. *Ati* (has the sense of) excess and crossing. *Svit* (is used in the sense of) interrogation and doubt. *Tu* (is used to denote) division and limitation.

4. *Sakṛt* (is used in the sense of) together with and once. *Ārāt* (has the sense of) near and far off. (The word) *paścāt* (is used in the sense of) western direction and the end. *Api* (has the sense of collection). *Uta* has the sense of option.

5. *Śaśvat* (is used in the sense of) repetition and together with. *Sākṣāt* (denotes) perception and identity. *Bata* (is used in the following senses) : grief, pity, pleasure, surprise and invitation.

6. *Hanta* (is used to express) rejoice, pity, beginning of a sentence and grief. *Prati* is used according to tradition in (the sense) of a representative both as repetition and as indicative etc.

7. *Iti* (is used in the sense of) cause, context, making explicit etc. and conclusion. *Purastāt* (is used to denote) in the east, at first, before and in front of. *Api* is also (used in the same sense).

8. *Yāvat* and *tāvat* (are used in the sense of) whole, end, measure and determination. *Atha* (is used to express) auspiciousness, continuity, beginning, query and whole.

9. *Vṛthā* (is used to convey) uselessness and devoid of injunction. *Nānā* (conveys) many and both. *Nu* (expresses) query and option. *Anu* (expresses) succession and resemblance.

10. *Nanu* (is used to indicate) query, determination, permission, pacification and invitation. *Api* (is used to denote) censure, collection, query, doubt and conjecture.

11. *Vā* (expresses) comparison and option. *Sāmi* (conveys) half and disgust. *Amā* (denote) togetherness and proximity. *Kam* (means) water and head.

12. *Evam* (is used to convey) similarity and such and such a manner. *Nūnam* (is used) in logic and determination. *Joṣam*

(is used to mean) silence and happiness. *Kim* (is used to convey) query and disgust.

13. *Nāma* (is used to mean) making explicit, conjecture, anger, approximation and censure. *Alam* conveys (the sense of) ornament, satiety, ability and prevention.

14. *Hūm* (is used to convey) doubt and inquiry. *Samayā* (denotes) proximity and middle. *Punaḥ* (conveys) not being the first and difference. *Niḥ* (expresses) certainty and prohibition.

15. *Purā* would (be used to indicate) continuity, long past, nearness and the future. The three (words) *ūrari*, *ūri* and *urari* (are used in the sense of) expansion and that which is agreed upon.

16. *Svaḥ* (is used in the sense of) heaven and other world. *Kila* (is used in the sense of) tidings and conjecture. (The word) *khalu* (is used to denote) prohibition, verbal embellishment, desire to know and pacification.[1]

17. (The word) *abhitaḥ* (is used in the sense of) proximity, both ways, quickness, whole and facing. *Prāduḥ* (is used to convey) name and explicitness. *Mithaḥ* (denotes) between one another and in secrecy.

18. (The word) *tiraḥ* (is used to denote) disappearance and horizontal. (The particle) *hā* (is used to express) pain, anger and grief. *Ahaha* (is used to denote) surprise and grief. (The particle) *hi* (is used to denote) cause and determination.

19. (The words) *cirāya*, *cirārātrāya*, *cirasya* and others (are used) in the sense of long time. *Muhuḥ*, *punaḥ punaḥ*, *śaśvat*, *abhikṣṇam* and *asakṛt* (again and again) have the same (sense).

20. (The words) *śrāk*, *jhaṭiti*, *añjasā*, *ahnāya*, *sapadi*, *drāk* and *maṅkṣu* are (used in the sense of) quickness. (The words) *balavat*, *suṣṭhu* and *kimuta* (denote) excessive. *Kim*, *kimu* and *uta* (are used in the sense of) option.

21. (The particles) *tu*, *hi*, *ca*, *sma*, *ha* and *vai* (are used) for completing a quarter of a verse. *Su* and *ati* (are used to denote) worship (reverence). *Divā* (is used to denote) at day. *Doṣā* and *naktam* (are used in the sense of) night.

22. *Sāci* and *tiraḥ* (are used) in the sense of horizontally. (The words) *pyāṭ*, *pāṭ*, *aṅga*, *he*, *hai* and *bhoḥ* (are used) in the

---

1. The *Purāṇa* reads wrongly *avasara*.

sense of calling a person. *Samayā*, *nikaṣā* and *hiruk* (have the sense of proximity).

23. *Sahasā* (is used in the sense of) unexpected. *Puraḥ*, *purataḥ* and *agrataḥ* (mean) in front of. *Svāhā*, *śrauṣaṭ*, *vauṣaṭ*, *vaṣaṭ* and *svadhā* (are used) in offering made to the gods.

24. (The words) *kiñcit*, *iṣat* and *manāk* (are used in the sense of) a little. *Pretya* and *amutra* (are used in the sense of) the other world. *Yathā* and *tathā* (convey) similarity. *Aho* and *ho* (indicate) surprise.

25-26. (The words) *tūṣṇim* and *tūṣṇikam* (are used in the sense of) silence. *Sadyaḥ* and *sapadi* (denote) the present moment. *Diṣṭyā* and *samupajoṣam* (convey) rejoice. (The words) *antare*, *antarā* and *antareṇa* (denote) 'in the middle'. *Prasahya* means 'by force'. The two (words) *sāmpratam* and *sthāne* (convey the sense) appropriate. *Abhikṣṇam* and *śaśvat* (mean) eternally.

27. (The words) *nahi*, *a*, *no* and *na* (indicate) non-existence. (The words) *māsma*, *mā* and *alaṁ* (are used in the sense of) restraining. *Cet* and *yadi* (are used to denote) alternative. The two (words) *addhā* and *añjasā* (are employed to convey) truth.

28. *Prāduḥ* and *āviḥ* indicate explicitness. *Oṁ*, *evaṁ* and *paramaṁ* (convey) opinion. (The words) *samantataḥ*, *paritaḥ*, *sarvataḥ* and *viśvak* (convey) all around.

29. *Kāmam* (is used to convey) permission unwillingly granted. An acceptance preceded by jealousy (is indicated by the word) *astu*. (The word *kāmam* is) also (used in the same sense). *Nanu* (indicates) a contrary opinion. *Kaccit* (indicates) affectionate enquiry.

30. (The words) *niḥ samam* and *duḥ samam* (are used to convey) condemned. *Yathāsvaṁ* and *yathāyatham* (convey the sense) of appropriate or befitting. *Mṛṣā* and *mithyā* (indicate) false. *Yathārtham* and *yathātatham* denote truth.

31. (The words) *evaṁ*, *tu*, *punaḥ*, *vai* and *va* are expressions (indicating) conclusion. *Prāk* (conveys) the thing that has taken place already. The two (words) *nūnam* and *avaśyam* (are used to indicate) certainty.

32. *Saṁvat* (is used to mean) the year. *Arvāk* (means) below. *Ām* and *evaṁ* (convey) approval. *Svayam* (means) by the

self. *Nicaiḥ* (means) low. *Uccaiḥ* (means) great. *Prāyaḥ* (denotes) a great quantity. *Śanaiḥ* (is used in the sense of) slowly.

33. The word *sanā* (denotes) eternal. *Bahiḥ* (conveys the meaning) outside. *Sma* (indicates) the past. *Astam* (denotes) invisible. *Asti* (conveys the sense) of reality. *U* is an expression of anger. *Ūm* (indicates) a query. *Ayi* (is an expression of) pacification.

34. *Hūm* (is used in) discussion. (The word) *uṣā* (has the sense of) end of the night. *Namaḥ* (conveys) obeisance. *Aṅga* (is used) in the sense of again. *Duṣṭu* (is an expression of) censure and *suṣṭu*, of praise.

35. *Sāyam* (conveys the sense) in the evening. (The words) *prage* and *prātaḥ* (convey the sense) 'in the morning'. *Nikaṣā* (conveys the meaning) nearby. (The word) *parut* (denotes) the last year and *parāri*, the year before the last. *Yati* (denotes the current year).

36. *Adya* (denotes) the present day. (The words) *pūrvedyuḥ* etc. (convey the sense of) the previous day etc. Similarly one should know that (the words *uttaredyuḥ*, *aparedyuḥ*, *adharedyuḥ*, *anyedyuḥ*, *anyataredyuḥ* and *itaredyuḥ* are formed) from *uttara* (tomorrow), *apara* (some other), *adhara* (the previous), *anya* (some other), *anyatara* (some other next) and *itara* (some other).

37. *Ubhayadyuḥ* and *ubhayedyuḥ* (convey the sense of) both the days. *Paredyavi* (means) on the next day. *Hyaḥ* (denotes) yesterday and *śvaḥ*, the day yet to come next. *Paraśvaḥ* (denotes) the day after tomorrow.

38. (The words) *tadā* and *tadānīm* (denote at that time). *Yugapat* (means) once. *Sarvadā* and *sadā* (mean) always. *Etarhi*, *samprati*, *idānīm*, *adhunā* and *sāmpratam* (mean) the present moment.

CHAPTER THREE HUNDRED AND SIXTYTWO

Words having many meanings

Fire-god said :

1. (The word) *nāka* (is used to denote) the sky and heaven. (The word) *loka* (means) the world and people. *Śloka* (is used to mean) a verse and fame. *Sāyaka* (has the meaning) an arrow and sword.

2. *Ānaka* (denotes) a *bheri* as well as *paṭaha* (two kinds of drums). *Kalaṅka* is a mark as well as a scandal. (The letter) *ka* in the masculine (is used to denote) wind, Brahmā and the Sun and *kaṁ* in the neuter (is used to denote) head and water.

3. (The word) *pulāka* (denotes) empty or bad grain, abridgement and rice-water. (The word) *kauśika* (is used in the sense of) Mahendra, *guggulu* (resin got from cow), owl, serpent and alligator.

4. A monkey and a dog (are denoted by the word) *śālāvṛka*. *Mānaṁ* is a means of measure. *Sarga* (is used in the sense of) one's nature, natural state, relinquishment, decision, chapter and creation.

5. (The word) *yoga* (is used in the sense of) an armour, means (expedience), contemplation and union. (The word) *bhoga* (has the meaning of) happiness and enjoying the company of a harlot. The word *abja* (is used to denote) conch and moon.

6. *Karaṭa* (denotes) a crow and the cheek of an elephant. *Śipiviṣṭa* (denotes) a leprous person. (The word) *riṣṭa* (is used in the sense of) prosperity, good and bad luck and *ariṣṭa*, good and bad luck.

7. (The word) *vyuṣṭi* (is used in the sense of) a fruit and plenty. (The word) *dṛṣṭi* (is used to denote) knowledge, eye and perception. (The word) *niṣṭah* (has the sense of) accomplishing, non-existence and destruction. (The word) *kāṣṭhā* (is used to denote) excellence, state and direction.

8. (The words) *iḍā* and *ilā* (convey the sense of) a cow, earth and speech. *Pragāḍham* (denotes) much and difficult. The word *dṛḍha* (means) capable of and stout.

9. *Vyūḍha* (has the meaning) placed in order and firmness. (The word) *Kṛṣṇa* (denotes) Vyāsa, Arjuna and Hari[1]. *Paṇa* (is used to denote) the stake in gambling etc., wages, price and a particular coin.

10. (The word) *guṇa* (is used in the sense of) the bow-string, quality of a substance, (qualities like) *sattva* (goodness), bravery[2] and treaty etc. (The word) *grāmaṇi* (is used to denote) excellent (person) and leader (in a village).

11. *Tṛṣṇā* (is used to convey) desire and desire to drink. (The word) *vipaṇi* (is used to denote) a merchant's shop. *Tikṣṇam* (is used to mean) poison, battle and iron in the neuter, but in all the three (genders) when (denoting) sharp-edged.[3]

12. (The word) *pramāṇa* (is used to mean) cause, limit in the *śāstra*, extent and the knower. *Karaṇa* is the excellent means. It is also (used to denote) the sense-organs. (The word) *iriṇam* (is used to convey) a barren land and a desert.

13. (The word) *yantṛ* (is used in the sense of) a mahout and a charioteer. (The word) *heti* (denotes) flame[4]. (The word) *śrutam* (is used to convey) scriptures and accurate knowledge. *Kṛtam* (is used to mean) the (first) *yuga* and enough.

14. *Pratita* (is used to mean) well-known and delight. *Abhijāta* (is used to denote) born in a good family and wise. (The word) *vivikta* (means) pure and devoid of men. *Mūrchita* (means) stupefied and elevated (prosperous).

15. *Artha* (conveys the sense) 'to be expressed', riches, an object, use and end. *Tirtham* (expresses the sense of) water tank, scriptures, water courses honoured by sages and preceptor.

16. *Kakudaḥ* (is used in the sense of) importance, the insignia of a king and a limb of a bull (hump on the shoulder) in the masculine and neuter. The feminine (word) *saṁvit* (conveys the sense of) knowledge, conversation, a disciplined action, battle and name.

17. (The word) *upaniṣat* (is used in the sense of) *dharma* and secret doctrine (such as) philosophy. (The word) *śarat* (has the

---

1. This line is not in the *Amara*.
2. The text wrongly reads *śukla* instead of *śaurya*.
3. The printed text wrongly reads *svara* instead of *khara*.
4. Vide *Amara* paṅkti 2476. The *Purāṇa* has omitted the other senses: ray of the Sun and weapon.

meaning of) a season and a year. (The word) *padam* (is used in the sense of) endeavour, protection, position, mark, foot and object.

18. (These are used) in all the three (genders): (The word) *svādū* (denotes) favourite and sweet. *Mṛdū* (denotes) not sharp and soft. *Sat* (is used to convey) truth, good people, existence, praiseworthy and respectable.

19. (The word) *vidhi* (is used to denote) an injunction and Brahmā. *Praṇidhi* (conveys the meaning of) request and a spy. *Vadhūḥ* (means) wife, son's wife and woman in general. *Sudhā* (denotes) plaster (used in temples etc.), nectar and the milk-hedge plant.

20. (The word) *śraddhā* (denotes) respect and desire. *Paṇḍitammanyaḥ* is one who thinks himself as learned and proud as well. *Brahmabandhu* (is used in the sense of) censure. *Bhānu* means ray as well as Sun.

21. *Grāvan* (is used to denote) a hill and a stone. (The word) *pṛthakjana* (denotes) a fool and also a low class man. (The word) *śikharin* (denotes) a tree as well as a mountain. *Tanu* (denotes) the skin and the body.

22. (The word) *yatna* (denotes) soul, firmness, intellect, nature and path of Brahman. *Utthānaṁ* (denotes) effort and remedial act for family. *Vyutthānaṁ* (denotes) rejection.

23. (The word) *niryātana* (is used to denote) revenge, gift and restitution of a deposit. *Vyasanam* (has the sense of) grief, fall and crime due to passion or wrath.

24. Hunting, dice-play, dreaming during the day, accusation, women, intoxication, the triple symphony (dance, music and instrumental music) and strolling about idly are the group of crime arising from passion.

25. Slandering, bravery, offence, hatred, jealousy, extravagance, reprimand and harshness are the eight crimes arising from wrath.

26. *Kaupinam* (is used to denote) a wrong deed, secret and organ of generation. *Maithunam* (is employed in the sense of) relating to union with wife and sexual union. *Pradhānam* (denotes) the superme spirit and intellect. *Prajñānam* (is used to mean) intellect and mark.

27. *Krandanam* (means) crying and calling. *Varṣma* (denotes) body and extent. *Ārādhanam* (means) accomplishing, attainment and satisfaction.

28. *Ratnam* (is used to mean) that which is excellent among its own class. *Lakṣma* (is used to denote) a mark and chief. *Kalāpa* (denotes) an ornament, peacock's plumes, quiver and a collection.

29. (The word) *talpam* (is used to denote) bed, an apartment on the roof and woman. *Ḍimba* (is used the mean) a child and a fool. (The word) *stambha* (is used to denote) a pillar of a building and dull. (The word) *sabhā* (is used to convey the meaning of) an assembly and member of a house.

30. *Raśmi* (is) a ray (of light) as well as rein (of horses etc.). (The word) *dharma* (is used to denote) merit and self-control etc. (The word) *lalāma* (conveys the meaning of) tail, mark (on the forehead of horses etc.), horse, ornament, prominence and banner.

31. (The word) *pratyaya* (is employed in the sense of) subject to control, oath, knowledge, faith and cause. (The word) *samaya* (is used to convey) an agreement, practice, time, a dogma and knowledge.

32. (The word) *atyaya* (is used to mean) transgression and crime. *Satyam* (means) an oath and truth. (The word) *vīryam* (is used in the sense of) strength, and greatness. *Rūpyam* (is used to mean) praiseworthy form.

33. *Durodara* (is employed to denote) a gambler and *durodaram* (to denote) the stake in gambling. (The word) *kāntāra* (is used to mean) a great forest or a difficult path, in the masculine and neuter.

34. (The word) *hari* (is used to denote) *Yama* (god of death), *Anila* (wind), *Indra* (ruler of the celestials), *Candra* (Moon), *Arka* (Sun), *Viṣṇu* and a lion etc. (The word) *dara* (is employed to mean) a hole and fear, in the masculine and neuter. (The word) *jaṭhara* (means) hard (besides stomach).

35. *Udāra* (is used to denote) giver and great. *Itara* (means) different as well as low. *Cūḍā* (denotes) crown and hair. The lock of hair (is called) *mauli*.

36. (The word) *bali* (is used to mean) tax, offering etc. (The word *balam* (is used to denote) an army and firmness.

(The word) *nivi* (is employed to mean) the knot on the waist garment of a women and ransom (against the prince etc. held as captive).

37-38a. (The word) *vṛṣa* (is used in the following senses): the scrotum (that discharges semen), rat, excellence, good deed and a bull. (The word)¦ *ākarṣa* (is used to denote) dice-play, the die and the board for dice-play. (The word) *akṣam* (means) an organ, and in the masculine, the dice, difference in the measure, dispute and the *vibhitaka* (one of the three myrobalans).

38b. (The word) *uṣṇiṣa* (is used to mean) crown etc.[1] *Karṣū* conveys the sense of a small river.

39. (The word) *adhyakṣa* (means) visible and one who presides over. (The word) *vibhāvasu* denotes the Sun and Fire. (The word) *rasa* (is employed to denote) (the sentiments) such as erotic and others, poison, splendour, qualities (such as sweet, sour etc.), passion and juice.

40. (The word) *varcas* (denotes) feces as well as splendour. (The word) *āga* (denotes) sin and crime. (The word) *chandas* (means) poetry and desire. *Sādhiyān* (is used to denote) good as well as strong. *Vyūha* (means) a collection as well as (strength). (The word) *ahiḥ* (denotes) Vṛtra as well as a serpent[2]. Fire, Moon and Sun (are referred to as) *tamonudāḥ* (destroyers of darkness).

CHAPTER THREE HUNDRED AND SIXTYTHREE

*The words denoting earth, city, forest and herbs**

Fire-god said:

1. I shall describe the words denoting earth, city, forest, herbs and lion etc. (The following words denote the earth): *bhūḥ*, *anantā*, *kṣamā*, *dhātri*, *kṣmā*, *jyā*, *kuḥ* and *dharitri*.

1. The crown and the turban. Cf. *Amara* Paṅkti 2776.
2. The *Purāṇa* omits this word. *Cf. Amara* paṅkti 2812.

*The *Purāṇa* summarises *Amara* kāṇḍas II. 2, II. 3 and II. 5

2. (The words) *mṛt* and *mṛttikā* (denote a piece of earth). Commendable earth (is denoted by the words) *mṛtsā* and *mṛtsnā*. (The land space on the earth is denoted by the words) *jagat, viṣṭapam, loka, bhuvanam* and *jagatī*.

3. (The words), *ayanam, vartma, mārga, adhva, panthā, padavī, sṛti, saraṇi, paddhati, padyā, vartani* and *ekapadi* (denote a path).

4-6a. (The words) *pūḥ, purī, nagarī, pattanam* and *puṭabhedanam* (denote a town). *Sthānīyam* is a big city surrounding big pathways. *Śākhānagaraṁ* is a suburb of a principal city. The suburb where the harlots dwell is *veśa*. *Āpaṇa* and *niṣadyā* (denote) the place for selling goods. *Vipaṇi* and *paṇyavīthikā* (denote) the market street. *Rathyā, pratolī* and *viśikhā* (denote) the pathways in the interior of a village. *Caya* and *vapram* (mean the earth dug up from a moat) in the masculine and neuter.

6b. *Prākāra, varaṇa* and *śāla* (denote the surrounding fence set up with poles, thorns etc.). A surrounding fence made up at the border (with bamboo, thorns etc.) (is called) *prācīnam*.

7-8. *Bhitti* and *kuḍyam* (denote a wall). That wall set with bone etc. inside (is known as) *eḍūkaṁ*. (The words) *vāsa, kuṭi, śālā* and *sabhā* (denote the assembly hall). *Sañjavanam* and *catuḥśālam* (is a group of four houses forming a court). *Parṇaśālā* and *uṭaja* (not feminine) denote a hermitage. *Caityam* and *āyatanam* (denote a sacrifiicial hall). *Vājiśālā* and *mandurā* (denote a stable).

9. The dwelling place of the rich (is) *harmyādi*. The place of the gods and kings (is called) *prāsāda*. (The words) *dvāḥ, dvāram* and *pratihāra* (denote a door), where the word *dvāḥ* is feminine. *Vitardi* and *vedikā* (mean a fence).

10-11a. (The words) *kapotapālikā* and *viṭaṅkam*, respectively masculine and neuter (denote a pigeonhouse made of wood etc.). *Kapāṭa* and *arara* are synonyms (meaning a door). *Niḥśreṇi* and *adhirohiṇī* (denote steps made with wood etc. for ascending). *Sammārjanī* and *Śodhani* (mean broom-stick). *Saṅkara* and *avakara* (denote sweepings).

11b-12. (The words) *adri, gotra, giri* and *grāvā* (denote mountains in general). (The words) *gahanam, kānanam* and *vanam* (denote a forest). (The words) *ārāma* and *upavanam* (denote) an artificial garden (that has been accomplished). The same that is fit for harem (is called) *pramadavanam.*

13. (The words) *vithi, āliḥ, āvaliḥ, paṅktiḥ* and *śreṇi* (denote a row). (The words) *lekhāḥ* and *rājayaḥ* (denote lines). A tree (that is seen) with fruits (produced) from flowers (is) *vānaspatyaḥ.* A tree (that is seen) with fruits not (produced) from flowers (is) *vanaspatiḥ.*

14. Those which end with fruit-bearing (are known as) *oṣadhi-s.* (The words) *palāśi, druḥ, druma* and *agama* (denote a tree). (The words) *sthāṇu, dhruva* and *śaṅku* (denote a cut tree). (The word) *sthāṇu* is optionally masculine. (The words) *praphulla, utphulla* and *saṁphulla* (mean a flower that has blossomed).

15-16a. (The words) *palāśam, chadanam* and *parṇam* (denote a leaf). (The words) *idhmam, edhaḥ* and *samit,* faminine (denote dry wood and grass). *Bodhidruma* and *caladala* (denote the holy fig tree). *Dadhittha, grāhi, manmatha, dadhiphala, puṣpaphala* and *dantaśaṭha* (denote the woodapple tree).

16b-17. (The words) *udumbara, hemadugdha, kovidāra* and *dvipatraka* (denote *udumbara*). The *saptaparṇa* (tree) (is also known as) *viśālatvak.* The *kṛtamāla* (tree is also known as) *suvarṇaka, ārevata, vyādhighāṭa, śampāka* and *cuturaṅgala.*

18. The *Jambira* (tree is also called) *dantaśaṭha.* The *Varuṇa* (tree is also called) *tiktaśāka. Punnāga* (tree is also called) *puruṣa, tuṅga, kesara* and *devavallabha.*

19-20a. *Nimbataru, mandāra* and *pārijātaka* (are the other names of) *pāribhadra* (tree). *Vañjula* and *citrakṛt* (are the other names of *tiniśa* tree). *Pitana* and *kapitana* (denote) the *āmrātaka* (tree). (The other names) of *madhūka* (are) *guḍapuṣpa* and *madhudruma.*

20b. *Guḍaphala* and *sraṁsi* (are the other names of) *pilu. Nādeyi* is the other name of *ambhuvetas.*

21. *Śigruḥ, tikṣṇagandhaka, akṣiva* and *mocaka* (are the other names of) *śobhāñjana.* If this (*śobhāñjana*) is red (it is called) *madhuśigruḥ. Ariṣṭa* and *phenila* are synonyms.

22. *Lodhra* (is also called) *gālava, śābara, tiriṭa, tilva* and *mārjana. Uddālaka* (is also known as) *śeluḥ, śleṣmātaka, śita* and *bahuvāraka.*

23. (The other names of) *vikaṅkata* (are) *sruvāvṛkṣa, granthila*

and *vyāghrapāt*. *Tinduka* (is also called) *sphūrjaka* and *kāla* (*skandha*)[1]. (The terms) *nādeyi* and *bhūmijambuka* (denote *nāgaraṅga*)[2].

24. *Kākatindu* and (*kāka*) *piluka* are synonyms. *Kramuka* and *paṭṭikākhya* would (denote *lohitalodhra*)[3]. *Kumbhi* (is also known as) *kaiḍarya* and *kaṭphala*.

25-26a. *Viravṛkṣa*, *aruṣkara* and *agnimukhi* (are the synonyms of) *bhallātaki* in (all the three genders). *Sarjaka*, *pitasāraka*[4] and *asana* (are synonyms of) *jiva* (*ka*). *Sarja* and *aśvakarṇa* (are synonyms of) *sāla*.[5] *Arjuna* (tree) (is also called) *virataru*[6], *indradruḥ*, and *kakubhaḥ*.

26b-27. *Iṅgudi* (is also known as) *tāpasataru*. *Śālmali* (is also known as) *mocā*. *Cirabilva*, *naktamāla* and *karaja* (are the other names of) *karañjaka*. (*Pūtika* is also known as) *prakirya* and *pūtikaraja*. *Markaṭi* and *aṅgāravallari* (are varieties of *karañja*)[7].

28. *Rohi*, *plihaśatru* and *dāḍimapuṣpaka* (are synonyms of) *rohitaka*. *Khadira* (is also known as) *gāyatri*, *bālatanaya* and *dantadhāvana*.

29. *Arimeda* and *viṭkhadira* (denote varieties of bad smelling *khadira*). *Kadara* (denotes) the white *khadira*. (*Eraṇḍa* is also called) *pañcāṅgula*, *vardhamāna*, *cañcu* and *gandharvahastaka*.

30-31a. *Piṇḍitaka* and *maruvaka* (are synonyms of *madana*). *Devadāru* (is also called) *pitadāru*, *dāru* and *pūtikāṣṭham*. *Priyaṅgu* (is also known as) *śyāmā*, *mahilāhvayā*, *latā*, *govandani*, *gundrā*, *phalini* and *phali*.

31b-32a. *Śoṇaka* (is also known as) *maṇḍūkaparṇa*, *patrorṇa*, *naṭa*, *kaṭvaṅga*, *ṭuṇṭuka*, *syonāka*, *śukanāsa*, *ṛkṣa*, *dirghavṛnta* and *kuṭannaṭa*.

32b. *Pitadru* and *sarala* (are synonyms). *Nicula*, *ambuja* and *hijjala* (are the synonyms of a kind of reed).

---

1. *Cf. Amara paṅkti* 725.
2. *Cf. ibid. paṅkti* 724.
3. *Cf. ibid. paṅkti* 730.
4. The *Purāṇa* wrongly reads *pitaśāla*. *Cf. Amara paṅkti* 735.
5. *Cf. Amara paṅkti* 737. The purāṇic reading is wrong.
6. *Cf. Amara paṅkti* 738.
7. *Cf. Amara paṅkti* 745.

33. *Kākodumbarikā* and *phalguḥ* (are the synonyms of *malayū*. *Ariṣta, picumardaka*[1], *sarvatobhadra* (are synonyms of) *nimba*. *Śiriṣa* (is also known as) *kapītana*.

34-35a. *Va (ba) kula* (is said to be *vañjula*. (*Kapilā*[2] is also called as) *picchilā* and *aguruśiṁśapā*. *Jayā, jayanti* and *tarkāri* (are synonyms of *vaijayantikā*[3]. *Kaṇikā* (is also known as) *gaṇikārikā*, *śriparṇam* and *agnimantha*. *Vatsaka* and *girimallikā* (are synonyms of *kuṭaja*).[4]

35b-36. *Kālaskandha* (is a synonym of) *tamāla*. *Taṇḍulīya* (is known as) *alpamāriṣa*. *Sinduvāra* (is also known as) *nirguṇḍi*. The same (*mallikā*) grown in the forest (is known as) *āsphoṭā*[5]. *Yūthikā* (is also known as) *gaṇikā* and *ambaṣṭhā*. *Navamālikā* (is also known as) *saptalā*.

37. *Atimukta* and *puṇḍraka* (are different varieties of *kunda*).[6] *Kumāri* (is also known as) *sahā* and *taraṇi*. Therein[7], the red variety is *kurabaka* and the yellow variety is *kuruṇṭaka*.

38. The blue *jhiṇṭī* (is also known as) *bāṇā*. (It is also known as *dāsi* and *artagala*[8].) *Jhiṇṭi* (in general is known as) *saireyaka*. If it is red, it is known as *kurabaka*. If it is yellow, it is known as *sahacarī* (and also as *sahacara*).

39. *Kitava* and *dhūrta* (are the other names of) *dhattūra*. *Rucaka* (is the other name of) *mātuluṅgaka*. *Samīraṇa, maruvaka, prasthapuṣpa* and *phaṇijjaka* (are the synonyms of *jambīra*)[9].

40-42a. *Kuṭheraka* (is the other name of) *parṇāsa*. *Vasuka* and *āsphoṭa* (are the synonyms of) *arka*. *Śivamalli* and *pāśupata* (are synonyms). *Vṛndā, vṛkṣādani, jīvantikā* and *vṛkṣaruhā* (are the synonyms of the plant that clings to a tree and grows). *Guḍūci* (has the other names) *tantrikā, amṛtā, somavalli* and *madhuparṇi*. *Mūrvā* (is also called) *moraṭā, madhūlikā, madhuśreṇi, gokarṇi* and *pīluparṇi*.

---

1. *Cf. Amara paṅkti* 773-*picumanda*.
2. *Cf. ibid. paṅkti* 773.
3. Cf. *ibid. paṅkti*. 779.
4. Cf. *ibid. paṅkti*. 781.
5. The *Purāṇa* mixes with the previous. *Cf. Amara paṅktis* 785 and 788.
6. *Cf. Amara. paṅkti* 792.
7. Refers to *amlāna*. *Cf. Amara. paṅkti* 796.
8. *Cf. Amara paṅkti* 797.
9. *Cf. ibid. paṅkti* 806-807.

42b-43. *Pāṭhā* (is also known as) *āmbaṣṭhā, viddhakarṇi, pracinā* and *vanatiktikā. Kaṭuḥ, kaṭumbharā, cakrāṅgi* and *śakulādani* (are the names of *kaṭurohiṇi*[1]). *Ātmaguptā, prāvṛṣāyi*[2] and *kapikacchu* (are the other names of) *markaṭi*.

44. *Apāmārga* (is also known as) *śaikharika, pratyakparṇi* and *mayūraka. Phañjikā*[3] and *brāhmaṇi* (are the other names of) *bhārgi. Dravanti, śambari* and *vṛṣā* (are synonyms).

45. *Maṇḍūkaparṇi, bhaṇḍiri, samaṅgā* and *kālameṣikā* (are synonyms of *mañjiṣṭhā*). *Rodani, kacchurā, anantā, samudrāntā* and *durālabhā* (are synonyms of *dhanvayāsa*)[4].

46. *Pṛśniparṇi, pṛthakparṇi, kalaśi, dhāvani* and *guhā* (are synonyms). *Nidigdhikā, spṛśi, vyāghri, kṣudrā* and *dussparśā* (are synonyms).

47. *Avalguja, somarāji, suvalli, somavallikā, kālameśi, kṛṣṇaphalā* and *pūtiphali* (are synonyms of) *vākuci*.

48. *Kaṇā, uṣaṇā* and *upakulyā* (are synonyms). *Śreyasi* and *gajapippali*[5] (are synonyms). *Cavyaṁ* and *cavikā* (are synonyms). *Kākaciñci, guñja* and *kṛṣṇalā* (are synonyms).

49-50. *Viśvā, viṣā* and *prativiṣā* (are synonyms). *Vanaśṛṅgāṭa* and *gokṣura* (are synonyms). *Nārāyaṇi* and *śatamūli* (are synonyms). *Kāliyaka, haridruḥ, dārvi, pacampacā, dāruśuklā*[6] and *haimavati*[7] (are synonyms of *parjani*). *Ugragandhā, ṣaḍgranthā, golomi* and *śataparvikā* (are the synonyms of) *vacā*.

51. *Āsphoṭā* and *girikarṇi* (are synonyms). *Siṁhāsya, vāsaka* and *vṛṣa* (are synonyms). *Madhurikā* (is also called) *misi* and *chatrā. Kokilākṣa* (is also known as) *ikṣura* and *kṣura*.

52. *Viḍaṅga* is known as *kṛmighna* (and is used) in the masculine and neuter. *Vajradru* (is also known as) *snuk, snuhi* and *sudhā*.[8] *Mṛdvikā* and *gostani* (are the other names of) *drākṣā. Balā* and *vāṭyālakā* (are synonyms).

---

1. *Cf. Amara. paṅkti* 819.
2. *prāvṛṣāyaṇī. cf. Amara* paṅkti 821.
3. *Amara paṅkti* 827 reads *hañjikā*.
4. *Cf. Amara paṅkti* 831-832.
5. *karipippalī. Cf. Amara paṅkti* 842.
6. *Amara paṅkti* 852 reads *dāru haridrā*.
7. *ibid.* reads *parjanī*.
8. *Amara paṅkti* 859 reads *guḍā*.

53. *Kālā* and *masūravidalā* (are synonyms of black *trivṛt*) *Trivṛt* (is also known as) *tripuṭā* and *trivṛtā*. *Madhukam*, *klītakam*, *yaṣṭimadhukam* and *madhuyaṣṭikā* (are synonyms).

54. *Ikṣugandhā* (is also known as) *vidārī*, *kṣīraśukla* and *kroṣṭrī*. *Gopī*, *śyāmā*, *śārivā* and *anantā* (are the other names of) *utpala-śārivā*.

55. *Mocā* and *rambhā* (are synonyms of) *kadalī*. *Bhaṇṭākī* and *duṣpradharṣiṇī* (are synonyms). *Sālaparṇī* (is also called) *sthirā* and *dhruvā*. *Śṛṅgī* and *vṛṣa* (are the synonyms of the herb) *vṛṣabha*.

56. *Gāṅgeruki* (is also called) *nāgabalā*. *Muṣa*(*sa*)*lī* and *tālamūlikā* (are synonyms). *Paṭolikā* (is also known as (*jyotsnī* and *jāla*. *Ajaśṛṅgī* and *viṣāṇikā* (are synonyms).

57. *Lāṅgalī* (is also known as) *agniśikhā*. *Tāmbūlī* and *nāga-vallī* (are synonyms). (The fragrant) *reṇukā* (is also called) *hareṇu* and *kauntī*. *Hrībera* (is also known as) *divyanāgaram*.[1]

58. (The other names of) *śaileya* (are) *kālānusārī*, *vṛddhā*, *aśmapāṣpam* and *śītaśivam*. *Murā* (is also known as) *tālaparṇī*, *daitya* and *gandhakuṭī*.

59. *Śukam* and *barham* (are other names of) *granthiparṇam* (as well as) *balā*[2]. *Tripuṭā* and *truṭi* (are the synonyms of *sūkṣ-mailā*)[3]. *Śivā* and *tāmalakī* (are synonyms of *bhūmyāmalakī*). *Hanu* and *haṭṭavilāsinī* (are synonyms).

60. *Kuṭannaṭam*, *dāśapuram*, *vāneyam* and *paripelavam* (are synonyms). *Jaṭāmāṁsī* (is also known as) *tapasvinī*. *Spṛkkā* (is also called) *devī*, *latā* and *laghu*.[4]

61. *Karcūraka* and *drāviḍaka* (are synonyms). *Gandhamūlī* is also known as *śaṭhī*. *Vṛddhadāraka* (is also known as) *ṛkṣagandhā*, *chagalāntrā* and *vegī*.

62. *Raktaphalā*, *bimbikā* and *pīluparṇī* (are the other names of) *tuṇḍikerī*. *Cāṅgerī*, *cakrikā*[5] and *ambaṣṭhā* (are synonyms). *Svarṇakṣīrī* (is also known as) *himāvatī*.

---

1. This name is not found in *Amara paṅkti* 892.
2. This term is not found in *Amara paṅkti* 913.
3. *Cf. Amara paṅkti* 899.
4. The purāṇic reading *laśuḥ* is obviously wrong.
5. *Amara paṅkti* 929 reads *cukrikā*.

63. *Sahasravedhī*, *cukra* and *śatavedhī* (are the other names of) *amlavetas*. *Jīvantī* (is also known as) *jivanī* and *jivā*. *Bhū(mi)-nimba* (is also called) *kirātaka*.[1]

64. *Kūrcaśirṣa* and *madhuraka* (are synonyms). *Candra*, *kapi-vṛka*,[2] *dadrughna* and *eḍagaja* are synonyms. Probably *varṣābhū* and *sobahāriṇī* are also synonyms (?).

65. *Kunandati*, *nikumbhastrā*, *yamānī* and *vārṣikā* (are synonyms).[3] *Laśunam* (is also known as) *gṛñjanam*, *ariṣṭa*, *mahākanda* and *rasonaka*.

66-67. *Badarā* and *gṛṣṭi* (are synonyms of) *vārāhī*. *Vāyasī* (is also known as) *kākamāci*. *Madhurā* (is also known as) *śatapuṣpā*, *sitacchatrā*, *aticchatrā*, *misi*, *avākpuṣpī* and *kāravī*. *Saraṇā*, *prasāraṇī*, *kaṭambharā* and *bhadrabalā* (are synonyms). *Karcūra* and *śaṭī* (are synonyms).

68. *Paṭola* is (also known as) *kulaka* and *tiktaka*. *Kāravella* (is also known as) *kaṭhillaka*. *Kūṣmāṇḍaka* (is otherwise called) *karkāru*. *Karkaṭī* (is known as) *urvāruḥ* and (used) in the feminine.

69. *Kaṭutumbī* (is also called) *ikṣvāku*. *Indravāruṇī* (is also known as) *viśālā*. (The other names of) *sūraṇa* (are) *arśoghna* and *kanda*. *Mustaka* and *kuruvindaka* (are synonyms).

70. *Veṇu* (is also called) *vaṁśa*, *tvaksāra*, *karmāra*, *maskara* and *tejana*. *Chatra*, *aticchatra*, *pālaghna*, *mālātṛṇaka* and *bhūstṛṇa* (denote different kinds of *jalatṛṇa*).

71a. *Tāla* is also called *tṛṇarāja*. *Pūga* (is also called) *ghoṇṭā* and *kramuka*.

71b. *Śārdūla*[4] and *dvipī* (are synonyms of) *vyāghra* (tiger). *Haryakṣa*, *kesarī* and *hari* (denote a lion).

72. (The words) *kola*, *potri* and *varāha* would (denote a boar). (The words) *koka*, *ihāmṛga* and *vṛka* (denote a wolf). *Lūtā*, *ūrṇanābha*, *tantuvāya* and *markaṭa* (denote a spider).

73. *Vṛścika* and *śūkakīṭa* (scorpion) (are synonyms). *Sāraṅga*[5] and *tokaka* are synonyms (denoting a *cātaka* bird). *Kṛkavāku* and

1. *kirātatikta*. *cf.* *Amara paṅkti* 934.
2. Corrupt reading for *kāmpilya* and *karkaśa*. *cf.* *Amara paṅkti* 941-2.
3. The Purāṇic reading is corrupt. *Cf.* *Amara paṅkti* 937-38.
4. The section on animals begins here.
5. From here begins the listing of synonyms of birds.

tāmracūḍa (are synonyms denoting a cock). *Pika* and *kokila* (are synonyms denoting a cuckoo).

74. *Karaṭa* and *ariṣṭa* (denote) a crow. *Baka* and *kahva* denote a crane. *Cakravāka* is also known as *koka* and *cakra*. *Kādamba* and *kalahaṁsaka* (are synonyms).

75. *Pataṅgikā* and *puttikā* (are synonyms denoting different kinds of honey-bees). *Dvirepha*, *puṣpaliṭ*, *bhṛṅga*, *ṣaṭpada*, *bhramara* and *ali* (denote a bee).

76. *Keki* (denotes a peacock). *Kekā* (denotes) the sound made by a peacock. (The words) *śakunti*, *śakuni* and *dvija* (denote a bird). *Pakṣati* is the base of the wing. It is in the feminine. *Cañcu* and *troṭi* (denote the beak). Both (the words) are feminine.

77-78. (The words) *uḍḍīnam* and *saṇḍīnam* (denote) the gait (of birds). *Kulāya* and *nīḍam* (denote a nest). They are (used) in the masculine and neuter. *Peśi*, *koṣa* and *aṇḍa* (denote an egg). If less than two, *aṇḍa* is used in the neuter. (The young one of a bird is denoted by the words) *pṛthuka*, *śāvaka*, *śiśu*, *pota*, *pāka*, *arbhaka* and *ḍimbha*. (The following words denote a collection): *sandoha*, *vyūhaka*, *gaṇa*, *stoma*, *ogha*, *nikara*, *vrāta*, *nikurambam*, *kadambakam*, *saṅghātaḥ*, *sañcayaḥ* and *vṛndam*. *Puñja*, *rāśi* and *kūṭakam* (are used to denote heap of grains).

CHAPTER THREE HUNDRED AND SIXTYFOUR

Words denoting men and the four classes of men

Fire-god said:

1. I shall describe the class of men, brahmins, *kṣatriya-s*, *vaiśya-s* and *śūdra-s*. (The words) *naraḥ*, *pañcajanāḥ*, *martyāḥ* (denote men). (The words) *yoṣit*, *yoṣā*, *abalā* and *vadhūḥ* (denote a woman).

2. A person seeking a lover, going to the place indicated (by the lover) (is called) *abhisārikā*. (The words) *kulaṭā*, *puṁścali* and *asatī* (mean a wanton woman). A nude woman (is called) *koṭavi*.

3. *Kātyāyanī* is middle-aged, (wears ochre garment and is without husband)[1]. One who lives in other's house (is called) *sairindhrī*. (She is independent and proficient in hair dressing etc.).[2] *Asiknī* is not old (and serves the harem). *Mālinī* is a woman in her monthly course.

4. *Vārastrī, gaṇikā* and *veśyā* (mean a courtezan). Brothers' wives are (mutually known as) *yātara*-s. Husband's sister (is known as) *nanānda*. (The descendants for seven generations are known as) *sapiṇḍa*-s and *sanābhi*-s.

5. (Sisters born of the same womb are called) *samānodaryaḥ, sodaryaḥ, sagarbhyaḥ* and *sahajāḥ*. (The words) *sagotra, bāndhava, jñāti, bandhu, svaḥ* and *svajana* are synonyms (denoting relatives belonging to the same clan).

6. (The words) *dampati, jampati, bhāryāpati* and *jāyāpati* (denote the husband and wife). (The outer skin of the embryo is known as) *garbhāśaya, jarāyu* and *ulbam*. (The foetus is called) *kalala*, in the neuter.

7. (The words) *garbha* and *bhrūṇa* are synonyms denoting (the young one in the womb). (The words) *klība, śaṇḍha* (are used to denote) a eunuch. *Uttānaśayā* and *ḍimbā* would (mean a child that sucks milk from the mother's breasts). *Bāla* (boy) (is known to be) *māṇavaka*:

8. (The words) *picaṇḍila* and *bṛhatkukṣi* (mean a person having a big belly). (The word) *abhraṭa* (is used to mean) a *natanāsika* (one having a flat nose). (A naturally deformed person is denoted by the words) *vikalāṅga* and *apogaṇḍa*. (The words) *ārogyam* (free from illness) would (also be known as) *anāmayam*.

9. (A deaf person is denoted by the words) *eḍa* and *badhira*. (The word) *gaḍula* (is used to denote) a hunch-back. (The word) *kuni* (is used to denote) a person having a maimed hand. (The words) *kṣaya, śoṣa* and *yakṣmā* (mean consumption). *Pratiśyāya* and *pinasa* (catarrh) (are synonyms).

10. *Kṣut, kṣutam* and *kṣava* (sneezing) (are synonyms). (The word) *kṣut* is feminine. (The words) *kāsa* and *kṣavathu* (meaning cough) are both masculine. *Śotha* (swelling) is also known as

1. The purāṇa omits the other characteristics. See *Amara paṅkti* 1108.
2. *Cf. Amara* paṅkti 1109.

śvayathu and *śopha*. *Pādasphoṭa* (sore on the foot) (is also known as) *vipādikā*.

11. *Kilāsam* and *sidhmam* (scab) are synonyms. *Pāma, pāmā* and *vicarcikā* (are used to mean) *kacchū* (scab). (The words) *koṭha, maṇḍalakam, kuṣṭham* and *śvitram* (white leprosy) (are synonyms). *Arśas* (piles) (is also known as) *durnāmakam.*

12. (The words) *ānāha* and *nibandha* (denote suppression of urine and feces). *Grahaṇīruk* and *pravāhikā* (denote diarhoea). (The words) *bījam, vīryam, indriyam* and *śuklam* (mean semen). (The words) *palalam, kravyam* and *āmiṣam* (denote flesh).

13. *Bukkā* and *agramāṁsam* (denote the lotus-shaped flesh in the heart). *Hṛdayam* and *hṛt* (heart) are synonyms. *Vapā* and *vasā* (denote the marrow of the flesh). The artery on the back of the neck (is known as) *manyā*. (The words) *nāḍi, dhamani* and *śirā* (artery) (are synonyms).

14-15. *Tilakam* and *kloma* (denote lump of flesh). *Mastiṣkam* (is the fluid on the fore-head). *Dūṣikā* (denotes) the rheum of the eyes. *Antra* (intestine) (is also known as) *purītat*. *Plīhā* and *gulma* (spleen) (are synonyms). (The words) *vasnasā* (in the masculine) and *snāyu* (in the feminine) (denote tendon). *Kālakhaṇḍam* and *yakṛt* are synonyms (denoting liver). *Karpara* and *kapāla* (denote skull), *kapālam* in the neuter. Bones (are in general denoted by the words) *kīkasam, kulyam* and *asthi.*

16. (The word) *kaṅkāla* (denotes) skeleton in the body. (The word) *kaśeruka* (denotes) back-bone. The skull-bone (is called) *karoṭi*, in the feminine. (The word) *parśukā* denotes the bones on the sides (of the body).

17. The limbs of the body (are denoted by the words) *aṅgaṁ, pratīka* and *avayava*. (The words) *śarīram, varṣma* and *vigraha* (denote a body). *Śroṇi-phalakam* (buttocks) (is also called) *kaṭa* (and that word is) masculine. *Kaṭi, śroṇi* and *kakudmatī* (hip) (are synonyms).

18. The hinder part of the waist of women (is known as) *nitamba*, in the neuter. The frontal part is *jaghanam*. The *kūpaka-s* (hollows below the loins) are in the *nitamba*. (The word is used) in the neuter. (The hollows above the loins are called) *kukundara-s*.

19. The fleshy portions in the hip are called) *sphicau* (*sphic*) and *kaṭiprothau*. (The organ of generation of woman is called)

upastha (because that is near) the two which are to be described now. In the case of women it is (called) *bhagam* and *yoni*. *Śiśna*, *medhra*, *mehanam* and *śepha* (denote penis).

20. (The words) *picaṇḍa*, *kukṣi*, *jaṭharam*, *udaram* and *tundam* (denote belly). *Stana* and *kuca* (mean breast). *Cūcuka* is the tip of breast. (The words) *kroḍam* and *bhujāntaram* denote chest. The word *kroḍam* is not masculine.

21. *Skandha*, *bhujaśiras* and *aṁsa* denote shoulder. (The junction of shoulder is known as) *jatru*. (Nail is denoted by the words) *punarbhava*, *kararuha*, *nakhara* and *nakha* (used) not in feminine.

22. *Prādeśika* is the span of the thumb and the forefinger. *Tālā* is the span of the thumb and the middle finger. *Gokarṇa* is the span of the thumb and the ring finger. The span of the thumb and the little finger is *vitasti* measuring twelve finger breadths.

23. The open hand with the fingers extended (is called) *capeṭa*, *pratala* and *prahasta*. *Ratni* (is the distance) from elbow to the end of closed fist. *Aratni* (is the distance) from elbow to the end of little finger.

24. Neck with three lines (is called) *kambugrivā*. (The words) *avaṭu*, *ghāṭā* and *vṛkāṭikā* (denote the backside of the union of head and neck). *Cibuka* (chin) is below the lips, then the two *gaṇḍa-s* (cheeks), the throat and chin.

25-26. The outer ends of eyes are (called) *apāṅga*-s. *Kaṭākṣa* (is used to denote) the look with *apāṅga*. (The words) *cikura*, *kuntala* and *vāla* (denote hair). (The words) *pratikarma*, *prasādhanam*, *ākalya*, *veṣa* and *nepathyam* (denote) beautification. It is perceivable and is produced by union with a play. *Cūḍāmaṇi* is the crest-jewel. The central gem in a necklace (is called) *tarala*.

27. (The ear-ornament is called) *karṇikā* and *tālapatra*. *Lambanam* or *lalantikā* (denote) a long necklace. (The words) *mañjira* and *nūpura* (denote the anklet) on the foot. *Kiṅkiṇī* and *kṣudraghaṇṭikā* (denote a small bell).

28. (The words) *dairghyaṁ*, *āyāma* and *āroha* (are used to denote the length of a cloth etc.). (The words) *pariṇāha* and *viśālatā* (denote the width). *Paṭaccaram* (denotes) a rag. *Saṁvyānam* (is the cloth worn) on the shoulder.

29. (The words) *racanā* and *parisyanda* (denote the arrangement of flowers etc.). (The words) *ābhoga* and *paripūrṇatā* (denote the fulfilling of all services). *Samudgaka* and *samputaka* (mean a casket). (The words) *pratigraha* and *patadgraha* (mean a spitoon).

CHAPTER THREE HUNDRED AND SIXTYFIVE

Words relating to the class of brahmins

Fire-god said :

1-3. (Words denoting genealogy are) *vaṁśa, anvavāya, gotram, kulam, abhijana* and *anvaya*. *Ācārya* is that person who expounds the scriptures. The person who instructs the priests in the sacrifice (is called) *vratī, yaṣṭa* and *yajamāna*. *Upakrama* (denotes) the beginning after having known (the course of action). Those having the same preceptors (are called) *satīrthyāḥ*. The members of an assembly (are called) *sabhya-s, sāmājika-s, sabhāsada* and *sabhāstāra-s*. (The priests who officiate in a sacrifices are known as) *ṛtvija-s* and *yājaka-s*. *Adhvaryu* is the priest associated with the *Yajurveda*. *Udgātṛ* is the priest proficient in the *Sāmaveda* and *Hotṛ* in the *Ṛgveda*.

4. *Caṣāla* is the wooden ring on the top of a sacrificial post. *Sthaṇḍilam* and *catvaram* are synonyms (denoting the ground made ready for a sacrifice). The transformation that occurs in milk by the addition of curd is known as *āmikṣā*.

5. Ghee together with curd (is called) *pṛṣadājya*. (The words) *paramānnam* and *pāyasam* (denote cooked rice mixed with milk). The animal that is killed in a sacrifice after being sanctified with formulae (is called) *upākṛta*.

6. (The words) *paramparākam, śamanam* and *prokṣaṇam* (convey) the sense of killing. (The words) *pūjā, namasyā, apaciti, saparyā, arcā* and *arhaṇā* are synonyms (denoting worship).

7. *Varivasyā, śuśrūṣā, paricaryā* and *upāsanā* (are synonyms meaning mode of worship). (The words) *niyama* and *vratam* (signify religious observance). (They are) not feminine. It consists of the meritorious deeds such as fasting and the like.

8. The first injunction is called *mukhya.* That which in inferior (subordinate) to that (is known as) *anukalpa. Kalpa* (the texts laying down injunctions) is known as *vidhi* and *krama. Viveka* is the power to distinguish between the world and the spirit.

9. The receiving of instruction in the scriptures after purification is known as *upākaraṇam.* (An ascetic is denoted by the words) *bhikṣu, parivrāṭ, karmandī, pārāśarī* and *maskarī.*

10. (The sages are in general denoted by the words) *ṛṣi*-s and *satyavacāḥ.* A student who has had the ceremonial bath (is called) *snātaka.* Those who have conquered the sense-organs (are known as) *yatinaḥ* and *yatayaḥ.*

11. The daily rite which depends on the body as means (is known as) *yama.* But *niyama* is that which depends on external conditions (and is voluntary). The state of *brahman* (is denoted by the words) *brahmabhūyam, brahmatvam* and *brahmasāyujyam.*

CHAPTER THREE HUNDRED AND SIXTYSIX

Words relating to kṣatriyas, vaiśyas and other classes

Fire-god said :

1. (The words denoting the warrior caste are) *mūrdhābhiṣikta, rājanya, bāhuja, kṣatriya* and *virāṭ.* A king who is respected by the vassals is known as *adhīśvara.*

2. (A king who holds way over the entire earth is known as) *cakravartī* and *sārvabhauma.* A king who is different from the above is a *maṇḍaleśvara.* (Minister or counsel is known as) *mantrī, dhisaciva* and *amātya.* (The chief counsel is known as) *mahāmātra* and *pradhānaka.*

3. A person who attends to disputes (is called) *prāḍvivāka* and *akṣadarśaka.* The man in charge of gold in a royal treasury (is called) *bhaurika.* (The words) *adhyakṣa* and *adhikṛta* are synonyms (denoting a superintendent). The person invested with the charge of the harem (is called) *antarvaṁśika.* (The words) *sauvidalla*-s, *kañcukin*-s, *sthāpatya*-s and *sauvida*-s (also denote the same).

4-6a. The words *ṣa* (*sa*) *ṇḍa* and *varṣavara* (denote the servants in the harem, who are eunuchs). (The words) *sevaka*, *arthi* and *anujivi* (denote a servant). A ruler of the region other than one's own is a *śatru* (enemy). One who is beyond that region is a *mitram* (friend). A person beyond that is *udāsina* (neutral). A king who is in the rear (of a kingdom) is *pārṣṇigrāha*.

6b-7. (A spy is denoted by the words) *cara*, *spaśa* and *praṇidhi*. The time that is to come is *āyati*. The present time is known as *tatkāla* and *tadātvam*. The fruit accruing in future (is called) *udarka*. (The fear that is caused) by such factors as excessive rains and fire (is) *adṛṣṭam*. (The fear that is caused) by one's own kingdom or other (is) *dṛṣṭam*.

8. (The words) *bhadrakumbha* and *pūrṇakumbha* (are synonyms meaning a pitcher that is full). (A vessel made of gold is called) *bhṛṅgāra* and *kanakālukā*. (A rutting elephant is called) *prabhinna*, *garjita* and *matta*. (A particle of water splashed by the trunk of an elephant is called) *vamathu* and *karaśikara*.

9. A goad is known as *sṛṇi*, in the feminine and *aṅkuśa*, in the masculine. (The words) *paristoma* and *kutha* (denote) the carpet on the back of an elephant in both (the genders). (A vehicle used by ladies for transport is called) *karṇiratha* and *pravahaṇam*. The words *dolā* (palanquin) and *preṅkhā* (swing) etc. (are used) in the feminine.

10. (The words) *ādhoraṇāḥ*, *hastipakāḥ*, *hastyārohāḥ* and *niṣādinaḥ* (denote mahouts). (Warriors are denoted by the words) *bhāṭāḥ*, *yodhāḥ* and *yoddhāraḥ*. (The words) *kañcuka* and *vāraṇa*[1] (mean armour). They are not feminine.

11. *Śirṣaṇya* (is used to denote) *śirastra* (helmet). (The words) *tanutram*, *varma* and *daṁśanam* (are used to mean armour). (The words) *āmukta*, *pratimukta*, *pinaddha* and *apinaddha* (are used to mean a person covered by armour).

12-14. An arrangement of army (for the sake of battle) is *vyūha*. (The words) *cakram* and *anikam* (denote an army). It is not feminine. The *patti* (consists of) an elephant, a chariot, three cavalrymen and five infantry. Three times the constituents of a *patti* and subsequently in the same way in order would be

1. *Amara paṅkti*. 15 93 reads *vāravāṇa*.

senāmukham, *gulma*, *gaṇa*, *vāhini*, *pṛtanā*, *camūḥ* *anikini*, *daśānikini* and *akṣauhiṇi*. A bow (is also known as) *kodaṇḍa*, and *iṣvāsa*. The tip (*koṭi*) (of a bow) is known as *aṭani*.

15. The middle of a bow (is called) *lastaka*. (The bowstring is called) *maurvi*, *jyā*, *śiñjini* and *guṇa*. (The words) *pṛṣatka*, *bāṇa*, *viśikha*, *ajihmaga*, *khaga* and *āśuga* (denote an arrow).

16. (The words) *tūṇa*, *upāsaṅga*, *tūṇira* and *niṣaṅga* (denote a quiver) both in the masculine and feminine. (The words) *asi*, *riṣṭi*, *nistriṁśa*, *karavāla* and *kṛpāṇa* (mean a sword).

17. *Tsaru* is the handle of a sword. *Īli* and *karavālikā* (denote a short sword). The words *kuṭhāra* and *svadhiti* (denote an axe). (The word *kuṭhāra* is used in) both (masculine and feminine). (The words) *churikā* and *asiputrikā* (denote a knife).

18. *Prāsa* is known to be *kunta* (meaning a spear). *Sarvalā* and *tomara* (mean an iron club) (used) in the masculine and neuter. (Bards who sing praises and wake up in the morning are called *vaitālika*-s and *bodhakara*-s. *Māgadha*-s (are bards in general). *Vandin*-s and *stuti* (*pāṭhaka-s*) (are bards singing in praise of the kings).

19. *Saṁśaptaka*-s are those who do not turn back from battle. (The words) *patākā*, *vaijayanti*, *ketanam* and *dhvajam* (denote a banner). (The word) *dhvajam* (is used) in the masculine and neuter.

20. (A fight with enthusiasm) I first, I first, (is known as) *ahaṁpūrvikā*, in the feminine. Where mutual ego is shown (I am capable) it is known as *ahamahamikā*.

21. (The words) *śakti*, *parākrama*, *prāṇa*, *śauryam*, *sthāma*, *saha* and *balam* (denote valour). *Mūrcchā*, *kaśmalam* and *moha* (denote stupefaction). *Avamardana* and *piḍanam* (mean devastation of grains etc. by the invading forces).

22. (The words) *abhyavaskandanam* and *abhyāsādanam* (mean encountering an enemy by trick), *Vijaya* and *jaya* (are synonyms meaning conquest). (The words) *nirvāsanam*, *saṁjñapanam*, *māraṇam* and *pratighātanam* (mean killing).

23. (The words) *pañcatā*, *kāladharma*, *diṣṭānta*, *pralaya* and *atyaya* would (mean death). (The words) *viṭ*, *bhūmispṛk* and *vaiśya* (denote a tradesman and agriculturist). (The words) *vṛtti*, *vartanam* and *jivanam* (mean livelihood in general).

24. *Kṛṣi* (agriculture) etc. are to be known (as the means of livelihood of a *vaiśya*). (The words) *kusīdam* and *vṛddhijīvikā* mean existing on interest by lending money). *Uddhāra* (means debt). (The word) *arthaprayoga*[1] (also means *kusīda*). *Kaṇiśa* (denotes) the ear of a corn.

25. *Kiṁśāru* (denotes) the beard of a corn. *Stamba* (means) a bunch of grass etc. (Paddy etc. are denoted by the words) *dhānyam*, *vrīhi* and *stambakari*. (The minute particles of straw) are known as *kaḍaṅgara* and *busam*.

26. Blackgram etc. are grains in the form of pods. Barley and other grains are in the form of beards. (Grains such as) *nīvāra* are wild grains (*tṛṇadhānya*). A winnowing basket is also known *prasphoṭanam*.

27. (A sack made of cloth to carry grains is known as) *syūta* and *praseva*. *Kaṇḍola* and *piṭa* (denote a cotainer made of bamboo etc). *Kaṭa* and *kiliñjaka* (relate to different varieties of reeds). These are similar. *Rasavatī*, *pākasthānam* and *mahānasa* (denote a kitchen).

28. The kitchen superintendent (is called) *paurogava*. (Cooks are denoted by the words) *sūpakāra*-s, *vallava*-s, *ārālika*-s, *āndhasika-s* *sūda*-s, *audanika*-s and *guṇa*-s.

29. (A frying pan is denoted by the word) *ambarīṣam*, in the neuter and *bhrāṣṭra*, in the masculine. (The words) *karkarī*, *ālu* and *galantikā* (denote a small pitcher). (A big pitcher is called) *aliñjara* and *maṇika*. *Suṣavī* (is the name of) black cumin seed.

30. (The words) *āranāla* and *kulmāṣam* (denote a kind of gruel). The words *vāhlika*, *hiṅgu* and *rāmaṭham* (denote asafoetida). (The words) *niśā*, *haridrā* and *pītā*, feminine (denote turmeric). (The words) *matsyaṇḍī* and *phāṇitam* (mean molasses).

31. Transformed milk (is called) *kūrcikā*. (The words) *cikkaṇam*, *masṛṇam* and *snigdham* (denote bland). (Rice parched and flattened is denoted by the words) *pṛthuka* and *cipiṭaka*. Fried and powdered barley (is called) *dhānā*, in the feminine.

32. (The words) *jemanam*, *leha* and *āhāra* (denote food). (The words) *māheyī* and *saurabhī* denote a cow. Those which are yoked (are called) *yugyaḥ*, *prāsaṅgyaḥ* and *śākaṭaḥ*.

---

1. *Cf.* *Amara paṅkti* 1714. The *Purāṇa* while making an extract mixes the two terms

33. (A cow) that has delivered a calf long time back (is called) *vaṣkayaṇi*, and (one) that has delivered recently (is called) *dhenu*. (The cow) that is attacked by a bull (for mating) (is called) *sandhinī*. A barren cow (is called) *vehat*.

34-35. (A person sustaining himself by buying and selling is called) *paṇyājiva* and *āpaṇika*. A thing left as trust (is called) *upanidhi* and the word is masculine. The words *vipaṇa* and *vikraya* (mean sale). The numerals one to eighteen (are to be used) in all the three (genders) and the numerals twenty onwards take only singular always. While counting number two takes the plural. Among them (the numerals) upto ninety are feminine.

36-37. (A unit measuring ten is called a *paṅkti*). Successive multiples of a *paṅkti* would be hundred, thousand etc. They are measured by *tulāṅguliprastha*[1]-s. Five *guñja*-s (make) one *ādyamāṣaka*. Sixteen (*māṣa*-s) (make) one *akṣa* (otherwise called) *karṣa*. The word is not feminine. Four *karṣa*-s (would make) one *palam*. An *akṣa* (measure) of gold (is known as) *suvarṇa* and *bista*. A *pala* (measure) of the same (is called) *kuruvista*.

38. One hundred *pala*-s (make) one *tulā*. That (word) is feminine. Twenty *tulā*-s would make one *bhāra*. (A *karṣa* measure of silver) is called *kārṣāpaṇa* or *kārṣika*. A *karṣa* (measure) of copper (is known as) *paṇa*.

39-40a. (The words) *dravyam*, *vittam*, *svāpateyam*, *riktham*, *ṛktham*, *dhanam* and *vasu* (denote wealth). (The words) *riti* and *ārakūṭa* (denote brass). It is not in the feminine. (The words) *śulbam* and *audumbaram* (are synonyms of) *tāmrakam* (brass). *Kālāyasam* and *aya* (are synonyms of) *loha* (iron).

40b. (The words) *kṣāra* and *kāca* (alkali) (are synonyms). (The words) *capala*, *rasa*, *sūta* and *pārada* (are synonyms denoting mercury).

41. The horn of the wild buffalow (is called) *gavalam*. *Trapu* and *piccaṭam*[2] (tin) (are synonyms). *Sisakam*[3] (denotes lead). (The words) *hiṇḍira*, *abdhikapha* (sea-foam) and *phena* (are

1. *tulā* is explained below; *aṅguli* is fingerbreadth and one *praṣtha* is equal to thirtytwo *pala*-s explained below.

2. The other equivalents are given in the next verse.

3. The *Purāṇa* wrongly mixes this word with the previous.

synonyms). (The words) *madhūcchiṣṭam* and *sikthakam* (bee-wax) are synonyms.

42. (The words) *raṅgam* and *vaṅgam*[1] (denote tin). (The words) *picu* and *tūla* (mean cotton). *Kunaṭī* (dentoes) *manaḥśilā* (arsenic) (especially the Nepalese variety). *Yavakṣāra* (nitre) would be (known as) *pākya*. (The words) *tvakkṣīrī* and *vaṁśa-rocanā* (denote a medicinal substance got from the bamboo).

43. *Vṛṣalāḥ, jaghanyajāḥ* and *śūdrāḥ* (are synonyms) (denoting the fourth class of men). *Caṇḍāla*-s and other low caste men (are known as) mixed (castes). *Kāru* and *śilpī* (denote the artisan). Their union (with those) of their own caste (is called) *śreṇi*, both in (the feminine and masculine).

44. (A painter is denoted by the words) *raṅgā-jīva* and *citrakāra*. (A carpenter is denoted by the words) *takṣā*, *vardhaki* and *tvaṣṭā*. (The words) *nāḍindama* and *svarṇakāra* (denote a goldsmith). (The words) *nāpita* and *antāvasāyī* (denote a barber).

45. (A shepherd is denoted by the words) *jābāla* and *ajājīva*. (A person living by serving the god is called) *devājīva* and *devala*. (Actors are denoted by the words) *jāyājīva*-s and *śailūṣa*-s. (The words) *bhṛtaka* and *bhṛtibhuk* (denote a person living on wages).

46. (A low person is denoted by the words) *vivarṇa*, *pāmara*, *nīca*, *prākṛta*, *pṛthagjana*, *nihīna*, *apasada* and *jālma*. (The words) *dāsera* and *ceṭaka* (are used to denote) a servant.

47. (The words) *paṭu*, *peśala* and *dakṣa* (mean a clever person). *Mṛgayu* is known to be *lubdhaka* (hunter). *Cāṇḍāla* (low class man) (is also known as) *divākīrti*. (The word) *pustam* (is used) in (the sense of) plastering.

48. A puppet (made of cloth etc.) is *pāñcālikā*. Any young animal (is known as) *varkara*. (The words) *mañjūṣā*, *peṭaka* and *peṭā* (denote a box). (The words) *tulya*, *sādhāraṇa* and *sama* (mean equal or similar). (The word) *pratimā* would (mean) *pratikṛti* (an image or statue). The *brahma* and other classes have been described so far.

---

1. *Cf.* the previous verse.

CHAPTER THREE HUNDRED AND SIXTYSEVEN*

The class of words dependent on the substantives for their genders

Fire-god said :

1. Listen to me ! I shall describe the genders of the substantives in general. (The words) *sukṛti*, *puṇyavān* and *dhanya* (denote a fortunate person). (A generous person is denoted by the words) *mahecchha* and *mahāśaya*.

2. (The words) *pravīṇa*, *nipuṇa*, *abhijña*, *vijña*, *niṣṇāta* and *śikṣita*[1] (a proficient person) (are synonyms). (A very liberal person is denoted by the words) *vadānya*, *sthūlalakṣya*, *dānaśauṇḍa* and *bahuprada*.

3. The words *kṛti*,[2] *kṛtajña*[3] and *kuśala* (mean a clever person). (The word) *āsakta* (means one drawn towards something). (The words) *udyukta* and *utsuka* (mean being drawn towards something by one's own desire). (The words) *ibhya*, *āḍhya* and *parivṛḍha* (denote a rich man). *Adhibhūḥ*, *nāyaka* and *adhipa* (mean a master).

4. (A person endowed with fortune is denoted by the words) *lakṣmivān*, *lakṣmaṇa* and *śrila*. (The words) *svatantra*, *apāvṛta* and *svairi* (denote an independent person). *Khalapū* would (mean) *bahukara* (a sweeper). (The words) *dirghasūtra* and *cirakriya* (denote a lazy person).

5. *Jālma* and *asamikṣyakāri* (mean a person acting without discriminating good and bad). One who is slow in doing things is known as *kuṇṭha*. (One who is proficient in doing things is) *karmaśūra* or *karmaṭha*. (The words) *bhakṣaka*, *ghasmara* and *admara* (denote a gluttonous person).

6. *Lolupa* (denotes a person having ardent desire). (The words) *gardhana* and *gṛdhnuḥ* (denote a greedy person). (A modest person is denoted by the words) *vinita* and *praśrita*. (The

---

*This chapter summarises *Amara*, *kāṇḍa* III, *paṅktis* 2030 ff.

1. Other words having the same meaning have been wrongly put in the next verse in the *Purāṇa*.

2. These words should be read with those in verse 2.

3. This word means a grateful person. Probably a mistake for *kṛtamukha*. Cf. *Amara*, *paṅkti*, 2033.

words) *dhṛṣṇuk* and *viyāta* (are synonyms of) *dhṛṣṭa* (immodest). *Nibhṛta*[1] and *pratibhānvita* (denote a person having imagination).

7. (The word) *adhira* (means a person afflicted by fear, hunger, thirst etc.). (A cowardly or timid person is denoted by the words) *bhīruka* and *bhīru*. (The words) *vandāru* and *abhivādaka* (denote a polite or respectful person). (The words) *bhūṣṇu, bhaviṣṇu* and *bhavitā* (mean a person desiring to become rich). A knower (is denoted by the words) *vidura* and *vinduka*.

8-9a. (The words) *matta, śauṇḍa, utkaṭa* and *kṣība* (denote an intoxicated person). *Caṇḍa* (means) *atyantakopana* (extremely short-tempered). *Devadrayaṅ* is a person adoring a deity. A person serving the world is *viśvadrayaṅ*. A companion, especially the husband (is denoted by the word) *sadhryaṅ*. A person serving crookedly (is called) *tiryaṅ*.

9b-10a. (The two words) *vācoyuktipaṭu* and *vāgmī* (denote a logician). A garrulous person (is denoted by the word) *vāvadūka*. (A person indulging in unrefined talks is denoted by the words) *jalpāka, vācāla, vācāṭa* and *bahugarhyavāk*.

10b-11. (One who is censured is called) *apadhvasta* and *dhikkṛta*. (The words) *kīlita* and *saṁyata* (denote a person) bound (with rope etc.). (The words) *ravaṇa*[2] and *śabdana* (denote a person making sound). (The words) *nāndivādī* and *nāndikara* are synonyms (denoting laudatory singer). (The words) *vyasanārta* and *uparakta* (denote a person afflicted by misfortune)[3].

12. (The words) *vihasta* and *vyākula* are synonyms (meaning a person who does not know what to do on account of grief. (The words) *nṛśaṁsa, krūra, ghātuka* and *pāpa* (mean a person bent on harming others). *Dhūrta* and *vañcaka* (mean a cheat). (The words) *mūrkha, vaidheya* and *vāliśa* (denote a fool).

13. (A miser is denoted by the words) *kadarya, kṛpaṇa* and *kṣudra*. (The words) *mārgaṇa, yācaka* and *arthī* (mean a beggar). (The word) *ahaṁyu* (means) an egoistic person. A person endowed with good fortune (is called) *śubhaṁyuḥ*.

14-15a. (The words) *kāntam, manoramam* and *rucyam* (are used in the sense of a beautiful thing). A thing that is desired

---

1. *Amara, paṅkti* 2075 reads *pragalbha*.
2. The *Purāṇa* wrongly reads *caraṇa*.
3. The next two words repeated from verse 10—obviously a mistake.

(is denoted by the words) *hṛdyam* and *abhīṣṭam*. (The words) *asāram* and *phalgu* (mean a worthless thing). (The word) *śūnyam* (means void). (An important thing or person is denoted by the words) *mukhya*, *varya* and *vareṇya*.[1] (The words) *śreyān*, *śreṣṭha* and *puṣkala* would (mean the outstanding). (The words) *prāgrya*, *agrya*, *agrīya* and *agriya* (also mean an important person).

15b-16. (The words) *vaḍram*, *uru* and *vipulam* (mean wide). (The words) *pīnam*, *pīva*, *sthūlam* and *pīvaram* (mean) stout. (The words) *stoka*, *alpa* and *kṣullaka* (are used in the sense of a little). (A minute thing is denoted by the words) *sūkṣmam*, *ślakṣṇam*, *debhram*, *kṛśam* and *tanu*. (The words) *mātrā* and *kuṭi* (in the feminine) and *lava* and *kaṇa* (in the masculine) (have the same sense). (The words) *bhūyiṣṭham*, *puruha* and *puru* (mean plenty).

17. (The words) *akhaṇḍam*, *pūrṇam* and *sakalam* (denote the whole). (The words) *upakaṇṭha*, *antika*, *abhita*, *samīpa*, *savidha*[2] and *abhyāsa* (mean near). (The word) *nediṣṭham* (means) very near.

18. (The word) *daviṣṭham* would (mean) very far. (The words) *nistala* and *vartula* (would mean) circular. (The words) *ucca*, *prāṁśu*, *unnata* and *udagra* (mean high). (An eternal thing is denoted by the words) *dhruva*, *nitya* and *sanātana*.

19. (The words) *āviddham*, *kuṭilam*, *bhugnam*, *vellitam* and *vakram* (denote the crooked). (An unsteady thing is denoted by the words) *cañcalam* and *taralam*. (The words) *kaṭhoram*, *jaṭharam*[3] and *dṛḍham* (mean hard).

20. (The words) *pratyagra*, *abhinava*, *navya*, *navīna*, *nūtana* and *nava* (mean fresh or new). (The word) *ekatāna* (means) concentrated on a single object. (The word) *uccaṇḍam* (means) quickly.

21. (The words) *uccāvacam* and *naikabhedam* (mean manifold ways). (The word) *sambādha* (means a narrow way). *Kalilam* (means a difficult path). (The words) *timitam*, *stimitam* and *klinnam* (mean wet). (The word) *abhiyoga* (means) *abhigraha* (an attack).

---

1. Some of the other words having the same meaning have been given in the *Purāṇa* in the next verse after a break.
2. The ptd. text of the *Purāṇa* reads *sannidha*.
3. Also spelt as *jaraṭham*.

22. (The word) *sphāti* (is used to mean) increase. (The word) *prathā* (is used to denote) fame. (The word) *samāhāra* (means) a collection. (The word) *apahāra* (means) *apacaya* (removal). (The words) *vihāra* and *parikrama* (mean movement on foot).

23. (The words) *pratyāhāra* and *upādānam* (are used in the sense of restraining. the sense-organs). (The extraction of extraneous objects from the body is denoted by the words) *nirhāra* and *abhyavakarṣaṇam*. (The words) *vighna*, *antarāya* and *pratyūha* would (mean an obstacle). (The words) *āsyā*, *āsyanā* and *sthiti* (are used in the sense of a seat).

24. (The words) *sannidhi* and *sannikarṣa* (would (mean proximity). (A difficult path is indicated by the words) *saṅkrama* and *durgasañcara*. (The words) *upalambha* and *anubhava* (convey the meaning of experience). (The words) *pratyādeśa* and *nirākṛti* (are used in the sense of rejection).

25. (The words) *parirambha*, *pariṣvaṅga*, *saṁśleṣa* and *upagūhanam* (denote embrace). An inference (is that which is gained) by means of *pakṣa* (subject of a syllogism), *hetu* (reason) and the like[1]. The words *ḍamara*[2] and *viplava* (are used) in (the sense of) frightening an enemy by shouts.

26. The knowledge about an object, that is not perceived, (arising) from the statement is said to be *śābdam*.[3] *Upamāna* (*ka*) (comparison) would be the cognition arising from seeing the resemblance in a similar (object).

27. *Arthāpatti* (presumption) would be the knowledge about a different thing which would not exist without (the thing seen) *Abhāva* (non-existence) is the cognition "it is not there" when the counter-correlative is not apprehended on the ground. Thus ends the genders of substantives told by Hari (Viṣṇu) for the sake of knowledge of men.

1. This is not found in *Amara*.
2. The printed text wrongly reads *bhramara*.
3. This and other terms of *Nyāya* given here are not found in *Amara*.

CHAPTER THREE HUNDRED AND SIXTYEIGHT

Constant dissolution, occasional and total dissolution

Fire-god said:

1-2. The dissolution of beings is of four kinds, such as constant dissolution of all beings (that takes place daily), the dissolution (known as) *Brāhma*, (otherwise known as) *naimittika* (*pralaya*), the *prākṛta pralaya*, occurring at the end of a thousand of four *yuga*[1] periods and the absolute dissolution (of all beings) by the union of all souls in the supreme soul by means of knowledge.

3-5. I shall describe to you the nature of the *naimittika* dissolution that occurs at the end of a *kalpa*[2] period. When the earth (has become) almost depleted at the end of a thousand of four *yuga* cycles, there would be a severe drought for hundred years. Then (all) the beings would perish. Then (lord) Viṣṇu, the lord of the universe, remaining in the seven rays of the Sun, drinks the waters. The water in the oceans, the earth and the nether world and the like gets dried up.

6-8. Then by the divine power (of lord Viṣṇu), the very same seven rays (of the Sun), nourished by the water, become seven Suns. O Twice-born ! They burn the three worlds completely together with the nether world. (The surface of) the earth would (appear) like the back of a tortoise. Then the terrible fire (of dissolution), a manifestation of (lord) Rudra, burns the nether worlds below in association with the breath of the serpent *Śeṣa*[3]. Then the all-pervading (fire) burns the (region) from the nether worlds to the surface of the earth and from there to the heaven.

9-11. Then all the three worlds appear like one blazing mass. Then the inhabitants of the two worlds, oppressed by the terrible heat, ascend to the Maharloka and to the Janaloka from

1. The four yugas—*kṛta, tretā, dvāpara* and *kali* are reckoned as equivalent to 1,728,000, 1,296,000, 864,000 and 432,000 years respectively.

2. One *kalpa* is equivalent to a day of Brahmā consisting of one thousand *yugas*.

3. The serpent having thousand hoods on whose body reclines (lord) Viṣṇu.

Maharloka. After the world is burnt (by the God) (assuming) the form of Rudra, there arise clouds of different shapes together with lightning from the breath of (lord) Hari (Viṣṇu). They rain for a hundred years and put down the fire that has arisen.

12-13. When the water rises upto the region of the seven sages (Great Bear), a hundred storms issue from the breath of (the lord) Viṣṇu and disperse those clouds. Then after having drunk the wind lord Hari lies down on that mass of water, having assumed the form of Brahmā, extolled by sea-dwelling persons who have gained supernatural powers and by sages.

14. (Lord) Madhusūdana (slayer of demon Madhu; i.e. Viṣṇu) lies down (on that mass of water) resting in the yogic sleep, which is his divine illusory form, contemplating His own form known as Vāsudeva.

15. He then lies down (in sleep) for a *kalpa*[1] (period) and after waking up, in the form of Brahmā, He creates. O Twice-born! Then (the universe) lies in an unmanifest state in the Prakṛti for two *parārdha*[2]-s.

16-19. One place is ten times the other place when expansion is made from one place. Then the eighteenth place would be said to be *parārdha*. The *prākṛta* dissolution is known to be twice the *parārdha*. O Twice-born ! When everything is burnt by contact with fire and on account of drought, (it is *prākṛta* dissolution). The modifications of *mahat* (one of the principles), (get merged into one) losing their separate existence, and get re-absorbed (into *prakṛti*) on account of the will of (lord) Kṛṣṇa. Water first swallows the qualities of earth such as smell and the like. Then earth (divested of) its characteristic of smell tends towards dissolution.

20. Then water having the characteristic of taste remains. It is drunk by light. When it is lost, fire glows on.

21. Then wind swallows light together with its characteristic of colour and form. When fire is lost, strong wind blows on.

22. The characteristic of wind, namely touch, is then consumed by ether. O Twice-born ! When wind is also lost, ether remains without any sound.

---

1. See p. 1028 fn. 1 above.
2. equal to 100,000,000,000,000,000 years.

23. (The characteristic) of ether is sound. Ether (together with its characteristic) is swallowed by *Bhūtādi* (i.e. A*haṅkāra* or Ego Principle in which the element of Tamas dominates). Ether born of Ego and *Bhūtādi* are swallowed by *Mahat* i.e. *Buddhi tattva* (the first evolute of *Prakṛti* in Sāṅkhya).

24-25. Earth gets merged in water, water in light, light in wind, wind in ether and ether in ego. O Twice-born ! that (ego) (gets merged) in the principle of *mahat* and (the principle of) *mahat* is swallowed by *prakṛti* (nature). The *prakṛti* (consists of two parts) such as manifest and unmanifest. The manifest (part of *prakṛti*) gets merged in the unmanifest.

26. The *puruṣa* (primordial being) is pure and is one undecaying (entity). He is also a part of the Supreme Soul. These *prakṛti* and *puruṣa* get merged in the Supreme Soul. There is no determination such as name, species and the like in that lord of all. (That Supreme Soul) is composed only of existence. He is to be known and (is of the form of) knowledge. (All) other souls (are merged) in (such Supreme Soul).

CHAPTER THREE HUNDRED AND SIXTYNINE

The description of absolute dissolution and the process of creation

Fire-god said :

1. I shall describe absolute dissolution. Absolute dissolution arises from knowledge after having known the sufferings caused by the mind etc. from one's disinclination.

2. The sufferings are of two kinds : physical and mental. The physical sufferings are manifold. O Twice-born ! Listen to me ! I shall describe them.

3-5. The (individual) soul after having discarded the sensual body enters the womb as a result of (the past) deeds. O Twice-born ! this body known as *ātivāhika* (that is carried forward) is peculiar to men alone. O Twice-born ! when the time for death comes the bodies of men are carried away by the servants of Yama (God of Death) along the path of Yama. O Sage! this is not the case with the other beings. Such a person would wander in heaven and hell like the *ghaṭayantra*[1].

6-7. O Brahmin ! This is a land of deeds and is known to bear fruits (of one's actions). Yama (God of Death) is the cause of one's birth. He determines the hell (to which one has to go) on account of the deed. Being awaited by them (men), Yama, makes them get their befitting places (dependent) on their (deeds). The beings which have got ethereal (bodies) reach the (befitting) wombs.

8-9a. A man is led by the messengers of Yama and he sees him (Yama). A pious man is honoured by him and a sinner is beaten. Citragupta[2] informs him the good or bad deed (done) in (every) house.

9b-12a. (The departed soul) dwells in the *Ātivāhika* (provisional) body and partakes the funeral oblations offered by the relatives. O Knower of virtue ! (After the funeral is over) (the soul) rejects that *preta* body (attained after death) and ascends to another region from that of the *preta*-s. It dwells (there) experiencing hunger and thirst and partakes the raw offerings (made to it by the relatives). A person does not get release from this newly acquired body without (eating) the funeral oblations. He partakes the ball-offerings there itself.

12b-13a. When the *sapiṇḍikaraṇa*[3] has been done, a (dead) man discards the *preta* body and gets a sensuous body after one year.

13b-14. Both the bodies are said to be sensuous and designated as inauspicious and auspicious. After having enjoyed by means of the sensuous body, one gets released from the bondage of deeds. Demons devour that body after that.

15. O Twice-born! A person who does sinful deeds, would enjoy (the fruits of good deeds at first) in the heaven. Then he takes a second body of sinners to experience (the fruits of sin).

---

1. A mechanism for drawing water from a well.

2. One of the assistants of Yama who records the virtuous and vicious deeds of men.

3. The rite performed at the end of one year or on the twelfth day after the death of a person to unite the dead with the departed ancestors.

16. After experiencing the fruits of sin one that has enjoyed heaven, is thereafter born in a pure and prosperous family.

17. A person doing pious deeds having (a little of) sin would first experience (the fruits of) the sin and when that body is dissolved would attain a beautiful body.

18. A person gets freed from hell even if a little of past deed still remains. There is no doubt that he would be born as an animal after getting liberated from hell.

19-20. The soul after having entered the womb dwells in the foetus. It gets hard in the second (month). The limbs (grow) in the third (month). Bones, skin and flesh (are formed) in the fourth (month). Hair grows in the fifth (month). Heart (is formed) in the sixth. The soul feels pain in the seventh.

21. Thus (the child) remains in the womb being covered with the placenta and having hands folded above the head. A eunuch stays in the middle (of the abdomen), a female (child) on the left side and a male (child) on the right side.

22. The child stays in the womb facing the back (of the mother). There is no doubt that it (the child) recognises the person in whose (womb) it stays.

23. It knows fully all the incidents of previous life from birth onwards. A person finds a great darkness and (experiences) suffering.

24. In the seventh month it partakes the food eaten by the mother. It becomes extremely restive in the eighth and ninth months.

25. It suffers when there is coition and physical exercise on the part of the mother. It becomes sick when (the mother is) sick, a moment (of agony) appearing as if lasting for a hundred years.

26. It is tormented by the (past) deeds and makes resolutions : "O Brahman ! After getting out from the womb I will gain knowledge relating to liberation (from this bondage)".

27. Being pressed down by the wind inside (mother's) womb, it gets out through the vagina. It gets afflicted in the first month (after birth) and feels pain when touched with the hand.

28. The auditory organs, minor organs and the state of being separate (are produced) in the body from the ether with

(its attribute of) sound. The process of breathing, movement and the feeling of touch are due to the wind.

29. Personality, sense of seeing, heat, celebrity, biles, intellect, colour, strength, shade, splendour and valour arise in the body from fire.

30. Sweat, the organ of taste, moisture, marrow, taste, blood, semen, urine and phlegm and the like are produced in the body from water.

31-33. The sense of smell, hair, nail, weight and firmness of the bones (are) from earth. The delicate organs, skin, flesh, heart, navel, marrow, ordure, fat, moisture and the upper part of the belly are got from the mother. Veins, arteries and semen are got from the father. Lust, anger, fear, joy, the states of being pious and not pious, form, voice, colour and the discharge of urine and the like are due to one's own (state).

34. Ignorance, negligence, idleness, thirst, hunger, infatuation, jealousy, defectiveness, grief, weariness and fear are qualities of *tamas* (temperament).

35. O Great sage! Lust, anger, valour, desire to do sacrifice, garrulousness, ego and contempt for others are qualities of *rājasa* (temperament).

36. Desire to be righteous, desire for emancipation, extreme devotion to (lord) Keśava (Viṣṇu), compassion and diligence should be termed as arising from *sāttvika* (temperament).

37. A person in whom wind predominates would be fickle, irritable, cowardly, garrulous, yielding to vices of *kali* (*yuga*) and dreams of flying in the air.

38. A person in whom bile predominates would be prematurely grey-haired, irritable, very learned, fond of battle and one who sees conflagrations in dream.

39. A person in whom phlegm abounds would be a steadfast friend, constantly enthusiastic, having firm limbs, endowed with wealth and one who perceives water and white colour in dream.

40-41. Serum is the life force in the body of beings. Blood (serves as) the anointment. Flesh causes urination and perspiration. Bones make (the body) firm. Marrow would fill up and increase potency. Semen gives potency. *Ojas* (virility) is the sustainer of life.

42. Virility is subtler and lesser yellow than semen and flows in the vicinity of heart. There are six parts of the body, viz, two thighs (legs), two hands, head and belly.

43-45. The six external layers of skin are the epidermis, (the layer) that contains blood, the next one that contains features of grace, the fourth one that bears the sacs (storing fluids), the fifth one that is the seat of abscesses and the sixth one that supports life. There are seven sheaths (namely) that which supports flesh, the second one, blood, that which is the prop for liver and spleen, the next one that holds fat and that which supports bone, that which holds marrow, phlegm and feces, situated in the abdomen. The sixth is that which holds bile and (the next one) that holds semen in the region of that sac.

CHAPTER THREE HUNDRED AND SEVENTY

The constituent parts of a body

Fire-god said :

1-2. The auditory organ, skin, the two eyes, tongue, nose, intellect, the five elements and their qualities (such as) sound, touch, colour, taste and smell, the anus, the organ of generation, the two hands, the two feet are the embodiments of sky. Their functions are emission, exhilaration, taking, movement and speech and the like.

3. Five among these are organs of action, five are organs of sense. The five great elements are objects of senses having the mind as that which governs.

4. The soul is unmanifest. The principles are twentyfour. The *puruṣa* is the supreme. (The soul exists) just like the fish in the water attached and detached.

5. The qualities *sattva*, *rajas* and *tamas* dwell in the unmanifest (*Prakṛti*). The inner being is the *puruṣa*. It is the Supreme brahman, the cause.

6-7. One who knows this Supreme *puruṣa*, attains the supreme position. There are seven sacs in the body: The first one is the sac of blood. (The other sacs) are those of phlegm, of undigested food and of bile. The fifth one is that of digestion. The receptacles for wind and urine (are the sixth) and seventh. The uterus is the eighth one in women.

8-9. The sac of digestion gets dilated by bile and the vagina by internal fire. The uterus would resemble lotus and expand during the menstrual period. There it holds semen together with blood. O Sage ! semen deposited in the vagina is led to the uterus in course of time.

10. Even during the menstruous period, the vagina would be surrounded by wind, bile and phlegm. It would not get dilated then.

11-12. O Fortunate one ! heart, lungs, liver and spleen are formed in due succession. O Knower of virtue ! spleen and liver of men are formed from the essence of the serum that gets condensed. Lungs (are formed) from the froth of blood.

13. Blood is then converted into bile and it is then known as *taṇḍaka*. Heart is formed from the spreading of fat and blood.

14. Intestines of mortals are formed from the spreading of blood and flesh. They should be known as three and a half *vyāma-s*[1] (long) in men.

15. They are three *vyāma*-s (long) in women according to those learned in scriptures. Its rise in passion is said to be from the union of blood and wind.

16. Heart assumes the shape of a lotus from the expansion of phlegm. That cavity hangs down and the soul remains therein.

17. All the feelings which accompany consciousness remain there. Spleen is to its left and liver is on the right.

18-19a. Lungs are on the right side of the (above) lotus. The sense organs are formed from the veins and arteries in the body which carry the phlegm and blood. They are the means to cognise objects.

1. A *vyāma* is a measure of length equal to the space between the tips of the fingers of either hand, when the arms are extended.

19b-20. The orb of the eyes is white. It is a paternal element and it owes its origin to the phlegm. The orb is black arising from wind and it is a maternal element. The entire skin is formed from the bile and it is formed from the father as well as the mother.

21-24. The tongue is formed out of flesh, blood and phlegm. The testes are from the marrow, blood, phlegm and fat. One has to know the ten vital places of life in the body (namely) head, heart, navel, throat, tongue, semen, blood, anus, pelvis and ankles. Sinews are said to be sixteen in the two hands, two feet, including four on the back and the neck. The membranes are sixteen from head to foot in the body. Flesh, sinews, arteries and bones are firmly placed around the wrist and ankles separately.

25. There are six brush (-like formations) in the hands, feet, neck and anus as pointed out by men.

26. There are four thread-like flesh formations in the region of the spinal column. There are ninety muscles, which bind them (in their places).

27-28a. There are seven *sivani*-s (a kind of thin muscles), among which five are on the head, one each in the penis and the tongue. There are sixtythree bones. Together with the minute ones there are sixtyfour in all. The teeth and nails are twenty.

28b-30. Hands, legs and the tips of these are the four places (of bones). Bones are sixty in the fingers, two on the heels, four at the ankles, four at the elbows, the same number on the shanks, two each at the knee, cheek and thighs which arise from the hip and shoulder. One has to know in the same way at the *akṣasthāna*, shoulder and hip.

31. There are one at the penis, forty-five on the back, and similar number of bones at the neck, collar bones and cheek.

32. The base of these which are two, have their places at the neck, eye, throat, nose and feet. The ribs together with the palate and lumps of flesh are seventytwo.

33. (There are) two temporal bones. There are four (bones) on the skull and the head. There are seventeen bones on the chest. There are two hundred and ten (bones) of the joints.

34. Among the sixty-eight in the arms sixty-one remain distributed. In the neighbourhood are eighty-three (bones). The sinews are nine hundred.

35. (There are) two hundred and thirty (bones) and seventy in the interior. Six hundred go upwards. (The bones) of the arm have been described.

36. The muscles are five hundred. Forty (among them) go upwards. There are four hundred in the arms and sixty in the interval.

37-39. There will be twenty-five more, ten more on the breast, thirteen in the organ of generation and four in the uterus in the case of women. There are thirty lakh veins in the bodies of men. There are also others numbering nine (thousand) and fifty-six thousand. They carry the (vital) fluid, the moisture and the fat inside the body just as the channels (carry water) to the basins (around plants).

40-43. O Great sage! There are seventytwo crores of hair. O Twice-born! The *añjali*[1] measure of marrow, fat, urine, bile and phlegm, feces, blood and fluids are in order one and a half times more than the preceding one respectively. The semen is half *añjali*. The *ojas* is half of that. Wisemen point out that the menstrual fluid (in women) is four times. Knowing that the body is a mass of dirt and impurity, one should discard and (take interest) in the soul.

CHAPTER THREE HUNDRED AND SEVENTYONE

The description of hells

Fire-god said:

1-2. I will describe to you the path (leading) to *Yama* (i.e. the world of God of Death) which have been pointed out (by the learned). The bodily heat getting intense and diffused by the deranged wind, obstructs the body as well as all the defects. Moreover it breaks the subtle places of life (in the body).

1. A measure of corn.

3-4. The wind excited by cold seeks an aperture (for its movement). The seven apertures are—two eyes, two ears, two nostrils and head. The eighth one is the mouth. Generally the lives of pious men escape through these holes.

5. (The lives) of doers of bad deeds (escape) through the anus and the organ of generation in the lower (region). The lives of yogins get out breaking the head by own will.

6-7. When the time for death has come, when the life force has approached the *apāna*[1], when knowledge has been engulfed by darkness and when the vulnerable spots (in the body) have been surrounded, the life is moved by the wind from the umblicus. Being affected thus it draws the eight fundamental attributes of vitality (life) within.

8-10. The accomplished beings and celestials witness with their spiritual vision, the exit (of life), the birth and the entry into the uterus. As soon as the life leaves the body it assumes a light body by means of *yoga*. When one is dead, the ether, wind and lustre go upwards from the body, the water and earth (go downwards) (and get merged in their respective elements). The messengers of Yama lead this light body.

11. The path to the place of God of Death is much dreadful. It extends over (a space of) eighty-six thousand (*krośas*). Being led thus, it partakes the food and water given by the kinsmen.

12. After having seen the God of Death, being directed by him on the words of Citragupta (the personal assistant of God of Death), a person is taken to the dreadful hells. A virtuous person is lead to the heaven by auspicious path.

13-14a. I shall describe the hells in which the sinners are placed and the sufferings (therein). There are twenty-eight important hells below the earth at the end of the seventh layer of the region covered by dreadful darkness.

14b-18. Ghorā is the name of the first hell. Sughorā is below that. The others are Atighorā, Mahāghorā, Ghorarūpā, the fifth, the sixth known as Taralatārā, the seventh one Bhayānakā, Bhayotkaṭā, Kālarātrī, Mahācaṇḍā, Caṇḍā, Kolāhalā, the one known as Pracaṇḍā, Padmā, Narakanāyikā, Padmāvatī, Bhīṣaṇā, Bhīmā, Karālikā, Vikarālā, Mahāvajrā, Trikoṇā,

1. One of the five winds in the body.

Pañcakoṇikā, Sudīrghā, Vartulā, Saptabhūmā, Subhūmikā and Dīptamāyā. The wicked suffer in these.

19. There are five foremost (divisions) among each one of the twenty-eight hells known as Raurava and others numbering one-hundred and forty.

20-22. Tāmisra, Andhatāmisra, Mahāraurava and Raurava, Asipatravana (forest of sword-like leaves), Lohabhāra, Kālasūtra, Mahānaraka, Sañjīvana, Mahāvīci, Tapana, Sampratāpana, Saṅghāta, Sakākola, Kuḍamala, Pūtimṛttika, Lohaśaṅku and Ṛjīṣa (are the sub-divisions). Śālmalī is the main river.

23. One should know that the hells are governed by dreadful looking serpents. They put the sinners in each one of the hells as well as in many of them.

24. Having their faces resembling cats, owls, frogs and vultures etc., they throw the man in caldrons of oil and then light the fire.

25-28. Some (are put) in frying pans, some in copper vessels, some others in iron caldrons and others among sparks of fire. Some are placed on the tip of pointed pikes. Some are pierced in the hell. Some are thrashed with whips. Some are made to eat molten iron. The men are made to consume dust, excreta, blood, phlegm etc. and made to drink hot wine by the messengers of God of Death. The men are again pierced. They are tortured by mechanical devices and (the bodies are) eaten by crows etc. Hot oil is sprinkled over them and the head is pierced repeatedly.

29-30. Wailing aloud 'Oh ! father!', (the men) denounce their (past) deeds. After having reached dreadful hells as a result of censurable great sins, the great sinners are reborn here when the (fruits) of the (past) deeds are exhausted. A killer of a brahmin is born in the womb of a deer, dog, pig and camel.

31. A drunkard (is born in the womb) of a Pukkaśa[1] or Mleccha[2]. A person stealing gold (gets) the state of an insect, worm or locust. A person defiling the bed of his preceptor (attains) the state of a clump of grass.

1. A mixed caste, an offspring of a hunter male and a *śūdra* woman.
2. A non-Aryan.

32. A killer of a brahmin would get consumption. A drunkard (would have) dark brown teeth (a dental disease). One who steals gold (would) have bad nails. A person violating the teacher's bed (would have) a skin disease.

33. A person commiting a sin by a particular limb would get that limb affected. A person stealing food would become dyspeptic. A person harming the articulation (of a man) (would be born) dumb.

34. A person stealing grains would have abnormal limbs. A miser (would be born as) having a fetid nose. A person stealing oil would become a bird. An informer would have an offensive breath.

35. A person abducting the wife of another and defiling a brahmin would be born as a *brahmarākṣasa* (a kind of ghost) in an uninhabited forest.

36. A person stealing gems (attains birth) in a low caste. (One who steals) perfumes (would be born) as the female of the muskrat. One who steals leaves, vegetables (would become) a peacock and one who steals grain (would become) a crow.

37-38a. (A person stealing) a domestic animal, milk, vehicle, fruit, honey, flesh, condiment, clothe or lotus and salt (would respectively be born as) a goat, crow, camel, monkey, fly, vulture, *gṛhakāka* (domestic crow), one afflicted by psoriasis and as cricket.

38b-39. Afflictions in mundane existence are said to be of three varieties namely, *ādhyātmika* (affecting mind and its faculties), *ādhibhautika* (caused by weapons etc.), and *ādhidaivika*, due to the planets, fire and gods. Men should nullify them by knowledge, by atonements, vows, making gifts and worship of (lord) Viṣṇu etc.

CHAPTER THREE HUNDRED AND SEVENTYTWO

The major and minor religious observances (yama-s and niyama-s)

Fire-god said:

1-2a. I shall describe to you the *yoga* having eight constituents in order to get free from the sufferings due to mundane existence. Knowledge makes Brahman manifest. There, *yoga* is the concentration of mind and the withdrawal of the mind (from all other objects). (It is) the highest (union) of the individual soul and the Supreme Brahman.

2b-3. O Brahmin ! Non-injury, truthfulness, non-stealing, celibacy and rejection of gifts are known to be the five major observances. These together with the minor observances yield enjoyment and emancipation. Purity, contentment, penance, study of one's own scriptures, worship of God are minor observances.

4-5a. Non-injury means not causing injury to the beings. Non-injury is the foremost virtue. Just as the footsteps of the travellers on foot could be contained in the footstep of an elephant, so also all the virtuous acts are said (to be included) in non-injury.

5b-7a. Injury (would) create anxiety, cause suffering, mental and physical pain (spilling of blood), slandering, great obstruction to beneficial thing, opening of vulnerable parts, denial of happiness, obstruction and killing. Thus it is of ten kinds.

7b-8. Truthfulness is defined as speech that would be extremely beneficial to beings. Speak the truth. Speak what is pleasing. But do not speak the truth that is not pleasing. Do not also tell a lie that would be pleasing. This is the eternal virtue.

9-10. Celibacy is the shunning of sexual enjoyment. It is eightfold. Men declare that sexual enjoyment is eightfold such as remembrance, praise, sport, seeing, talking in secret, resolve, endeavours and the final consummation.

11-12a. Celibacy is at the root of action and an action becomes fruitless otherwise. Even the elders in age and wisdom, such as Vasiṣṭha, Candramas, Śukra, the preceptor of gods (Bṛhaspati), and Pitāmaha (Brahmā) were captivated by women.

12b-14a. The three kinds of wine are known as *gauḍī* (from molasses), *paiṣṭī* (from flour) and *mādhvī* (from honey). The fourth sort of wine is known as woman by which the world has been deluded. One gets intoxicated just after seeing a woman, but one gets intoxicated by wine only after drinking. Since a woman is like wine by being looked at, one should not look at her.

14b-15a. A person who forcibly takes away another's possession, whatever it may be, would certainly attain the state of lower animals. (Similar would be the result) for eating (stealthily) the butter offered as oblation.

15b-17a. (A mendicant) may accept a loin-cloth as covering, clothing, wallet that prevents cold and a pair of sandals. But one should not covet anything beyond these. Dress etc. are put on (the body) for the sustenance of the body. Body is associated with virtue. Hence it should be protected with care.

17b-18. Purity is said to be twofold—external and internal. External purity is to be maintained by means of earth and water and the internal by cleaning the feelings. One who is pure in both these respects is said to be pure, and not otherwise.

19-20a. Contentment is said to be the feeling of satisfaction with whatever one gets. Penance is the concentration of the mind and senses on a single object. The conquest of senses and mind is said to be the foremost among all virtues. Penance which fulfils all desires is threefold, namely, oral consisting of repetition of sacred formulae etc., mental (consisting of) eschewing desires, and physical (consisting of) the worship of gods etc.

20b-31. The *Vedas* begin with *praṇava* (the syllable *oṁ*) and also end with the *praṇava*. *Praṇava* is the entire collection of words. Hence one has to repeat *praṇava*. (It is composed of) the syllables *a*, *u* and *m*, (the latter) being half a syllabic instant. The three syllabic instants (represent) the three *Vedas*. The three worlds *Bhū* etc. are its qualities. (It also represents) the three states such as waking, dreaming and deep sleep. (It is also equated with) the gods Brahmā, Viṣṇu and Maheśvara. (The divine forms) such as Pradyumna, Śrīvāsudeva etc. (have all come) duly from the syllable *oṁ*. (The *praṇava*) to which a syllabic instant is not added or that which is bereft of a syllabic instant or more is not auspicious. One who has learnt the syllable *oṁ* is a sage and none else. The fourth syllabic instant is endowed with the *gāndhārī* (accent) and is indicated on the head. It is the fourth one, the Supreme Brahman, like the lamp in a pot. One has to contemplate always (that Brahman) resting in the lotus of the heart. *Praṇava* is the bow, the (individual) soul is the arrow and Brahman is said to be its target. It should be known with all assiduity and one should become united like the arrow. This single syllable is Brahman. It is the supreme entity. A person who knows this syllable would get what he wishes (to get). The goddess Gāyatrī is its metre. The lord within is known to be its sage. The Supreme Soul is its deity. This application would yield enjoyment and prosperity. '*Bhūḥ*, to the soul of fire' is (the formula of) the heart. '*Bhuvaḥ*, to the soul of Prajāpati' is (the formula of) the head. '*Svaḥ*, to the soul of Sun' is said to be the armour of the tuft. '*Oṁ bhūr bhuvaḥ svaḥ*' is the armour. 'To the soul of truth' (is) the weapon. After having placed (lord) Viṣṇu, one should repeat (this formula) for the sake of enjoyment and emancipation.

32-33. One should offer oblations of sesamum and clarified butter etc. One would obtain all things. A person who repeats the syllable twelve thousand times everyday would have the manifestation of the Supreme Brahman (in front of him) in twelve months. By the repetition (of the syllable) one crore times (one would gain perfections) such as *aṇimā* (subtlety) etc. One would gain the grace of the (goddess of) learning (by repeating this) a lakh times.

34. Sacrificial rites for (lord) Viṣṇu are of three kinds, Vedic, Tāntric and mixed. One should worship (lord) Hari (Viṣṇu), by one of these three methods that is desired.

35. The position which one gains by prostrating flat on the ground like a stick and worshipping (lord Viṣṇu), (he would) not (gain) by means of (performing) hundreds of sacrificial rites.

36. The import of these explained here would become manifest to those great men who have extreme devotion for the god and also for the preceptor as for the god.

CHAPTER THREE HUNDRED AND SEVENTYTHREE

Description of āsanas (different physical postures) and control of breath

Fire-god said :

1-3a. (The term) *āsana* denotes postures such as the 'lotus'[1] etc. Sitting in that posture one should contemplate the Supreme (Being). After having established oneself firmly in that posture in a pure place which is neither too much raised nor too much lowered, on the skin of an antelope and the *kuśa* (grass), one should concentrate after controlling the mind and the senses. Seated in that posture one should practise *yoga* for the sake of the purification of the self.

3b-6. The body, head and neck should be held erect and firm without movement and one should look at the tip of the nose. One should not look in any other direction. One should protect the testicles and the penis with the heels, and place (the heels) on the thighs, keep the hands across with effort and place the back of the right palm on the left (palm). After raising the face slowly and holding the mouth forward (one should practise the control of breath). *Prāṇa* is the wind in one's body and its *āyāma* is its retention.

7. (Holding and) closing (one of) the nostrils with the finger (exhale and) empty the air from the chest with the other nostril. Because of emptying it is known as *recaka* (exhalation).

8. Fill the inside with external air like a leather bag till it gets fully filled and remains steady. It is known as *pūraka* (filling) because of filling to the full.

9. When one neither lets off the air inside nor inhales the air but remains steady like a completely filled pot, (it is called) *kumbhaka*.

10-11. (Again *prāṇāyāma* is divided into three classes) : *Kanyasa* (the shortest one) is inhaling once for a duration of twelve *mātrā*-s (moments). *Madhyama* (the middle one) is inhaling twice lasting for a duration of twenty-four moments. *Uttama* (the longest) is inhaling thrice lasting for a period of thirty-six

1. See verses 3b ff below.

moments. *Uttamottama* (the foremost one) is that which produces sweat, shivering and stiffness.

12-13. One should not tread on untrodden ground. (By doing so) (one would be liable to get) hiccough, breathing (trouble) etc. When the vital air is conquered there would be little defect in the feces, urine etc. (One would gain) health, quick gait, enthusiasm, clarity of voice, grace in strength and colour and the loss of all defects.

14. That (*prāṇāyāma*) which is not accompanied by, muttering (of prayer, divine name etc.) and contemplation (is known as) not impregnated. That which is accompanied (by muttering of 'om' etc. is known as) impregnated. An impregnated (*prāṇāyāma*) should be practised foremost for the subjugation of the senses.

15. When the senses are conquered along with the acquisition of knowledge and detachment and one has acquired mastery in *prāṇāyāma*, everything else would then become conquered.

16. The senses are really everything (which leads) to heaven or hell. By controlling them or leaving them unbridled (one would go) to heaven or hell.

17-18. The body is said to be like a chariot and the senses (are) its horses. The mind is said to be the charioteer. *Prāṇāyāma* is known to be the whip. With the reins of knowledge and detachment and by getting rid of illusion, the mind attains steadiness by means of *prāṇāyāma* alone.

19. (The practice of) *prāṇāyāma* (gives) the same benefit that would accrue to a person who drinks drops of water through the tip of a *kuśa* (grass) month after month for whole period of one hundred years.

20. *Pratyāhāra* is said to consist in the withdrawal and restraining of the senses which are ordinarily immersed in the ocean of objects.

21. One should pull up the self by one's own effort just as a man sinking in the water (is pulled out). (One should cross) the rapid current of the river of enjoyment of objects by resorting to the tree of knowledge.

CHAPTER THREE HUNDRED AND SEVENTYFOUR

Contemplation

Fire-god said :

1. The root *dhyai* is known (to be used) in (the sense of) contemplation. A constant meditation on (lord) Viṣṇu without digression of mind is said to be contemplation.

2. Contemplation is said to be that power of the soul equal to the thought of the (Supreme) Brahman by means of one's own will unconditioned by any category.

3. (In other words) contemplation is said to be that thought found to be together with a similar thought resting on an object to be contemplated and which is free from the thought of any other kind.

4. It is said to be contemplation when the mind thinks constantly of a thing that is to be contemplated at any fixed place.

5. A person who discards his body (with his mind) endowed with such contemplation would elevate his family, kinsmen and friends and would become (lord) Hari (Viṣṇu).

6. The position which one attains by contemplating (lord) Hari with faith for a moment or half in this manner, could not be got by (performing) all great sacrificial rites.

7. A person who knows the truth should apply himself to (the practice of) *yoga*, after having known the four (things) such as the contemplator, contemplation, the thing to be contemplated and that which is the benefit of the contemplation.

8-9a. A person would obtain release (from bondage of mundane existence) by practising *yoga* (and would also gain) eight (kinds of) great powers[1]. (A person who is) endowed with knowledge and detachment, earnestness, forbearance, devotion to (lord) Viṣṇu and is always enthusiastic is deemed to be the Supreme Soul after such contemplation.

9b.-10a. The Supreme Brahman is both embodied and not embodied. Contemplation is (the constant) thought about that

---

1. These are the eight miraculous powers such as *aṇimā* (becoming minute as an atom) etc.

(lord) Hari. (Lord) Hari, the omniscient and supreme should be known as endowed with parts and without parts.

10b. The benefit of contemplation is the gain of powers such as *aṇimā* (ability to become minute like an atom) and the like (as well as) emancipation.

11-12a. (Lord) Viṣṇu associates (us) with the fruit and hence one should contemplate the Supreme Lord. One should always think of the lord while moving, standing, sleeping, waking, opening and closing the eyes, whether one is clean or not clean.

12b-14a. After having established (lord) Keśava (Viṣṇu) in the mind residing inside the body one should worship Him as seated on the pedestal of one's lotus-like heart, by means of the *yoga* (union) of contemplation. This sacrifice (in the form) of contemplation is supreme, pure and is devoid of all defects. By worshipping thus one gets released (from bondage of existence) and not by external cleanliness and sacrificial rites.

14b. (Because contemplation) is free from the defect of violence, it is the means of purifying the mind.

15-16a. Hence the sacrifice in the form of contemplation is the highest as it yields final beatitude. Hence after having discarded the temporal impure external means such as the sacrificial rite etc., one should intensively practice *yoga*.

16b-17. First of all one should contemplate in the heart the three qualities, unmanifest, free from any modification and endowed with the objects of enjoyment and (the feeling of) pleasure after having covered (the quality) *tamas* by means of *rajas* and then *rajas* by means of *sattva*.

18-19a. Then one should first contemplate the three spheres such as black, red and white in order. The Supreme Soul, the twenty fifth principle, that is beyond the limiting adjunct of *sattva* (quality), should be contemplated. After having discarded the impure thing, pure thing should be thought of.

19b-21. A glorious divine lotus exists above the Supreme Being. It measures twelve inches wide. It is pure, blossomed and white. Its stalk is eight finger-breadths (long). It had its origin from the bulbous root of the navel. The eight petals of the lotus should be known as the eight qualities such as *aṇimā*. Its pericarp, filament and stalk are knowledge and detachment.

22. Its root is the *dharma* (characteristic) of (lord) Viṣṇu. Such a lotus should be meditated upon. Its characteristic, namely, knowledge and detachment, is wholly composed of the foremost glory of (lord) Śiva.

23-24a. After having known the lotus posture completely, one would have the end of all miseries. One should meditate on the lord (in the form of) the syllable *Oṁ*, that is spotless, of the size of a thumb and of the form of the wick of a pure lamp.

24b-25a. Otherwise one should contemplate (the lord) as resembling the form of an asterism, as having the form of a cluster of *kadamba* (flowers) and illumined by a cluster of rays.

25b-26a. One should contemplate and repeat the syllable *Oṁ* that is supreme, undecaying (symbolizing) the lord, the principal entity, that transcends the *puruṣa* and dwells in the lotus (of the heart).

26b-28. (Yogins) want to contemplate on gross things first for making the mind firm. One would be able to get steadiness in (contemplating on) minute things also after gaining firmness (in the above). A stalk ten finger-breadths long is at the root of the navel. A lotus of twelve finger-breadths and having eight petals (is supported) by the stalk. Orbs of sun, moon and fire (are situated) in the pericarp and the filament.

29-32a. (Lord) Viṣṇu having four arms bearing conch, disc, mace and lotus and stationed at the centre of an orb of fire, or (lord) Hari having eight arms bearing a bow, rosary, bracelet, noose and goad etc., and of a golden complexion, white complexion, wearing the *śrivatsa*[1] (mark on the chest), the *kaustubha* (gem), a garland of wild flowers and a gold necklace, and shining with ear-ring (in the shape) of a fish (should be contempleted). (He should also be imagined) as wearing a sparkling gem (studded) crown and silk robes and endowed with all kinds of ornaments. Otherwise (one may contemplate a form) of the size of twelve finger-breadths as one would like.

32b. (One should also repeat the formula) "I am Brahman, light, soul, Vāsudeva (name of Viṣṇu, as manifested in the form of Kṛṣṇa), the liberated, *Oṁ*".

1. The curling hair on the chest.

33. When one has become tired of contemplation, one may repeat the formula. When one has got tired of repetition one may meditate. (Lord) Viṣṇu gets pleased quickly with a person engaged in the repetition (of a formula), contemplation and the like.

34. The merits of (performing) sacrificial rites are not worth even a sixteenth part of the merits of the rites of repeating (a formula). Diseases, calamities and (evil influences of) planets do not approach a person repeating (a formula). One would get the benefit of devotion, liberation and conquest over death by means of the repetition of a formula.

CHAPTER THREE HUNDRED AND SEVENTYFIVE

Fixing-up of the mind in the object of contemplation

Fire-god said :

1. *Dhāraṇā* is the fixing-up of the mind firmly on (the object) to be meditated upon. Like *dhyāna* (contemplation), it is also twofold according as the object is an embodied or an unembodied form of (lord) Hari.

2. The mind does not get shaken from the object that lies outside. That period for which the mind remains in a state of obsorption in a particular place without being distracted (is known as) *dhāraṇā*.

3. *Dhāraṇā* is said to be that period for which the mind remains absorbed (in the contemplation) of god, without deviating from its object.

4. *Dhāraṇā* has a duration of twelve *yāma*[1]-s. Twelve *dhāraṇā* -s (are equal to) *dhyāna*. It is said to be *samādhi* which consists of twelve (such) *dhyāna*-s.

5. If a person practisting *dhāraṇā* discards his life, he attains supreme position in the heaven after elevating twenty-one (generations of his) family.

1. One *yāma* is equal to three hours.

6. When a particular part of the body of a *yagin* gets affected by disease, (the yogin) should fix up the mind on that particular part as though pervaded by the mind.

7-10. (*Dhāraṇā* is fourfold namely) *āgneyi*, *vāruṇi*, *aiśāni* and *amṛtātmikā* (respectively) belonging to Agni, Varuṇa and Īśāna and (the fourth) of the nature of ambrosia. O Foremost among the twice-born ! (In the āgneyī), the *śikhā* (formula of the tuft) of (lord) Viṣṇu ending with *phaṭ* should be repeated. The glorious tip of the spear that is cleaved by the *nāḍi*-s (arteries) should be pierced with that. O Great sage ! The votary should think of all those from the big toe to the skull as surrounded by orbs of rays spread across lower and upper parts (of the body) by excessive lustre. One's own body that has been (conceived mentally as) burnt to ashes should be withdrawn into one's self. O Twice-born ! The cold, phlegm etc. and sin get destroyed thereby.

11-15a. (The *vāruṇi dhāraṇā* is explained now). One should think of the head, neck, *dhira* (?) and *kāra* (?) (as existing) in the face bent downwards. Then after conceiving the mind as unbroken and concentrated, the entire earth should be thought as being filled with showers of snow produced by glittering spray. (The mind) should be brought down from the *Brahmarandhra*[1] to the *Mūlādhāra*[2] through the path of *suṣumnā*[3] by means of shaking and as remaining in the orb of the full moon should be flooded with nectar-like water (produced) by contact with snow. A votary who is afflicted by sufferings such as hunger, thirst and the like should bear this *vāruṇi* (*dhāraṇā*) vigilantly for the sake of pleasure.

15b-20. I have described to you the *vāruṇi dhāraṇā*. Listen to me ! (I shall now describe) the *aiśāni dhāraṇā*. One should contemplate the grace of (lord) Viṣṇu, after having nullified the (airs) *prāṇa* and *apāna*[4] in the lotus, that is verily Brahman, in the sky, until one's thoughts cease. Then one has to repeat the great truth. The lord (should also be contemplated) as pervading

---

1. An aperture in the crown of the head through which the soul is said to escape after the death of a person.
2. A mystical circle above the organs of generation.
3. One of the arteries in the human body.
4. The printed text wrongly reads *aprāṇa*.

everything, as half moon, supreme, tranquil, without any semblance and unstained. Until a person knows one's real form through the words of his preceptor the entire unreal world (movable and immovable) appears as real. When that Supreme Principle is realised all the entities from the world to the *brahman*, the knower, the means of knowledge and the things to be known, the shaking of the lotus in the heart by means of contemplation, repetition, offering oblation, worship etc. and everything, (would appear) like the sweet cakes given by the mother. (The whole thing) may also be done with the formula of (lord) Viṣṅu. I shall describe to you the *amṛta-dhāraṇā* (now).

21-22. (In the *amṛta-dhāraṇā* the votary) should contemplate a lotus resembling the full moon held in the clenched hand of the votary. (Then the votary) should contemplate with effort a region of the full-moon having the spendour of a lakh moons filled with the waves (of bliss) of (lord) Śiva as situated on the head. (Then he should think of the same as filling) in the lotus of the heart. (Then the votary) should think of his body at its centre. The votary would become free from distress by means of the *dhāraṇā*-s and the like.

CHAPTER THREE HUNDRED AND SEVENTYSIX

Deep meditation (samādhi)

Fire-god said :

1. The deep meditation is said to be that contemplation in which the consciousness alone appearing in its spiritual aspect, remains like the ocean of coagulated milk made immobile and ceases to be operative.

2. A *yogin* is said to be in deep meditation if he remains steady in contemplation with the mind deeply absorbed, like fire (kept) in a windless (place).

3-4. He does not hear or smell or see or spit out. Moreover, he does not feel the touch. His mind does not make any resolve. He does not think and remains like a log of wood without knowing anything. A person who is absorbed in the lord thus is stated to be in deep meditation.

5-10. Just as a lamp remaining in a windless (place) does not shake, this is said to be similar. For a *yogin* who is in deep meditation, contemplating himself as (lord) Viṣṇu, divine portents occur indicating success. The essential ingredient of the ear gets fallen. There would be pain in the teeth and the limbs. The celestials beseech that *yogin* with divine pleasures. The kings (approach) him with gift of land. The rich offer wealth. The *Veda*-s and all other *śāstra*-s become manifest themselves. He gains mastery over the metres as well as poetry in abundance. Excellent medical recipes, medicinal herbs and all sculpture and other arts become known to him. The virgins of the world of Indra and qualities such as imagination (also come to him). (Lord) Viṣṇu gets pleased with one who discards these as grass.

11-12a. (Such a yogin) endowed with the wealth of powers such as *aṇimā* (becoming subtle like an atom) etc., after having imparted knowledge to the pupil and after having enjoyed the pleasures as much as desired and after having discarded the body, should abide in his self that is of the form of knowledge, bliss and Brahman.

12b-13. Just as a dirty mirror is not capable of knowing the self (i.e., the reflection of the self), so also the soul experiences pain in the body because it is connected with all (things). A person united with *yoga* does not experience the pain of all.

14. Just as the single *ākāśa* (space) becomes distinct in the pot etc., so also the single soul (remains) in many as the Sun (is reflected) in the reservoirs.

15. The Brahman, sky (ether), air, lustre, water and earth, the materials on earth, these worlds, this soul and the movable and immovable (objects) have all (come) from Him.

16-18a. Just as a potter (makes) a pot by the conjunction of clay, rod and the wheel and just as a person building a house makes a house with grass, earth and wood, so also the soul creates itself (its body) in different wombs making use of the materials (five elements) and combining them. (The soul) gets fettered by its (past) deeds, faults and ignorance by its own will.

18b-21. The (individual) soul is released (from bondage) by means of knowledge. A *yogin* does not fall sick because of his virtue. Just as a lamp is maintained (to burn) by the combination of the wick, base and oil, (so) (the body) also undergoes changes. The life goes away premature. Like a lamp the soul that is inside the heart, has many rays—white, black, tawny, blue, red, yellow and brown. A person who remains (firm) above all these, pierces the region of the Sun, crosses the world of Brahmā and attains the highest state.

22-23. One reaches the abodes of the celestials by means of the other hundred rays which are situated above. Those rays of different forms which are below have soft lustre. He moves around here by means of them for enjoying (the fruits) of (his past) deeds.

24-25. All the organs of sense, mind, organs of action, ego, the earth etc. (are known as) the *kṣetra* ('field'). The unmanifest soul is said to be the knower of the *kṣetra*. The lord who is in all the beings is existent, non-existent, as well as both existent and non-existent.

26-27a. The intellect has its origin from the unmanifest. Then the ego and the (five elements) sky etc. come into being. They have twenty-one qualities. Sound, touch, colour, taste and smell are their characteristics.

27b-28. That (quality) which rests on a particular thing gets absorbed in that particular thing. *Sattva*, *rajas* and *tamas* are also stated to be its qualities. He wanders like a wheel being possessed by *rajas* and *tamas*.

29. The one who is without a beginning and the first is (said to be) the Supreme Being. That which is knowable by means (of knowledge) and the senses is said to be a modification (of that self).

30. The *Veda*-s, *Purāṇa*-s, learning, *Upaniṣad*-s, verses, aphorisms, expositions and all other words are from Him.

31. Those who perform the *agnihotra*[1] rite for progeny,

1. A short rite invoking Fire-god.

pass through the path of the manes, the *upavithi* and that of (sage) Agastya towards the heaven.

32-35a. Those who are given to charity and are endowed with eight qualities, the eighty-eight thousand sages, who kindle the household fire are born again as the upholders of virtue. They reach the celestial world by the path of the seven sages and the serpents. Only so many sages devoid of all beginnings remain in each one of the places endowed with penance, celibacy, discarding association and learning till all the beings get destroyed.

35b-36a. The study of the *Veda*-s, sacrificial rites, celebacy, penance, restraint, earnestness, fasting and truth are the causes for (gaining) knowledge of the soul.

36b-40a. All those who adhere to truth have to practise profound meditation in this way only. It should be seen, thought about and heard by the twice-born. Those twice-borns who thus find (the truth) by resorting to the forest and meditation and are endowed with truth and extreme earnestness, will become united with pure white lustre in course of time. Then those people reach the celestial world, the Sun, lightning (and attain) the world of Brahmā. They are not reborn here.

40b-42a. Those men, who gain heaven by means of sacrificial rites, penance and gifts, reach the world of manes, the moon, the sky, air, water and earth through smoke, night, dark fortnight and the *dakṣiṇāyana* (the period when the Sun moves towards the south). They are again born here and again return.

42b-44. Those who do not know the two courses of the soul would become a serpent or a cricket, or a worm or an insect. The individual soul would become immortal by contemplating the Brahman resembling a lamp in the heart. Even a householder who accepts wealth acquired in the right way, remaining steady in knowledge about the truth, getting delighted in (seeing) guests, who performs ancestral rites and speaks truth, would get release (from bondage).

CHAPTER THREE HUNDRED AND SEVENTYSEVEN

Knowledge of Brahman

Fire-god said :

1. I shall describe the knowledge about Brahman for the sake of getting released from the ignorance of mundane existence. A person gets released (by constantly thinking), "I, this soul, is verily the Supreme Brahman."

2. The body is not the soul because that is perceived like a pot etc. It is known certainly while sleeping and at the time of death that the soul is different from the body.

3. If the body is the soul it should behave like one which does not undergo any change etc. The organs such as the eye and the like are only instruments (of knowledge) and hence are not the soul.

4. The mind and the intellect also are not the soul. They are only instruments like a lamp (for supplying light). The life-breath is also not the soul as (no ?) consciousness manifests during deep sleep.

5-6a. The consciousness is not experienced during waking and dreaming (states) because it is mixed up. Since the life-breath devoid of consciousness is known during deep sleep, the soul is not the same as the organs which belong to the soul (as instruments) (and so are not identical with it).

6b-7. The ego is also not the soul because of its non-constancy like the body. This soul which is distinct from the above-mentioned categories remains in the heart of all (beings). (The self) is the seer and enjoyer of all things like a glowing lamp in the night.

8-10a. A sage should contemplate thus at the time of commencing deep meditation :- Sky (came) from Brahman, air from sky, fire from air, water from fire, earth from water and the subtle body from that (earth). The quintuplated forms of the five elements came from the free forms of the five elements. After having meditated upon the gross body, one should think of getting absorbed in Brahman.

10b-13. The elements have been quintuplated and the Virāṭ (the first creation of Brahman) is known to be their effect. This gross body is the product of the ignorance of the soul. Wise men know knowledge through the senses as the waking state. The world has attachment for it. These three are not creation. The effect of the elements which are not quintuplated is said to be the *liṅga*. The union of the seventeen (categories) is known as the 'golden egg.' The body is stated to be the subtle mark of the soul.

14. Dream is the recollection of experience occurring in the waking state. The soul also would resemble it. (The soul that has not been fettered) with the universe (is known as) *taijasa*.

15. There is one single cause of the two known as the gross and subtle body. The soul, that is knowledge and possessing lustre, is said to be inferred from that.

16-17. It is not *sat* (existence), not *asat* (non-existence), not *sadasat* (existence as well as non-existence). It is neither composed of components, nor devoid of components. It is neither separated, nor not separated. It is both separated and not separated. It is inexplicable and is the creater of bondage and mundane existence. That single Brahman (is obtained) by means of knowledge and is never obtained by means of actions.

18. (The means of the knowledge of the soul) by all means is to control the senses which are the cause of the bondage of the soul. The place of the intellect is deep sleep. It affects the two.

19. This wise soul is known to be the *praṇava* composed of the three syllables. The syllables *a*, *u* and *m* combined (is the *praṇava*).

20. It is the witness of all things as 'I'. It is of the form of consciousness alone in the waking, dreaming and other states. Ignorance and bondage in mundane existence etc. are not its work.

21. It is eternal, pure, free from bondage, truth, bliss and without a second. I am Brahman. I am Brahman. I am the supreme splendour and the ever free *Oṁ*.

22. I am Brahman, the supreme knowledge—this contemplation destroys the bondage. Brahman is eternal, bliss, truth, knowledge and endless.

23. This soul is the Supreme Brahman. "You are that Brahman." This individual soul is instructed by the preceptor, (to identify himself with Brahman) as "I am Brahman."

24. That Brahman is the Sun. I am that partless being. *Oṁ*. The knower of Brahman gets freedom from the worthless mundane existence. He would become Brahman.

CHAPTER THREE HUNDRED AND SEVENTYEIGHT

Knowledge of Brahman

Fire-god said :

1. I am Brahman, the Supreme Light devoid of earth, water and fire. I am Brahman, the Supreme Light devoid of wind and sky.

2. I am Brahman, the Supreme Light devoid of the primary undertaking. I am Brahman, the Supreme Light bereft of the first creation and the soul.

3. I am Brahman, the Supreme Effulgence devoid of waking place. I am Brahman, the Supreme Lustre devoid of the feeling of universality.

4. I am Brahman, the Supreme Light devoid of the syllable '*a*'. I am Brahman, the Supreme Effulgence devoid of speech, hands and feet.

5. I am Brahman, the Supreme Lustre devoid of anus and penis. I am Brahman, the Supreme Light devoid of ears, skin and eyes.

6. I am Brahman, the Supreme Effulgence bereft of taste and form. I am Brahman, the Supreme Lustre devoid of all smells.

7. I am Brahman, the Supreme Light without tongue and nose. I am Brahman, the Supreme Effulgence bereft of touch and sound.

8. I am Brahman, the Supreme Effulgence bereft of mind and intellect. I am Brahman, the Supreme Lustre devoid of consciousness and ego.

9. I am Brahman, the Supreme Effulgence free from (the vital winds) *prāṇa* and *apāna* (in the b·dy). I am Brahman, the Supreme Lustre bereft of (the vital winds) *vyāna* and *udāna* (in the body).

10. I am Brahman, the Supreme Light devoid of (the vital wind) *samāna* (in the body). I am Brahman, the Supreme Effulgence devoid of old age and death.

11. I am Brahman. the Supreme Effulgence bereft of grief and ignorance. I am Brahman, the Supreme Light free from hunger and thirst.

12. I am Brahman, the Supreme Lustre devoid of all modifications of sound. I am Brahman, the Supreme Effulgence bereft of the golden egg.

13. I am Brahman, the Supreme Light devoid of the dreaming state. I am Brahman, the Supreme Effulgence devoid of luminosity etc.

14. I am Brahman, the Supreme Light free from harm etc. I am Brahman, the Supreme Lustre devoid of knowledge relating to an assembly.

15. I am Brahman, the Supreme Lustre bereft of inference. I am Brahman, the Supreme Light devoid of the qualities such as *sattva* (goodness) and the like.

16. I am Brahman, the Supreme Effulgence devoid of the feeling of *sat* and *asat* (existence and non-existence). I am Brahman, the Supreme Light, bereft of all components.

17. I am Brahman, the Supreme Lustre devoid of difference and non-difference. I am Brahman, the Supreme Light devoid of the location of deep sleep.

18. I am Brahman, the Supreme Effulgence free from the feeling of being learned. I am Brahman, the Supreme Light free from the syllables such as '*ma*'.

19. I am Brahman, the Supreme Lustre free from the means and objects knowledge. I am Brahman, the Supreme Light free from knowledge and knower.

20. I am Brahman, the Supreme Effulgence devoid of being a witness etc. I am Brahman, the Supreme Light devoid of effect and cause.

21. I am Brahman devoid of body, organs, mind, intellect,

life-breath and ego. I am Brahman, the fourth state that is free from (the states of) waking, dreaming and deep sleep.

22. (I am) eternal, pure, wise and free, truth, bliss and without a second. I am Brahman. (I am) Brahman endowed with knowledge and absolutely free. *Oṁ*. I am Brahman, the Supreme Effulgence, deep meditation and the supreme being that confers emancipation.

CHAPTER THREE HUNDRED AND SEVENTYNINE

Knowledge of Brahman again

Fire-god said :

1. (The votary) reaches the region of the gods by (performing) sacrificial rites and the region of *Virāṭ* by (doing) penance. By renouncing actions (one would gain the place) of *Brahmā*. By detachment (one would get) absorbed in nature.

2. Liberation is got by means of knowledge. These are known to be the five courses. Detachment is turning away from the feelings of happiness, torment, grief etc.

3. Renunciation is giving up all actions already performed together with those yet to be performed. (By such means) one would get free from the difference of change beginning with the unmanifest and ending with discrimination.

4. Knowledge is said to arise from knowing (the soul) as different from the animate and inanimate things. The Supreme Soul, the Supreme Lord is the sustainer of all things.

5. He is glorified in the *Veda*-s and the philosophical treatises by the name of (lord) Viṣṇu. That lord of the sacrificial rites (known as) *Yajñapuruṣa* is worshipped by those who are engaged in that.

6. That embodiment of knowledge is perceived by those who have abstained from (doing actions) by means of association with knowledge. That Supreme Being (is referred to) as speech (consisting of the sounds) short, long and protracted etc.

7. O Great sage ! The action that is the means of attaining Him is said to be knowledge. The knowledge is said to be two-fold : that which is explained in the *Āgama*[1]-s and (that which is obtained) from discrimination.

8. The Śabdabrahman (Brahman composed of sound) is an embodiment of the *Āgama*-s and the Supreme Brahman is the knowledge arising from discrimination. One should know the two Brahmans—the Śabdabrahman and the Supreme Brahman.

9. Learning in the form of the *Veda*-s and the like (is known as) *aparam* (not the supreme). The imperishable Brahman is the supreme (learning). This (Brahman) is denoted by the term "*Bhagavān*" (prosperous) in service, worship and other acts. (The letters of the word mean as follows :)

10. The syllable '*bha*' has two senses—*bhartā* (protector) and *sambhartā* (one who collects or hoards). O Great sage ! The letter '*ga*' (means) the leader, the conveyor and the creator.

11. The word '*bhaga*' (which is the combination of the letters *bha* and *ga*) means the six : the entire wealth, valour, fame, fortune, knowledge and detachment.

12. All the things exist in (lord) Viṣṇu. That Supreme Spirit is threefold. In the same way (the word) *Bhagavān* (is used) in the case of (lord) Hari and elsewhere as a courtesy.

13. He knows the creation, destruction, the coming and going of the beings, true knowledge and nescience and hence is designated '*Bhagavān*'.

14. The term '*Bhagavān*' connotes knowledge, power, supreme opulence, strength and splendour in entirety without the bad qualities fit to be avoided.

15-16a. In olden time, Khāṇḍikya Keśidhvaja imparted to (King) Janaka[2], the *yoga* (as follows) : The seed of the origin through ignorance is twofold : the notion of self in things which are not the self and the notion that self and body are identical.

16b-20. The soul enshrined in the body made of five

1. The sacred texts explaining the nature of Śiva or Viṣṇu and the methods of worshipping them.

2. The famous king of Mithilā; known for his knowledge; became an anchorite in later days.

elements and engulfed in illusion and darkness entertains the bad thought 'I am this'. In the same way a person (entertains the thought) in the sons, grandsons etc. and their progeny. The learned (entertain) similar notion with respect to the physical bodies of others. A man does work for the welfare of all the bodies (men). But a person (begins to think) that those bodies are different; it becomes a cause for the bondage. This spotless soul is verily of the form of liberation and knowledge. Impiety of the form of painful experience belongs to the *prakṛti* and not to the soul. Just as water cannot be united with fire and a union is brought about by means of the intervening vessel, (pain and illusion though they do not belong to the soul, appear as though associated with the soul).

21. O Great sage ! The sounds such as '*ka*' etc. (are said to be) the result of its action. In the same way, the soul uniting with *prakṛti*, is endowed with the feeling of the self.

22. (The self seems) to enjoy all the bodily attributes. But it is different from them and it is without any modification. The contact (of the mind) with the things is for bondage and one should withdraw his mind from the things of the senses.

23. After having withdrawn it from the things, one should think of (lord) Hari, the one identical with Brahman. O Sage ! It leads a person meditating on Brahman to gain the state of Brahman.

24-25a. After due thought (one should strive) by means of one's own effort. (The attraction of Brahman) would be like the magnet (drawing) the iron. It is said to be *yoga* which is the union of the distinct mental path with Brahman dependent on one's effort.

25b-27a. (The mind) steady in a state of deep meditation, attains the Supreme Brahman. By means of self-control, by withholding the senses from the objects, conquering the winds by doing retention of breath, regulation of breath and subjugating the senses by means of withdrawal of breath, one should make the mind steady in the auspicious repose.

27b-28. Brahman, that is to be resorted to by the mind, is twofold, namely, embodied and not embodied. (The sages) Sanandana and others were endowed with the thought of being Brahman, while the gods and other created beings (gained elevation) by means of action.

29-32. In the case of the golden egg etc., it is twofold such as due to knowledge and action. The mental activity is said to be threefold. The whole universe is contemplated as Brahman. That knowledge which is of the form of pure existence, beyond the reach of expression, that which does not possess the sense of being different and which could be known by the soul is designated as Brahman. That is the Supreme Form of (lord) Viṣṇu, devoid of form, unborn and indestructible. It is difficult to contemplate at first (the formless). Hence one has to meditate on the embodied form (at first). Such a person would become indistinct from the Supreme Soul by attaining the state of absence of the attitude of possession. (The feeling of) his difference would be due to his ignorance.

CHAPTER THREE HUNDRED AND EIGHTY

Knowledge of non-dual Brahman

Fire-god said :

1-5. I shall impart the knowledge of the non-dual Brahman which was expounded by Bharata. He (Bharata) performed penance at Śālagrāma (name of a place) worshipping Vāsudeva (Kṛṣṇa, a manifestation of Viṣṇu) etc. Because of the company of a deer, (the sage) thinking of the deer at the end of his life, became a deer (in the next birth). But because he carried the memories of his past birth even after being born as a deer, (he) discarded his life by means of *yoga* and regained his self. Having attained identity with the non-dual Brahman, he wandered in the world like an inert thing. An attendant of king Sauvīra advised (him) to serve (the king) for wages and led him to the camp. Being prompted by the words of the servant, the wiseman accepted to serve and carried the palanquin in order to destroy (the past deed) of the self. While others (carrying the palanquin) moved fast, he was lagging behind. Seeing the others moving fast and himself (moving) slow the king said to him :

The king said :

6. Are you tired ? you have borne my palanquin only for a short distance. You seem to be stout. Are you not able to stand the fatigue ?

The brahmin said :

7. I am not stout. I have not borne your palanquin. I am neither tired nor fatigued. O King ! You are a person to be borne.

8-10. The pair of feet rest on the earth, the two shanks on the pair of feet, the two thighs on the pair of shanks, which in turn are the support for the belly. Then the region of the chest, the two arms and the pair of shoulders are resting on the belly. This palanquin is on the shoulder. What has the feeling of 'mine' done here. This body remaining on the palanquin is beheld as yourself. There (the terms) 'you' and 'I' (are worldly conventions). This may be described in another way.

11-14. O King ! I, you and others are being borne by the elements. This conglomeration of *guṇas* ('qualities') fallen in the stream of *guṇas* goes on. O Ruler of earth ! These 'qualities' of goodness etc. are bound by the (past) deeds. The *karma* (past deed) is acquired by ignorance in all the creations without any exception. The soul is pure, imperishable, calm, devoid of *guṇas* and superior to *parkṛti*. Among all the creations, this alone does not have growth or decay. O King ! Just as it does not have growth, so it does not also have decay. Hence how is it that you have said 'you are stout' !

15-18. This palanquin is resting on the earth, shank, feet, hip, thigh and belly etc. and similarly on the shoulder. Hence (my) feeling is same as yours. O King ! By means of bearing the palanquin (I have become similar) to the other beings. Whether originated from a mountain, other materials or a house or originated from the earth, as the *puruṣa* (soul) is different from the physical causes. How can there be a big burden to be borne by me? O King ! With what material the palanquin has been made, the other worldly things have been made with the same material. In this respect, yourself, myself and all others have been made similar.

19. After having heard these words, the king held his feet, beseeched him to forgive (and said) : "Be pleased. Lay off this palanquin and speak to me who is listening to you. Who are you? For what reason have you come here ?"

The brahmin said :

20-21. Listen to me. It is not at all possible to tell you who I am. Everywhere the act of coming is for the sake of enjoying (the fruits of past deeds). Every being reaches a place etc. to enjoy the pleasure or pain arising from (the past) pious or impious (deeds) resting on place etc.

The king said :

22. O Brahmin ! How is it not possible to say that I am that person who is here. O Twice-born ! It is not wrong (to apply) this word 'I' to mean the self.

The brahmin said:

23-28. It is not wrong to use the word 'I' to denote the self. But it is fallacious to think and say that a thing that is not the self is the self. When there is a single soul enshrined in all the bodies, it is meaningless to ask who you are and who I am. O King ! You, this palanquin, these palanquin bearers going in front, and this world of yours are not said to be existence. Wood (the material for making the palanquin) is got from a tree. O King ! Is this palanquin on which you are placed designated as a tree or as wood ? A sensible man does not say that the great king is seated on a tree. So also (seeing) you on a log of wood, all do not say that you are on a palanquin. (In reality) the palanquin is a combination of wood in a particular design. O Excellent king ! Look at the palanquin in its distinctive feature.

29. A man, a woman, cow, horse, elephant, bird, tree should be known as worldly convention to denote the bodies due to the effect of (the past) deeds.

30. O King ! the tongue, teeth, lips and palate say 'I'.

They are not 'I' because all these are means of making an utterance.

31. For what reasons does speech itself says 'I' ? Even then it is false and not proper to say speech is not I.

32. O King ! because (limbs such as) the head, anus etc. of men are different from the body, how can I denote them as 'I'?

33. O Excellent king ! Only if something different from me exists, it is possible to say 'This is I and that is another'.

34. In fact, there is no difference such as immobile, animal, tree and different bodies etc. These are all the effects of past deeds.

35. O King ! A person (designated) as a king and those (designated) as the soldiers of the king, that and other appellations are not real.

36. You are a king to the world, a son to (your) father, a foe to an enemy, husband to (your) wife, father of a son. O King ! How shall I call you?

37. O Lord of the earth ! Are you this head? Do not the head and belly belong to you? Are not the feet etc. yourself? Or do they not belong to you?

38. You are different from all the constituent parts. O King! Think seriously as to who you are.

After having heard that, the king said to that anchorite brahmin (who was a manifestation of lord) Hari (as follows):

The king said:

39. O Twice-born ! Once I endeavoured to ask sage Kapila (to explain to me) what was beneficial (to a man). You are a part of that sage Kapila. You are giver of knowledge on earth for my sake. (Release) the wave of knowledge from the ocean (of knowledge). Impart to me whatever is beneficial to me.

The brahmin said :

40-44. You are again asking (me) what is beneficial. You are not asking about the reality. O King ! All those things which are beneficial are unreal.. After having propitiated the gods, (men) desire for abundant wealth, desire for sons and for kingdom. O King ! What is the benefit? The wise (hold) that the communion with the Supreme Being is the only good. Acts such as the (performance of) sacrificial rites (would not confer this union). One would not get wealth (by such union). The union of the self with the Supreme Being is said to be the foremost thing. The (Supreme) Soul, which is one, is all-pervading, even, pure, without characteristics, superior to nature, devoid of birth, growth etc., omnipresent and undecaying. It is wholly of the form of supreme knowledge and that lord is not associated with qualities, kinds etc.

45-47. O King! Listen to me! I shall describe to you the dialogue between Nidāgha and Ṛtu[1]. Ṛtu was the son of Brahmā and was a wiseman. Nidāgha, the son of Pulastya, was his disciple After gaining knowledge from him, (Nidāgha) came to the city and was living there. Once Ṛtu, while walking along the banks of (river) Devikā, thought of him. After one thousand celestial years had passed, (Ṛtu) had gone to see Nidāgha. After doing Vaiśvadeva[2] (worship) Nidāgha took food and asked him "You have eaten. Have you been satisfied? Is that satisfaction eternal?"

Ṛtu said:

48-55. O Brahmin! A person feeling hungry would get satisfied after eating food. I had no hunger. Why do you ask me about getting satisfied? O Twice-born! Hunger and thirst are said to be the properties of the body and hence do not belong to me. Because you have asked me I shall say that I am always satisfied since I am the (Supreme) Spirit, omnipresent and all-pervasive like the sky. Hence I am the inner self of all the beings. How then can I be restricted to this? I neither go, nor come, nor am confined to a particular place. You are not different from me, nor am I different from yourself. Just as a mud house is strengthened by plastering with mud, so also this body made of earthly (element) (is held fast) by infinitesimal particles of earthly (materials). O Twice-born! I am Ṛtu, your preceptor, come to impart to you wisdom. I have come here and I shall go now as soon as you know the highest truth. You know that there is only one and there is no difference in the entire

1. The text consistently reads Ṛtu; probably a mistake for Ṛbhu.
2. A daily rite to please all gods performed before taking food.

universe. (All the things) are the manifestation of the Ṣupreme Being known as Vāsudeva (name of Kṛṣṇa, manifestation of Viṣṇu).

Ṛtu went again to that city after one thousand years. He said to Nidāgha staying at a lonely place on the outskirts of the city, "Why do you stay at a lonely place?

Nidāgha said:

56. O Brahmin! There is a strong rumour that the king would go round (the city) to see the beauty of the cīty. Hence I am staying here.

Ṛtu said:

57-60. Who is a king here and who are the other subjects? O Excellent Twice-born! Tell me this. You are conversant (with these)! O Foremost among twice-borns!"

(Nidāgha said): "He is the king who rides that elephant in rut rising from the peak of the mountain and others are (those) moving around him. O Brahman! That which is under is the elephant and one who is above is the king." Ṛtu asked (again): "Who is the elephant and who is the king?"

Nidāgha said (the same thing again). Ṛtu made Nidāgha to lie crawling on fours and rode him (and said), "I am above like the king and you are below like the elephant."

61-62. Ṛtu said to Nidāgha, "How shall I name you then?" Being told thus Nidāgha prostrated and said, "You are certainly my preceptor. My mind has not been (made free from the dualistic bias by anyone else". Ṛtu said to Nidāgha, "I had come here to impart to (you) knowledge relating to Brahman. I have shown to you the highest truth, verily the essence, that is one without a second."

The Brahmin said:

63-65. Nidāgha also became converted to non-dualism by the counsel (of Ṛtu). He then perceived all beings without any difference in his own self. He attained liberation by means of knowledge. You will also similarly obtain liberation. You and I and all other beings are (lord) Viṣṇu from whom all has come. Just as the single sky is perceived variedly as yellow, blue etc., so also the single soul (is perceived) as separate on account of erroneous perception.

Fire-god said:

66. The king gained liberation by means of the knowledge imparted by Bharata. Contemplate that the knowledge of Brahman is the enemy of the tree of ignorance of mundane existence.

CHAPTER THREE HUNDRED AND EIGHTYONE

The essence of the Bhagavadgītā

Fire-god said:

1. I shall describe the essence of the (*Bhagavad*) *gītā*, that is foremost among all the *gītā*-s and which Kṛṣṇa imparted to Arjuna in olden days and which yields enjoyment and emancipation.

The Lord said:

2. One should not feel grief-stricken by the thought that the life is extinct or not extinct. The soul within the body is birthless. The soul neither gets old nor dies. It cannot be differentiated. Hence one should discard (the feeling of) grief etc.

3-5a. Brooding on the objects (of senses), man gets attachment for them. From attachment (arises) desire, then (comes) anger and delusion (proceeds) from anger. Confused memory (arises) from delusion and one gets ruined on account of the confusion. Association with bad elements is destroyed by means of association with good elements. The desire for gaining liberation destroys the desire (to enjoy pleasures). By discarding desire one gets firm on his own self. He is said to be a man of steady wisdom.

5b-7a. That which is night to all beings, in that the disciplined man wakes; that in which all beings wake, is night to the sage cognizing (the soul). There is nothing to be done by him who feels happy in his (own) soul. For him there is no object to acquire by doing (an action) ; nor is there any (loss) by not doing (an action).

7b-8a. O Mighty-armed ! The knower of the truth relating to the nature of *guṇas* and action knows that *guṇas* (as senses) merely abide with the *guṇas* (as objects) and does not get entangled.

8b-9a. By the raft in the form of knowledge one goes beyond all pain. O Arjuna ! The fire of knowledge burns all the deeds to ashes.

9b-10a. One who dedicates his deeds to Brahman discarding all attachment, is not stained by sins just as a lotus by water.

10b-12a. A person united to *yoga* would perceive himself in others and others in his self and would view all as equal. A person fallen from *yoga* would be born in the house of prosperous and pious persons. O Son ! A person doing auspicious things does not suffer.

12b-13a. Verily this divine illusion of mine, consisting of the qulities, is difficult to surmount. Only those who resort to me cross over this illusion.

13b-14a. O Foremost among the Bharatas ! Four types of men worship, namely, a man in distress, a man seeking knowledge, a man seeking wealth and a man imbued with wisdom. (Among them) the wiseman (is) ever steadfast.

14b-18. The imperishable is the Supreme Brahman. Its dwelling in the individual body is said to be *adhyātman*. The offering which causes the origin of beings is called *karma*. The perishable nature is *adhibhūta*. The *puruṣa* (the being) is *adhidaivata*. I alone am the *adhiyajña* here in this body, O Best among the embodied ! Whoever, at the time of death, remembers me alone, attains oneness with my state without any doubt. A man would attain the same state which he thinks of at the end after discarding the body. Fixing the life-energy in the middle of the eye-brows (a person) reaches me uttering the one-syllabled '*Om*', the Brahman, and then discarding the life, (and knowing that) (the things) beginning with Brahmā and ending with a tuft of grass are all my magnificence.

19. All glorious and noble beings are known to be a part

of Myself. One who knows that the universe is a manifestation of me, gets released.

20. One who knows the body as the field is said to be *kṣetrajña* (knower of the field). The knowledge about the field and the knower of the field is deemed by Me (lord) as knowledge.

21-22. The great elements, egoism, intellect, unmanifest (principle), the ten (organs of) senses, one (mind) and the five objects of senses, desire, hatred, pleasure, pain, the aggregate, consciousness and firmness—all these have been described briefly as the *kṣetra* (field) with its modifications.

23-27. Humility, modesty, non-injury, forbearance, uprightness, serving the preceptor, purity, steadfastness, self-control, not having desire for the objects of senses, absence of egoism, cognizing the evil in birth, death, old age, sickness and pain, non-attachment, non-identification (of the self) with son, wife, home and the like, constant equanimity towards desirable and undesirable happenings, exclusive unswerving devotion to Me (god), resorting to solitary places, distaste for an assembly of men, constancy in knowledge about self, viewing things in accordance with the knowledge of truth—these are declared as knowledge. Ignorance is the opposite of these.

28. I shall describe that which has to be known, by knowing which one enjoys immortality. The Supreme Brahman is without a beginning. It is said to be neither existence, nor non-existence[1].

29-31. With hands and feet everywhere, with eyes, heads and mouths everywhere and with ears everywhere[2]—(He) remains enveloping all. Shining by the functions of all the senses, (He) is without all the senses. (Although) unattached, (He) is the supporter of all (beings). (Although) devoid of qualities, (He) is the person experiencing them. He is outside and within (all) the beings. He is movable as well as immovable. He is incomprehensible because of his subtlety. He is far and near.

1. The textual reading is wrong. It has been corrected as in *BG* XIII. 12.

2. The textual reading has been corrected on the basis of *BG* XIII.13.

32-33. He is undivided and yet He seems to be existing in beings as divided. He should be known as the supporter of beings. He devours and is mighty (generator). The light of all lights, He is said to be beyond darkness. (He is) the knowledge, the knowable and the goal of knowledge, remaining in the hearts of all (the beings).

34-35. By means of meditation some behold the self in the self by the self. Others (see the self) by *sāṅkhya-yoga* (deliberation) and yet others by *karma-yoga* (action). Still others, not knowing thus, worship (Him) as they have heard from others. They too cross death quickly by their devotion to what they have heard.

36. Knowledge arises from *sattva* (goodness), greed from *rajas* and error, delusion and ignorance from *tamas*.

37. One who simply stands composed (thinking) that the *guṇas* exist in him and is not shaken (by them) and remains equanimous towards respect and insult, friend and foe, (is said to be) free from *guṇas*.

38. The imperishable *aśvattha* (holy fig tree) is said to be having its roots above and branches below. Its leaves are the *Veda*-s. One who knows it is the knower of the *Veda*-s.

39. There are two (types of) beings in this world, the divine and the demoniacal. Non-injury etc.[1] and forbearance belong to one born for a divine state.

40. Neither purity, nor (right) conduct belong to one born for a demoniacal state. As anger, greed and sex lead to hell, one should reject the three.

41-42. Sacrificial rites, penance and charity are known to be of three varieties due to the (three) qualities, *sattva* etc. The food that augments life, purity, strength, health and pleasure (is known to be) *sāttvika*. The food that is pungent and dry and productive of pain, grief and disease (is) *rājasa*. The food that is impure, rejected, putrid and tasteless (is said to be) *tāmasa*.

43. The sacrificial rite is said to be *sāttvika* if it is performed as laid down without desiring reward. (A sacrifice is) *rājasa*,

1. See *BG* XVI. 2-3 for other characteristics.

if it is (done) for the sake of gaining a fruit. If it is for vanity it is *tāmasa*.

44. Physical penance is said to be that which is accompanied by faith, sacred formula and the like. Worship of the gods etc. and non-injury etc. are said to be verbal penance.

45. A speech that does not cause excitement, truthfulness, practice of the study of the scriptures of one's own school and sacred repetition (are said to be austerity of speech). Mental (austerity) consists of purity of disposition, silence and self-control[1].

46-47. The *sāttvik* austerity (is done) with no desire (for any fruit), the *rājasa*, with the intention of gaining an object and the *tāmasa* for harming others. The *sāttvika* charity is that which is performed at the right place etc. with a sense of duty. *Rājasa* (charity) is that (performed) with a view to receive in return. It is said to be *tāmasa* (when performed) at a wrong place and insultingly.

48. "*Om tat sat* (*Om*, that and real)" has been declared to be the triple designation of Brahman. Sacrificial rites, charity and such other deeds confer enjoyment and emancipation to men.

49. The threefold fruit of action—disagreeable, agreeable and mixed—accrues after death to a person who does not relinquish (karma) but never to those who renounce.

50-51. The *tāmasika* action (arises) from an action associated with delusion, the *rājasa* action from pain, fear etc., and the *sāttvika* from non-desire. These (following) five are the five causes of an action—the body, the agent, the various instruments such as the senses, the different[2] functions of various sorts and the presiding deity, the fifth.

52-53a. The knowledge that (everything is) one is *sāttvika*. The knowledge that it is separate is *rājasa*. That which is contrary to reality is *tāmasa*. The *sāttvika* action is without any

1. The text has carelessly abridged *BG* XVII.15-16.
2. The printed text wrongly reads *trividhāḥ* for *vividhāḥ*. *Cf. BG* XVIII.14.

desire. The *rājasa* action is with desire. The *tāmasa* (action) is from ignorance.

53b-54. A *sāttvika* agent would be equanimous towards success and failure. A *rājasa* (doer) (would be) deceitful. A *tāmasa* (doer would be) languid. The understanding at the beginning of an action is *sāttviki*. That which is only at the time of an action would be *rājasi*. The contrary (would be) *tāmasi*.

55-56a. The firmness of mind (towards pleasure and pain etc.) would be *sāttviki*. The desire (of the mind) for satisfaction is *rājasi*. Grief etc. is *tāmasi*. There would be pleasure at the beginning from *sattva*. The pleasure that comes at the end is *rājasa*. Pain at the beginning and end is *tāmasa*.

56b-58. All the beings had their origin from that by which this (universe) has been pervaded. One finds success by worshipping (lord) Viṣṇu by one's action. A person who knows the world from *Brahmā* to a tuft of grass as (lord) Viṣṇu by means of his action, mind and speech in all the states gains success always. The devotee of the lord (would) certainly (be) a *bhāgavata*.

CHAPTER THREE HUNDRED AND EIGHTYTWO

The Yamagitā

Fire-god said:

1. I shall describe to you the *Yamagitā* expounded to Naciketas. It would confer enjoyment and emancipation to the pious desiring emancipation who read and listen to this.

Yama said:

2. Alas! man himself being non-eternal, desires for eternal seats, beds, vehicles, clothes, houses etc. on account of ignorance.

3. It has been said by (the sage) Kapila (in olden days). that always having non-attachment for pleasures and viewing one's own self (critically) are most excellent for men.

4. (The sage) Pañcaśikha has said that impartiality to

wards all, attitude of non-possession, not being attached (to worldly pleasures) are most excellent for men.

5. Gaṅgāviṣṇu has declared that a true knowledge (of the miseries) of the stages (of life) beginning with that of embryo and including birth, childhood and old age etc. is most excellent for men.

6. Janaka has stated that remedying the pains such as the *ādhyātmika* (bodily and mental) and the like from the beginning to the end is most excellent for men.

7. Brahmā holds that the most excellent thing for men is to perceive the oneness of the Supreme Being appearing as different (in different beings).

8. Jaigīṣavya has said that the highest good lies in discharging one's duties as laid down in the *Ṛg*, *Yajur* or *Sāma* (*veda*) without attachment and with a sense that they have to be done.

9. Devala is said to hold the view that the most excellent thing for men would be to abandon all actions for the sake of the happiness of the self.

10. (Sage) Sanaka has declared that the knowledge (gained) from renunciation of desires leads one to Brahman, the supreme place, and that those who entertain desires (do not get) this knowledge.

11. (Lord) Hari has said that the foremost among the excellent is to transform the actions done with attachment into those of non-attachment. This is verily non-action, the Brahman.

12. The elevated person who has gained knowledge does not become different from Brahman, known as (lord) Viṣṇu, the supreme and indestructible.

13. A person would gain by (doing) austerities whatever he mentally desires such as knowledge of Brahman, knowledge of worldly existence, faith in god, good fortune and a beautiful form.

14. There is nothing to be contemplated equal to (lord) Viṣṇu. There is no austerity superior to fasting. There is no fortune equal to health. There is no river equal to the (river) Gaṅgā.

15-16. There is no kinsman other than (lord) Viṣṇu, the lord of the universe. A person who meditates on (lord) Hari as (existing) below, above, in front and in the body, senses, mind etc. and passes away would become (lord) Hari. That which is the Brahman, from that all the things (have emanated) and in that all the things exist.

17. (Lord) Viṣṇu dwells in the hearts of all in the form of higher and lower, as un-understandable, indefinable and well-established.

18. Some (people) invoke that lord Viṣṇu as the lord of sacrifices. Some (invoke) Him as (lord) Hari, some as (lord) Hara (Śiva) and some others as Brahmā.

19. Some (invoke) Him by the names of Indra etc. and others as Sun, Moon and as the eternal time. People state that the whole earth, from Brahmā to a tuft of grass, is Viṣṇu.

20-21a. A person who has attained (lord) Viṣṇu, the Supreme Brahman, never returns (to worldly existence). A man may acquire such a state by making great gifts such as gold, bathing in sacred waters, meditation, austerities, worship, wealth and listening to sacred texts.

21b-22. Know the soul as traveller, the body as chariot, intellect as charioteer and mind as reins. The senses are said to be horses and the objects the pasture ground for them.

23-24a. People name the soul united with the mind and senses as the enjoyer. He who is not wise and whose mind is not always associated (with the soul), does not reach the Supreme Brahman and is born in the world.

24b-25a. He who is wise and whose mind is united (with the soul) always, attains the place (of Brahman) and is not born in this world again.

25b-26a. A person who has knowledge as the charioteer and mind as the reins, reaches the end of his journey and (gets) the highest region of (lord) Viṣṇu.

26b-28a. The objects (of senses) are higher than the respective organs; the mind is higher than the objects; the intellect is higher than the mind; the self (is higher) than the intellect and (the principle of) *mahat* is higher than the self. The unmanifest is higher than the *mahat*. The *Puruṣa* (the spirit) is higher than the unmanifest. There is nothing higher than the Supreme Spirit. It is the ultimate end and course.

28b-30. This self hidden in all the bodies does not reveal itself. The subtle one is perceived by men having sharp intellect and subtle vision. A wiseman should restrain his speech in the mind, that knowledge in the self, that knowledge in the great self and place it at the end in the self. After having known the union of Brahman and the self by means of moral duties etc., one would become Brahman.

31-32. Non-injury, truthfulness. non-stealing, celibacy, refraining from receiving gifts (are known) as the *yama*-s (moral abstentions). The *niyamas* (observances) (are) five—purity, happiness, austerity, study of the *Veda* (of one's school) and worship of God. The (physical) postures are such as the *padmaka* etc. *Prāṇāyāma* (is) conquest of wind. *Pratyāhāra* is the restraining of the mind in the self.

33. *Dhāraṇā* consists of fixing of the mind on an auspicious object. O Twice-born ! It is said to be the *dhāraṇā* by the wise because the mind is steady.

34. The continuous fixing-up of the mind in the same place is known as *dhyāna* (contemplation). *Samādhi* is the state of (having the attitude) "I am Brahman".

35. Just as the space enclosed by a pitcher becomes one with the sky when the pitcher is destroyed, in the same way the liberated soul becomes Brahman.

36. The individual soul deems itself as Brahman by (means of) knowledge (alone) and not by any other (means). The individual soul gets released from ignorance and its effect and becomes undecaying and immortal.

Fire-god said:

37. O Vasiṣṭha ! I have expounded (to you) the *Yamagitā* which yields enjoyment and emancipation to the readers. The eternal union is stated to be the total occupation of the intellect by Brahman (as outlined) in the philosophical thought.

CHAPTER THREE HUNDRED AND EIGHTYTHREE

The Glorification of the Agnipuraṇā

Fire-god said:

1-4. I have expounded to you the *Āgneyapurāṇa* of the form of Brahman. It with extension and without extension consists of the two *vidyā*[1]-s. The learning consists of the *Ṛg*, *Yajur*, *Sāma* and *Atharva* (*veda*). Viṣṇu is the creator of the world. Prosody, phonetics, grammar, lexicon, astronomy, etymology, *dharmaśāstra* (treatises on religious duties), *mīmāṁsā* (inquiry), *nyāya* (logic), science of medicine, archery, science of music and science of statecraft are all (known as *parā*) *vidyā*. The other one beyond the *Veda*-s is lord Hari known as *aparā vidyā* (that which has nothing superior to it). Highest knowledge is the supreme undecaying thing.

5-6. One who has the feeling that all the things are (the manifestations of lord) Viṣṇu, is not affected by the *Kali* (era). One would not incur any sin by not performing the great sacrificial rites or not offering the obsequial rites to the manes if he worships (lord) Kṛṣṇa with devotion. One does not get ruined by intensive contemplation of (lord) Viṣṇu, who is the cause of all things.

7. A person whose mind has been drawn towards the objects arising from defects due to other rituals, gets released from sins, even after doing a sin, by contemplating (lord) Govinda (Kṛṣṇa).

8. It is contemplation where there is Govinda. It is a narrative where there is Keśava. That is an action which is devoted to Him. What is the use of others which are repeatedly spoken about.

9. He is not a father who fails to describe this supreme knowledge spoken by me to the son and he is not a preceptor who fails to impart (this) to his pupil.

10. O Twice-born! One could get a son, wife, wealth, prosperity, friends and other things by wandering in this world, but not this knowledge.

1. explained below.

11. What is the use of son and wife? What (comes out of) friend, land and relatives? Such knowledge is the supreme relative, which liberates a person.

12. There are two courses for the beings—divine and demoniac. Constant devotion to (lord) Viṣṇu is divine and the contrary is demoniac.

13. This, which has been expounded to you, is sacred, healthy, praise-worthy, capable of destroying bad dreams, giving pleasure and satisfaction and liberation to men.

14. In whatever houses transcripts of the *Āgneyapurāṇa* are kept, disturbances never approach them.

15. What is the good of pilgrimages, or making gifts of cows, or sacrificial rites or fasting, when people hear the *Āgneya* (*purāṇa*) daily?

16. A person who gives a *prastha* (measure) of sesamum or a *māṣa* (weight) of gold, would obtain equal (merit) by listening to one verse of the *Agni* (*Purāṇa*).

17. The reading of a chapter of this (*Purāṇa*) is more commendable than making a gift of a cow. A sin done in the course of a day and night by a person is destroyed by his desire to listen to this (*Purāṇa*).

18. (The benefit) that would accrue by making a gift of hundred tawny cows at Puṣkara[1] in (the month of) *Jyeṣṭha* (June-July), that benefit would be obtained by reading the *Āgneyapurāṇa*.

19. The piety of two kinds—being engaged and being withdrawn—does not become equal to this sacred text of *Agnipurāṇa*.

20. O Vasiṣṭha ! A devoted man would get liberated from all sins by either reading the *Agnipurāṇa* daily or listening to it.

21-22. Where there is a copy of the *Agnipurāṇa*, in that house there would not be any difficulty, mishap or fear of theft, or fear of miscarriage of foetus, or possession of children by the spirits. There would not be the fear of the evil spirits and the like, where there is (a copy of) the *Agnipurāṇa*.

23. By listening to this (*purāṇa*), a brahmin would become learned in the *Veda*-s, a *kṣatriya* (would be) a monarch, a *vaiśya* would gain wealth and a *śūdra* would get health.

---

1. A holy place of pilgrimage in Rajasthan.

24-25. O Brahmin ! A devotee of Viṣṇu, having equanimity would get all his afflictions destroyed by reading or listening to the *Agnipurāṇa*. (Lord) Keśava would destroy all the misfortunes that would be celestial, terrestrial or earthly such as bad dreams, evil incantations and other mishaps (of such a person).

26-28. The reading or listening to the text is more meritorious for a man than performing a sacrificial rite. A person who listens to the sacred *Agnipurāṇa* in the *Hemanta* (early winter) after offering worship with perfumes and flowers would get the benefit of (performing) *Agniṣṭoma* (rite). (A person would get the benefit of performing) the *Puṇḍarīka* (rite) in *Śiśira* (advanced winter), *Aśvamedha* (rite) in the spring, *Vājapeya* (rite) in the summer and *Rājasūya* in the rainy season. (One would get) the benefit (of making a gift) of thousand cows in the autumn by reading this (*Purāṇa*).

29. O Vasiṣṭha ! He who devoutly recites the *Agnipurāṇa* in front of (lord) Hari, would be deemed as worshipping (lord) Keśava with the rite of knowledge.

30. He who has a book of the *Agnipurāṇa* in his house would be victorious. In whose house the transcribed (*Purāṇa*) is worshipped, (that person) has enjoyment and emancipation on his hand.

31. Thus (lord) Hari (Viṣṇu) has expounded to me in days of yore in the form of the destructive fire at the end of the world. The *Āgneyapurāṇa* consists of two sorts of knowledge. O Vasiṣṭha! You would impart to the devotees these two kinds of knowledge.

Vasiṣṭha said :

32-33a. O Vyāsa ! I have narrated to you the *Āgneyapurāṇa*, consisting of two sorts of knowledge, obtained from (lord) Viṣṇu, the Supreme Brahman, and as expounded to me by Agni (Fire-god) in the presence of the celestials and sages. It makes everything known.

33b-35a. O Vyāsa ! He who reads or listens to or writes or causes to write or causes to listen to or causes to read or worships or carries this *Agnipurāṇa*, known as the Brahman and expounded by Agni (Fire-god) in days of yore, would be liberated from all sins and would attain heaven after obtaining the desires.

35b-36. After having caused the excellent *Purāṇa* to be copied, he who gives (the copies) to brahmins, would attain the world of Brahmā and elevate hundreds of his family. He who reads a verse (from this *Purāṇa*) would become free from the mire of sin.

37-38. Hence, O Vyāsa ! This Purāṇa making everything explicit should always be read to the disciples in the company of the sages such as Śuka and others who are desirous of hearing. *The Āgneya(purāṇa)* read and contemplated would be auspicious and confer enjoyment and emancipation. Obeisance to that Fire-god who has sung the *Purāṇa*.

Vyāsa said :

39-44a. O Sūta (redactor) : This *Āgneya*(*purāṇa*) which is of the form of *parā* and *aparā vidyā* and the supreme position was sung by (sage) Vasiṣṭha in days of yore and it has been expounded to you by me. The fortunate ones would attain a form difficult to get. Those who meditate upon this *Āgneyapurāṇa*, the Brahman, would reach (lord) Hari. Those who seek knowledge (would get) knowledge. Those who wish for kingdom would obtain kingdom. Those without progeny get children. Those without resort would reach a resort. Those who seek fortune and those who desire for liberation get them. Those who transcribe and those who cause it to be transcribed become sinless and gain fortune. O Sūta ! Think of the form of the *Āgneyapurāṇa* (expounded) by Śuka, Paila and others. There is no doubt that you would gain enjoyment and emancipation. You recite the *Purāṇa* to the disciples and devotees.

Sūta said :

44b-47a. I have heard the *Āgneyapurāṇa* with respect by the favour of Vyāsa. The *Agni* (*purāṇa*) is a manifestation of the Supreme Brahman. You and other sages such as Śaunaka and others had worshipped lord Hari in the Naimiṣa forest. They were steadfast. The *Agnipurāṇa* is spoken by Agni and conforms to the *Vedas*. This (*Purāṇa*) endowed with the two (sorts of) *brahmavidyā* confers enjoyment and emancipation.

47b-51. There is nothing richer in substance than this. Nothing is a better friend than this. There is no greater work than this. There is no better course than this. There is no greater treatise than this. There is no greater scripture than this. There is no superior knowledge than this. There is no *smṛti* (textbook of piety) than this. No *āgama* (texts dealing with worship) is superior to this. No knowledge is greater than this. No exposition excels this. There is nothing extremely auspicious excelling this. No philosophic exposition is greater than this. This is the foremost *Purāṇa*. There is no object more difficult to obtain than this on the earth. All the lores have been expounded in this *Purāṇa*.

52. All the manifestations (of lord Viṣṇu) such as the fish and the like, *Gītā*, *Rāmāyāṇa* ((epic story of *Rāma*), *Harivaṁśa* (Account of the successors of lord Kṛṣṇa), *Bhārata* (the legend of the patricidal war between the Kauravas and Pāṇḍavas) and fresh creation have been described.

53-55. The *vaiṣṇava āgama* (mode of worship relating to Viṣṇu) such as worship, initiation and installation (of the idol), investiture with the sacred thread, the characteristic of the idols and temples etc. and formulae yielding enjoyment and emancipation, texts dealing with worship relating to Śaivite gods and their substance, (the. worship) of the goddess and Sun, different circles, *vāstu* (relating to the ground), different types of formulae and secondary creation of the primordial egg and the like have been sung.

56. The geography of the world with the continents, mountain ranges and rivers and the greatness of the sacred places of pilgrimage such as Gayā, Gaṅgā, Prayāga etc. have been told.

57. The galaxy of stars, astronomy and prognostication for victory in battle have been described. The different periods of Manu and the duties of different classes of men have been explained.

58. Pollutions, purification of things and expiations have been explained. The duties of kings, the making of gifts and different kinds of austerities have been described.

59-60. Disputes, appeasing rites, the application (of the formulae) of the *Ṛgveda* etc., the Solar and Lunar dynasties, archery, medical science, science of music, statecraft, *mimāṁsā* (inquiry), *nyāya* (logic), the greatness and number of *Purāṇa*-s, prosody and grammar have been explained.

61. Poetics, lexicography, phonetics and rules relating to performance of rites have been described. The casual, natural, and absolute destructions have been explained.

62. *Vedānta* is said to be the knowledge about Brahman and *yoga* as having eight constituents. The eulogy, greatness of the *Purāṇas* and the eighteen lores have been expounded.

63. The *Ṛgveda* etc. (are known to be) the *parāvidyā* (that which has something superior to it) and the *aparāvidyā* (that which has nothing superior to it) is the undecaying Supreme Brahman. The form of Brahman is said to be cosmic and acosmic.

64. This *Purāṇa* (having an extent) of fifteen thousand (verses)[1] is always read by the celestials in the celestial world as having one hundred crore (verses).

65. Fire-god has sung it here after shortening it for the sake of the welfare of the world. O Sages, Śaunaka and others! You know that all the things (are manifestations of) Brahman.

66. One may listen to, cause to be heard, read, cause to be read, transcribe, cause to be transcribed, worship or sing (its glory).

67-68. The king should take effort to honour the reader of this *Purāṇa*. After having honoured him by (making) gifts of cows, land and gold and the satiating gifts of clothes and ornaments, one would get the fruits of listening to (the recitation of) the *Purāṇa*. At the end of (the reading of) the *Purāṇa*, the twice-born must be fed.

69-71. (He who does as above) would become spotless, gain all the riches and attain heaven along with his ancestors. He who gives leaves (paper) for (copying) the book, thread for stitching together the leaves and the cloth for binding would attain heaven. He who gives (the book as a gift) would

1. But this *Purāṇa* here contains about 8000 verses only.

reach the world of Brahmā. He who has the book in his house does not have the fear due to portents. (Such a person) would get enjoyment and emancipation. You all remember the *Āgneyapurāṇa* as a form of the lord. After having been honoured by them (Śaunaka and others) Sūta went away and Śaunaka and others reached (lord) Hari.

INDEX